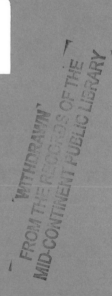

Oz

And
Beyond

And
Beyond

The Fantasy World of
L. Frank Baum

MICHAEL O. RILEY

UNIVERSITY PRESS OF KANSAS

To apply for membership in the International Wizard of Oz Club, write to the International Wizard of Oz Club, Inc., P.O. Box 266, Kalamazoo, MI 49004-0266. For general inquiries, contact Fred M. Meyer, P.O. Box 95, Kinderhook, IL 62345.

Design by Patrick Dooley.

Published by the University Press of Kansas (Lawrence, Kansas 66049), which was organized by the Kansas Board of Regents and is operated and funded by Emporia State University, Fort Hays State University, Kansas State University, Pittsburg State University, the University of Kansas, and Wichita State University

Library of Congress Cataloging-in-Publication Data

Riley, Michael O'Neal.
    Oz and beyond : the fantasy world of L. Frank Baum / Michael O'Neal Riley.
        p.   cm.
    Includes bibliographical references and index.
    ISBN 0-7006-0832-X (alk. paper)
    1. Baum, L. Frank (Lyman Frank), 1856–1919—Criticism and interpretation.
    2. Children's stories, American—History and criticism.   3. Fantastic fiction,
    American—History and criticism.   4. Oz (Imaginary place).   I. Title.
    PS3503.A923Z85   1997
    813'.4—dc21   97-276

British Library Cataloguing in Publication Data is available.

Printed in the United States of America
10 9 8 7 6 5 4 3 2 1

The paper used in this publication meets the minimum requirements of the American National Standard for Permanence of Paper for Printed Library Materials Z39.48-1984.

Contents

CONTENTS

Preface

THE FIRST OZ BOOK, *THE WONDERFUL WIZARD OF OZ*, WAS PUBLISHED IN 1900; therefore, Oz is just as old as the twentieth century. Actually, this could be labeled the century of Oz, at least by American children and other lovers of fantasy. For roughly the first half, there was a new Oz book to look forward to at each Christmas season. (From 1913 until 1942, that publishing event was as inevitable as the holiday itself.) By 1951, the series had reached a total of thirty-nine books, and Oz had become such a large and well-populated place that Jack Snow could publish his fanciful *Who's Who in Oz* (1954), which at nearly three hundred pages still left out a large number of the characters and did not attempt to list the places in that amazing country. Snow also included brief biographies of the five authors of Oz books and the four illustrators. With only one more title published in 1963 (which added two more authors and another illustrator), the "official" Oz canon was completed at forty books. The canon, in this instance, refers to the original Oz book and those sequels published by the Reilly & Britton (later Reilly & Lee) Company of Chicago.

When the majority of the books in the original series went out of print in the 1960s, the rich store of Oz history became largely unavailable to the general public, which limited the acquaintance that most new readers had with Oz to those characters and incidents in the original book and in the version of the story presented in the classic MGM film.

If the first half of the century could be called the era of "Oz the Series," the second half could be called the era of "Oz the Movie." Although the film had been made in 1939, had been successful then, and had been rereleased to theaters, it was only with its historic first showing on television in 1956 and the subsequent annual showings that its version of Oz captured the minds and hearts of generations of American children so completely. Between the original book and the film, there can be few Americans—or, for that matter, few people in any part of the world with access to books and television—who do not know the story of Dorothy and her three companions and their quest for qualities that only the humbug wizard can give them. So ingrained in the American consciousness is Oz that the story and characters are often used as though they were myth. Political cartoons frequently refer to the story; public figures are often compared to the Wizard; adult novels treat Oz as source material; theaters present musical and nonmusical stage versions; and films ranging from fairly faithful adaptations to disturbing, adult visions of a dark future claim Oz as source and inspiration.

Nevertheless, Oz was not an anonymous creation from our folklore. Its creator was Lyman Frank Baum (1856–1919). But who was he, and what exactly did he create? The first question has been answered in several biographies and biographical essays, beginning with Martin Gardner and Russel B. Nye's *The Wizard of Oz and Who He Was* (1957). The second question is the one that this book attempts to answer.

As I grew up, I was lucky to be able to experience the Land of Oz both as it was presented in the entire official Oz series and as it was depicted in the film. I was exposed to the combined imaginations of the seven authors and the visual images of the five illustrators, as well as the vision of the writers and designers of the film. But the many versions of Oz are not always consistent, and this is noticeable even to a child. Talented authors continued the Oz series after Baum's death, but they had their own styles and ideas about how to develop the series. I loved them all, but I began to try to identify just what part of that massive edifice Baum himself had created, and I wondered where he might have gone with the series had he lived longer.

This study is the result of those investigations that began so long ago. It quickly became apparent that Baum's Oz cannot be fully understood without reference to all his fantasy writings. His imaginary countries are related, and it turns out that Oz is only a part of his fantasy world; therefore, this study deals with all his fantasies. However, it deals only incidentally with the later Oz authors and not at all with the MGM film. I believe that this concentrated approach makes it possible to demonstrate that Baum had a more consistent and disciplined imagination than is generally recognized. In fact, Baum's ability to create believable and interconnected imaginary worlds that are larger than any of the individual stories that take place in them compares favorably with the creative genius of J. R. R. Tolkien. What I believe emerges by the end of this study is more than the picture of Baum's entire fantasy world, for this book is also the story of a mind—the chronicle of the growth and development of the creative imagination of one of America's greatest writers for children.

In addition, by identifying just what Baum did create, we may be more able to appreciate the creative talents of the later Oz authors. In many important instances, they were not merely imitating Baum, but taking Oz in new and different directions that were uniquely their own. It is my hope that this study of Baum's original conception of Oz will reveal a depth to his imagination not generally recognized before and that it will also inspire more detailed studies of the individual contributions of the authors who continued the Oz series.

I have had the help and encouragement of many people while working on this book. I want to thank Robert Detweiler and the late Lore Metzger and Arthur Evans for guiding me with wisdom and kindness through the initial phase of this project. I also thank Rolf Knieling for his help in preparing and proofing the original typescript. For help during the second phase, I am indebted to Walter Reed for his advice and to Douglass Parker for his insightful criticism and very helpful suggestions. I owe special thanks to June Mann for her technical help in preparing the manuscript, as well as thanks to Ralf Thiel and Keith Anthony. I also want to express my great appreciation to Editor-in-Chief Michael Briggs of the University Press of Kansas for his belief in this book and to Melinda Wirkus, Susan Schott, Patrick Dooley, and all the other people at the press who have made getting the book published such a pleasant experience. The encouragement of my colleagues at Castleton State College has been much appreciated as well. And finally, I owe an incalculable debt of gratitude to Douglas G. Greene for his advice, suggestions, and unfailing enthusiasm at all stages of the project.

All illustrations for *Oz and Beyond* were reproduced from first or early editions of Baum's books in the author's collection.

Illustrations

For my parents,
my mother, Elaine Brown Riley,
and my late father, Harold Edward Riley,
who made my childhood
a loved and magical time
and who gave me the freedom
to wander in worlds
of the imagination.

Copyright page from The Emerald City of Oz *(1910) by John R. Neill.*

Prologue

American Arcadia

Imagination has given us the steam engine, the telephone, the talking-machine and the automobile, for these things had to be dreamed of before they became realities. So I believe that dreams—day dreams, you know, with your eyes wide open and your brain-machinery whizzing—are likely to lead to the betterment of the world. The imaginative child will become the imaginative man or woman most apt to create, to invent, and therefore to foster civilization. A prominent educator tells me that fairy tales are of untold value in developing imagination in the young. I believe it.

L. Frank Baum,
"To My Readers" in
The Lost Princess of Oz (1917)

L. Frank Baum's *The Wonderful Wizard of Oz* is now considered the quintessential American fairy tale and occupies much the same place in our literature as Lewis Carroll's *Alice's Adventures in Wonderland* does in British literature. In fact, Baum is the only American author of fairy tales whom Humphrey Carpenter in *Secret Gardens: A Study of the Golden Age of Children's Literature* allows to have equaled the achievements of the great British writers.[1] And, according to Brian Attebery's study *The Fantasy Tradition in American Literature,* Baum's story was not only the most successful American fairy tale, but also the first: "Coming out of nineteenth-century fairy tales, but an evolutionary step above them, the first unquestionably American fantasy appeared in 1900, L. Frank Baum's *The Wizard of Oz.*"[2]

Successful fantasy is one of the rarest and most elusive of literary creations and one of the most difficult to approach by a critical method because its particular appeal, magic, or success often depends on extra-literary elements and can—and sometimes does—exist in spite of sloppy writing, two-dimensional characters, and faulty plots. According to J. R. R. Tolkien, "Faërie cannot be caught in a net of words; for it is one of its qualities to be indescribable, though not imperceptible." He also stated that "fairy-stories were plainly not primarily concerned with possibility, but with desirability. If they awakened *desire*, satisfying it while often whetting it unbearably, they succeeded."[3] Various writers and critics have tried to define the extraliterary element: Tolkien called it "Sub-creation," "the making or glimpsing of Other-worlds";[4] C. Warren Hollister described it as "three-dimensionality," that "experience of going into another universe where everything is brighter and more fragrant, more dangerous, and more alive";[5] and Humphrey Carpenter wrote that it is the "search for an Arcadia, a Good Place, a Secret Garden."[6] All these brief definitions put the emphasis very much on "place."

It is, though, not enough for this place, this Other-world, to be arbitrarily different from the real world; it must be a fully realized, consistent world that is as much subject to laws (however strange or wonderful) as our own. George MacDonald, one of the great nineteenth-century British writers of fairy tales, explained:

> *The natural world has its laws, and no man must interfere with them in the way of presentment any more than in the way of use; but they themselves may suggest laws of other kinds, and man may, if he pleases, invent a little world of his own, with its own laws; for there is that in him which delights in calling up new forms—which is the nearest, perhaps, he can come to creation.*[7]

As satisfying and desirable as the alternative world may be in itself, it can also have implications beyond its boundaries. Tolkien called these implications the three faces of fairy stories: "the Mystical towards the supernatural; the Magical towards Nature; and the Mirror of scorn and pity towards Man." And he went on to explain: "The essential face of Faërie is the middle one, the Magical. But the degree in which the others appear (if at all) is variable, and may be decided by the individual storyteller."[8] If most of the enchantment and interest of fantasy lies in the middle face, much of its power comes from the other two: the look back at the world of man and the realization that the stories are sometimes, as Carpenter suggests, "commenting, often satirically and critically, on real life";[9] and the look beyond the fantasy world to the mystical or the religious experience, "a piercing glimpse of joy, and heart's desire, that for a moment passes outside the frame, rends indeed the very web of story, and lets a gleam come through."[10]

In what, at first, seems like a strange inversion where the background comes to the foreground, all the comments quoted have pointed to the creation of a believable Other-world—a world that is often only glimpsed—as a major, if not *the* major, element of successful fantasy. What, then, of plot, characters, and narrative style? They are, of course, important, and when all the elements work together, the result is something exceptional, such as MacDonald's "The Golden Key," Carroll's *Alice's Adventures in Wonderland,* Baum's *The Wonderful Wizard of Oz,* or Tolkien's *The Lord of the Rings.* But let the believability of the Other-world fail or even falter badly and nothing can save the story, for fairy tales are concerned with magic and enchantment: without that believable Other-world, the Magical face of Faërie becomes only realism; the Mystical, allegory; and the Mirror toward Man, satire.

However natural it may be to link Baum with other great writers of fairy tales like George MacDonald, Lewis Carroll, and J. R. R. Tolkien (and Baum is a part of that tradition), he differs from them in two important respects: the very special effect of his stories on many readers and the existence of his total Other-world outside any one of his stories. In those respects, Baum resembles the author of a very different kind of "fantasy," Sir Arthur Conan Doyle. Doyle's Sherlock Holmes and Baum's Oz exist, as just about the sole inhabitants, in that rarefied realm of fictional creations that have taken on a life of their own, independent of their creators; that have sparked the imaginations of readers to seemingly endless discussions of the mysteries, inconsistencies, and lapses in the stories; and that have inspired authors, both amateur and professional, to write more stories about them as though they were adding to the history of a real person or a real place.

5

Of course, despite the similar effects on their readers, a fictional character and a fictional place cannot be compared, but the parallel between Doyle and Baum is in the *way* in which they created and developed that character and that place; neither exists as a whole in any one story or book. Baum built up his imaginary Other-world, like Doyle built up the character of Sherlock Holmes, in each new story and book, each one adding scraps of information that expanded or otherwise altered the reader's mental picture. Christopher Morley noticed this about Doyle's creation and, speaking for the league of Holmes devotees, wrote: "We read the stories again and again; perhaps most of all for the little introductory interiors which give a glimpse of 221B Baker Street."[11] And even though Morley was referring to the life and character of Holmes primarily and the London of the 1890s only secondarily, there is a strange correlation between his phrases and those that other writers have used to describe the extraliterary element of fantasy; Holmes is the "living" element of Doyle's stories just as the imaginary world is of Baum's.

In L. Frank Baum's first published book for children, a collection of stories entitled *Mother Goose in Prose* (1897), the final story concerns a little girl named Dorothy who, in a rural, vaguely American landscape, has a magical encounter with a rabbit who tells her of his adventures in the castle of Santa Claus. It is a slight tale, and probably its only significance within the context of the book is that it is one of the few of the stories that has a recognizably American ambience. However, its significance for Baum's subsequent career is very much greater because the story contains seeds that took root and continued to grow until in Baum's last fantasy, *Glinda of Oz* (1920), published the year after his death, another—or perhaps the same—Dorothy, a mortal, American child, has become a princess of one of the most detailed, satisfying, and magnificent fairylands ever to be created: the Land of Oz, the center of a whole continent of fantasy countries whose histories, geographies, and strange and interesting inhabitants are detailed. Along the way, Baum had also created a distinctly American form of fantasy and had provided this raw, new country with a mythology—an American mythology.

6

This study intends to rediscover Baum's original Other-world by extracting those glimpses—those "introductory interiors"—from his fantasy works and by tracing the sometimes rocky road of its development. Because of Baum's importance to the history of American children's literature and to the fantasy tradition in America, there are significant reasons why such a study should be done.

1. By the time of Baum's death in 1919, he had written fourteen full-length Oz books, six small Oz booklets for younger readers, and a series of twenty-seven newspaper stories about his Oz characters. Baum also shared with Doyle the experience of having the very "life" he had given to one of his creations, like the Frankenstein monster, take over, change, and direct the course of his life and work to such a great extent that he, like Doyle, tried to destroy his creation—Doyle by "killing" Holmes in "The Final Problem," and Baum by making his fairyland of Oz invisible and closed to the outside world in *The Emerald City of Oz*. Both attempts were unsuccessful, and both creations continue today as healthy and strong as they were in their authors' lifetimes.

Although Oz came to dominate Baum's life, the Oz books were not his only fantasies, and Oz was only a part of the vast continent of Baum's imagination. He managed to publish ten full-length fantasies, four volumes of short stories, and approximately twenty miscellaneous fairy tales chronicling other parts of his imaginary world before the overwhelming popularity of Oz, coupled with circumstances in his personal life, forced him to become reconciled to being, above all other things, the "Royal Historian of Oz." Therefore, Baum's imaginary world does not exist in its totality in his Oz books; rather, it was built up through the entire course of both his Oz and his non-Oz fantasies.

While the full-length Oz books have always been available, most of Baum's other fantasies were out of print (as some of them still are) and not easy to find for many years. For that reason, it is often very difficult for the general reader today to form an accurate picture of Baum's entire Other-world.

2. Baum's original conception should be reexamined because

much of it has been so expanded and embellished in the books published since his death that in many instances it is almost unrecognizable. Because of the popularity of the Oz books, his publisher elected to continue the series with other authors, who had very different approaches to fantasy. Such was the strength of Baum's world that the series lasted for twenty-five more books until the original impulse had become stretched so thin that the series finally collapsed (as a professional publishing venture) from its own weight. The Epilogue to this study will discuss the evolution of Oz after Baum's death and, as nonprofessional publishing ventures, the continued publication of books in the series because there still exists, just as in Baum's lifetime, a host of readers who demand "more about Oz."

3. Baum's vision has educated the imaginations of generations of American children. Because he had a unique way of looking at the world around him, America can never again be a country without magic. Wherever he looked—at the settled areas of the Northeast, at the booming midwestern city of Chicago, at the frontier towns of the Dakota Territory, at the endless prairie of Kansas and Iowa, at the American deserts, or at the Mediterranean-like paradise of southern California—his imagination filled those places with magic, enchantment, and wonderful beings. He put wizards in our cities, magic and enchantment on the prairie, and fairies in the forests, oceans, and skies. By doing those things, he helped create a sense of wonder in the children and gave them, as Attebery put it, "a new freedom of the imagination."[12]

4. Baum was able to experience the United States in more variety and depth than most other people of his generation. He lived and worked from New York City to Los Angeles: he was an actor in New York, a playwright and actor who toured most of the Northeast and Midwest, a storekeeper and newspaper publisher in a frontier town, a traveling salesman throughout most of the Midwest, a technical-magazine editor in Chicago, and a film producer in Hollywood—to name only a few of his many endeavors. And the development of his fantasy world reflects directly and indirectly his encounters with America, as well as the circumstances and other interests of his life.

8

5. Baum's was a vision that should not be diluted or lost because its importance to American society has only increased with the passing years. Carpenter called *The Wizard of Oz* a "subversive tale" and wrote:

> *Only with* The Wonderful Wizard of Oz, *published in the first year of the new century, did the United States produce a fantasy which, like its great British counterparts, examined society critically in fairy story terms. Baum's was an isolated voice . . . ; no one managed to equal his achievement for more than half a century after the first appearance in print of Dorothy, the Tin Man, the Scarecrow, and the Cowardly Lion. America was still possessed with the kind of optimism that had infected British society around the time of the Great Exhibition; and optimistic societies do not, apparently, produce great fantasies.*[13]

Optimistic societies that are pleased with themselves and their prospects have no reason to look for an "Arcadia" or a "Good Place," and Baum was no reactionary who longed for some past golden age. He eagerly embraced the discoveries and inventions of his own day (they seemed as much like fairy tales to him as his own stories) and incorporated many of them into his tales, mixing magic and machines in a way that had not been done before. But his *was* an isolated voice because his vision was not blinded by the spirit of optimism to the potential dangers inherent in some of those discoveries or to the flaws in the American Dream.

Baum believed in dreams and imagination; he believed that they "are likely to lead to the betterment of the world,"[14] but the operative word is "betterment." His imagination enabled him to look past the newness of the discoveries and inventions to their future uses and abuses, and his clear-sightedness forced him to realize that the human spirit had not kept pace with technological progress. Because of that perspicacity, many of the themes he dealt with in his books are startlingly modern: the spoiling of the environment, the protection of human freedom in a technological age, the frightening emphasis placed on destruction rather

THE
EMERALD CITY
OF
OZ

than creation, and the inability of people to control some of the forces they unleash.

In Baum's early stories, his Other-world seems very close to the real world, just down the road or around a corner; but later, as his Other-world becomes more and more a picture of what America was capable of, but falling short of, it begins receding farther and farther from the every-day one. Some of Baum's ideas and criticisms of the American Dream are still too radical to be fully accepted, but it is easy to understand why, as shown in Raylyn Moore's book *Wonderful Wizard, Marvelous Land*, the generation of the 1960s rediscovered Baum and embraced him as one of their own.[15] Baum's isolated voice still tells us that a society cannot be self-satisfied, that unless it recognizes its flaws and looks for that "Good Place," there will not be progress in the most important area of all—the minds and hearts of its people.

6. After the long period between Edward Wagenknecht's short study, *Utopia Americana* (1929), and Martin Gardner and Russel B. Nye's essays in *The Wizard of Oz and Who He Was* (1957) when only a few important articles about Baum appeared, an increasing number of books and articles dealing with Baum and his works have been published (for a detailed list, see the Bibliography). Of the books, the official biography, *To Please a Child*, by Baum's son Frank Joslyn Baum and Russell P. MacFall, appeared in 1961; Michael Patrick Hearn's *The Annotated Wizard of Oz* in 1973; Raylyn Moore's *Wonderful Wizard, Marvelous Land* in 1974; Hearn's Critical Heritage Series edition of *The Wizard of Oz* in 1983; and Angelica Shirley Carpenter and Jean Shirley's *L. Frank Baum* (a biography for younger readers) in 1992. Two beautifully illustrated books, David L. Greene and Dick Martin's *The Oz Scrap Book* (1977) and Allen Eyles's *The World of Oz* (1985), give brief overviews of the entire Oz series. Baum and Oz have been given considerable attention in two im-

John R. Neill's fanciful half-title illustration for The Emerald City of Oz *(1910). Baum attempted to end the Oz series with this book.*

11

portant critical studies: Roger Sale's *Fairy Tales and After* (1978) and Brian Attebery's *The Fantasy Tradition in American Literature* (1980), in which Baum is given credit for having founded a tradition of American fantasy. There have also been many articles dealing with individual aspects of his works.

No study, however, has examined his fantasy solely from the standpoint of his Other-world or examined that Other-world as a whole. Understandably, because Oz is what Baum is best remembered for, the tendency has been to concentrate on his masterpiece, *The Wonderful Wizard of Oz,* or to deal with his Oz series without giving much emphasis to his non-Oz fantasies. Yet Baum's Other-world includes much besides Oz, and Oz itself was not a static creation; it developed and changed over the course of the books in the series. Therefore, considering Oz only as an inert, unchanging imaginary world can lead to confusion and sometimes misunderstanding. For example, when comparing Mo, Baum's first imaginary country, with Oz, Martin Gardner wrote: "There are many ways in which Mo resembles Oz. . . . Its human inhabitants do not grow old or die. . . . It is a land without money or poverty."[16] The reader familiar with Baum's fantasies knows that Gardner, who is an authority on Oz, was referring to Oz as it had developed by the end of Baum's series, but a new reader would assume that Baum originally created Oz and Mo as similarly styled fairylands, which is certainly not the case. They were quite different in almost all major respects; Oz began to resemble the earlier country only after the series was well advanced.

Because Baum did alter his conception of Oz several times, problems such as this do crop up especially when dealing with books in the series other than *The Wizard,* and this study traces the growth of Oz and of Baum's other imaginary countries through *all* the stages of their development and through the steps by which they were drawn together into a single Other-world. Therefore, this book, which attempts to bring some order and clarity to Baum's extraordinary imaginary creations and thus reduce possible confusion, is intended as a supplement to the many excellent studies of Baum that have been done.

My approach will be to examine each of Baum's relevant fantasies (whether book-length or short story), to analyze the glimpses of his Other-world, and to piece together a picture of the way in which that world emerged, was changed, was modified, or was enlarged from its beginning until Baum's death. I will also point out how that world and its development reflected the circumstances of Baum's life and his experiences of America. For the purposes of this study, all his works of fantasy are of equal importance, and there will be little attempt at critical evaluation of the books because some stories that critics count among his weakest from the standpoint of plot, characters, and theme are among his strongest from the standpoint of the development of his Other-world.

To be able to draw correlations between the developments in Baum's fantasy world and the events in his real life, I will include necessary biographical details at the appropriate places in the various chapters. In one major instance, however, that is impossible. Baum did not publish his first book for children until he was forty-one years old; he had always loved children and had often told them stories, but of all the career projects he had been involved in, the career of being America's most beloved author of children's books was the one he fell into almost by accident. Yet very many of the experiences and jobs he had had and the skills he had acquired in his first forty years were important to the later development of his fantasy world. Therefore, before the exploration of his imaginary continent can begin, it will be necessary to present a very brief survey of the first part of Baum's life.

Chapter One

Charmed Youth and Years of Struggle
1856–1895

"[Children's] joy is in being alive, and they do not stop to think. In after years the doom of mankind overtakes them, and they find they must struggle and worry, work and fret, to gain the wealth that is so dear to the hearts of men."

"Yet every man has his mission, which is to leave the world better, in some way, than he found it. I am of the race of men, and man's lot is my lot."

With that he gave them all a loving look and turned away. There was no need to say good by, but for him the sweet, wild life of the Forest was over. He went forth bravely to meet his doom—the doom of the race of man—the necessity to worry and work.

L. Frank Baum,
The Life and Adventures of Santa Claus (1902)

L. Frank Baum's life followed a course as strange and convoluted as any plot he ever devised. If one imagines a story constructed of elements mixed together indiscriminately from a Horatio Alger tale, Mark Twain's *The Gilded Age*, and Booth Tarkington's *The Magnificent Ambersons* and leavened with fair-size amounts of Thomas Edison, P. T. Barnum, and David Belasco, one may begin to have an idea of what his life was like.

Lyman Frank Baum was born on May 15, 1856, in the village of Chittenango, New York, a few miles east of Syracuse. Frank was the seventh of nine children born to Benjamin Ward and Cynthia Stanton Baum, but four of the children died in infancy and Frank himself was born with "a seriously defective heart."[1]

His father and his uncle Lyman Baum (for whom he was named) owned and operated a factory located on the edge of the village that made "tight barrels and butter firkins."[2] Three years after Frank's birth, the discovery of oil in Titusville, Pennsylvania, caused a dramatic upswing in the Baum family fortunes. Benjamin Baum immediately saw the new industry's need for good barrels, and he soon recognized the even greater possibilities inherent in becoming part of the oil industry. He began developing his own oil fields. By the time Frank was four years old, his family was no longer merely comfortable; they were affluent and on their way to becoming wealthy.

In 1860 Benjamin bought "a residential farm property just north of Syracuse" that consisted of a large house and fifteen acres of land.[3] Cynthia Baum called the estate Rose Lawn because the gardens were filled with rosebushes. The family also acquired a large town house in Syracuse, but except "in cold weather, or when social obligations called them," they were at Rose Lawn.[4] The country estate, which has been compared with Mark Twain's description of the Bolton estate in *The Gilded Age*, proved to be an ideal and idyllic place for the children to grow up.[5] Rose Lawn and Frank's happiness there were reflected in several of his later books; he described it in *Dot and Tot of Merryland:*

> *The cool but sun-kissed mansion seemed delightful after the stuffy, formal city house. It was built in a quaint yet pretty fashion, with many wings and gables and broad verandas on every side. Before it were acres and acres of velvety green lawn, sprinkled with shrubbery and dotted with beds of bright flowers. In every direction were winding paths, covered with white gravel, which led to all parts of the grounds, looking for all the world like a map.*[6]

The one great shadow on Frank's childhood was heart disease, which he suffered from all his life: "In early manhood, heart attacks several times caused him to fall unconscious. Later in life he would walk the floor in agony, tears streaming from his eyes as he fought the pangs of angina pectoris."[7] His poor health caused him to receive most of his education from private tutors, except for a year at the Syracuse Classical School and two unhappy years at Peekskill Military School.[8] Nevertheless, his physical handicap does not seem to have had any emotional ill-effects. Being limited to more sedate kinds of activity—reading and dreaming among them—may, indeed, have developed those very qualities of imagination and vision in which he later excelled. He could not join in the more boisterous games of the other children, but he was far from an inactive child; he was always becoming interested in something new and dreaming up new projects.

The unusual and important thing about those youthful projects is that they were not the passing fancies of an idle child in delicate health. He mastered each one to a degree that some internal idea of excellence demanded, and rather than discarding any of them, each became part of the pattern of his life. Some hobbies, after their initial appearance, never regained dominance but always remained part of the background: breeding prize chickens, collecting stamps, studying music, and gardening. Other projects persistently remained central, leading to his successful career: printing and writing. And one interest often outshone all the others and kept bursting in, for good or ill, throughout his life: his love of the theater.

Young Frank was meant to take over the agricultural part of his father's business interests,[9] but he early began to develop those interests that were very far removed from agriculture. Surprisingly, those new, and sometimes unusual, activities did not seem to cause conflict within the family. Perhaps Frank's fragile health caused his parents to be more indulgent with him, to allow him a greater range of self-expression. They had lost four of their children at, or soon after, birth and probably were fearful that they would lose him also, but young "Frankie" Baum (as he was listed in the 1860 census) was not growing up to be another Georgie Amberson Minafer.[10] He always took the responsibility for his projects and always justified his parents' faith in him.

The most significant of his youthful enterprises was his involvement with printing. In 1870, when he was fourteen, he became fascinated by a print shop and immediately decided to become a newspaperman when he grew up. His father bought him the best amateur printing press and equipment available, and before long Frank produced the first issue of the *Rose Lawn Home Journal,* an amateur newspaper that he continued to publish for two years. Besides the obvious benefits to him from such a

17

hobby—the valuable experience in writing and editing—it also showed Baum's determination to excel at whatever he attempted because printing is a craft that requires skill, immense patience, and much hard work before it will yield satisfactory results. But he persevered, and the surviving copies of the newspaper exhibit competence in typesetting and design.[11] After he stopped publishing the *Journal,* he began a new paper that combined his printing skills with his interest in stamps. The *Stamp Collector* lasted about a year, until in 1873 he acquired a better press and, with Thomas G. Alvord, Jr., the New York lieutenant governor's son, began publishing another paper, the *Empire.*[12]

Frank seemed destined to achieve his ambition of becoming a newspaperman, but in 1874 there occurred an event that changed the course of his life. As one of his many business interests, Benjamin Baum had acquired a small chain of theaters, and it was at one of those theaters in Gilmore, Pennsylvania, that Frank first saw a company perform some of Shakespeare's plays.[13] He became completely stage-struck and decided almost immediately that acting was the career for him.

Although his lasting fame would ultimately come from another source, his love for the theater—its glamour and its illusion—remained with him for the rest of his life and affected just about everything he did, especially his writing career. It is very possible that the theater was largely responsible for his continuing the Oz series; it is certain that it had much to do with the contents of at least three of the Oz books.

Young Baum began the pursuit of his new ambition with his usual zeal and with many things in his favor. He had grown up into a strikingly handsome young man (even in his last years, he remained a handsome and distinguished-looking man); he had a good voice; he had a charming and engaging manner; and he had ambition, intelligence, and discipline. But his first experience was not a happy one.

When Frank approached the manager of a rather seedy, provincial theater company, he was too inexperienced with the world to disbelieve the manager when he told Frank that he would engage him to play the leads in all of Shakespeare's plays *if* Frank supplied all his own costumes, which would cost several thousand dollars. With great enthusiasm, Frank approached his parents with the plan. The elder Baum was an intelligent man and a good businessman who had had dealings with "show folk," yet he did agree to finance his son, perhaps believing that the resulting disillusionment would get the acting business out of Frank's blood. Therefore, equipped with a wardrobe of beautiful and expensive costumes, Frank embarked on his first encounter with the stage. It did not work out the way he had hoped. One actor after another in the company began borrowing the fine costumes from him until, at the end of the run, he had no costumes left and had had only a couple of walk-on parts.[14] One wonders if the many confidence men and humbugs in his writings stemmed from this incident.

It was a bitter experience, especially for a youth who had known only the kindness and fair-play of his family; it was an experience that would have killed many a youth's interest in the stage. Chastened, he returned home and worked for the next two years as a clerk in one of the family businesses: Neal, Baum and Company, "importers and jobbers of dry goods."[15]

He had not lost his interest in printing, but lacked the time necessary to pursue it. However, in later years his experience with the craft stood him in good stead (as did, oddly enough, his experiences with dry goods). Actually handling the type and creating designs gave him firsthand knowledge of what goes into making a book, as well as an understanding of the limitations and possibilities of type design that later played an important part in making his children's books some of the most innovative and beautiful ever published. He was never content with merely enjoying the finished product, with merely enjoying the surface illusion. It was the same with printing as it was with acting: he wanted to know what went on behind the scenes; he wanted to be the creator of the illusion himself.

Baum's interest in the stage had not been killed, only dampened for a little while, and in 1878 he joined a legitimate company in New York City. The company was Albert M. Palmer's Union Square Theater, which had the facilities to teach new actors. Frank, using the stage name Louis F.

Baum, soon had a role in Bronson Howard's *The Banker's Daughter*, which
turned out to be one of the most successful of the company's productions.
The play opened on November 30, 1878, and ran for a hundred performances, which was quite a respectable run at that time.[16]

For some reason, this success was not followed by another acting
job, and Frank took his first professional job as a newspaperman in New
York; but soon after, through his father's influence, he got a job on a newspaper in Bradford, Pennsylvania.[17] It may have been that his father wanted
to get him out of the big city, but it was not to lure him away from the
theater. After Frank had worked on the Pennsylvania newspaper for about
a year, his father wisely made him the manager of his string of theaters—
letting Frank do what he most wanted to do and still keeping him within
the family circle. And after Frank had proved himself in that position, his
father deeded the theaters to him.[18] One can imagine the elder Baum's
sigh of relief that his talented, but mercurial, son was at last settled in a
profession he loved, and one that would also provide for his future security.

Managing the theaters, however, was not all that Frank did; he
also acted in them. His company produced versions of some of Shakespeare's plays, and Baum was finally able to appear in Shakespeare—he
even played Hamlet![19] Also, being aware of the tastes of the audiences of
the provincial theaters, he undertook to supply original plays for his theaters. In 1882 two of his plays were produced. The second, *Matches*, did
not cause much of a stir, but the first, *The Maid of Arran*, an Irish melo-
drama based on the novel *A Princess of Thule* by William Black, proved to
be a hit. Baum not only wrote the play, the lyrics, and the music, but also
played one of the leads![20]

This period of his professional life also proved to be an important
time in his personal life. During the Christmas holidays of 1881, which
he spent with his parents in Syracuse, he met Maud Gage, the daughter of
the well-known suffragette Matilda Electa Joslyn Gage, co-author with
Susan B. Anthony and Elizabeth Cady Stanton of the four-volume *History of Woman Suffrage*.[21] Miss Gage was someone whom Frank wanted to
know better.

During the summer of 1882, *The Maid of Arran* played in New York City for a week and then began a tour of the Northeast. Whenever possible, Baum returned to Fayetteville, New York, to improve his acquaintance with Maud. By the end of the summer, he had proposed. Even though Frank came from a wealthy and prominent family, it was not a time when parents approved of a daughter marrying an actor. But Matilda Gage, standing by her lifelong convictions of the rights of women, let her daughter choose for herself. Maud said yes.

The Maid of Arran was already scheduled for an autumn tour of the Midwest, but Frank temporarily left his company to marry Maud in early November. After a brief honeymoon in Saratoga Springs, he and his bride rejoined the tour in Michigan, and in December the company moved into Kansas. Early in the tour, Frank had had his first view of Chicago and had been favorably impressed, but Maud was not pleased with what she saw on the second half. She wrote to her brother, who was living in the Dakota Territory: "I don't see how you can like the West. I wouldn't be hired to live there. . . . I never in my life was in such a wild rough place as Sioux City."[22] She also did not like living out of a trunk. In early 1883, after the tour ended, Maud decided that they should have a home, and Frank agreed to a more settled way of life. The couple rented a house in Syracuse, and Baum left the company but continued to work on plays for possible production. By late April, Maud knew that she was pregnant, and in July, Frank rejoined the family business.[23]

Frank Baum and Maud Gage had very different personalities, but they complemented each other and theirs became a happy partnership rather than a marriage typical for that time. Also, Frank took an equal part in the raising of their children, and the loneliest times in his future life were those when circumstances prevented him from being with his family. But he gladly turned over all practical matters to Maud, who was better equipped by temperament to deal with them, and she, in turn, never discouraged him from following his dreams.

Their first child was born in December 1883, and Christmas must have been an especially happy and joyful time that year. Frank's

21

parents, brothers, and sisters were nearby to help celebrate the season, and the young couple's house had become the scene for many pleasant parties. There was Rose Lawn to look forward to when the weather was better, and parties and gatherings in the great Syracuse town house. The theaters were bringing in a good income, as was Frank's job in the family business. Maud was happy with her home, and Frank was getting his creative fulfillment from the work he was doing on new plays for his company. They were immensely proud of their new son, and the future seemed without worry.

What Frank did not know was that this Christmas was to be the high point of his early life, and the last one for a very long time that was to be serenely happy. The Baums were a perfect example of the general idea of the American Dream, which promised that any man who was willing to work, who was ambitious, and who had his wits about him could make a success. But there were other parts of the American experience that were usually glossed over and not talked about: the fierce competition; the men with ambition who were struggling to realize the dream, but by dishonest means; and the dark secret of the dream, that it was not a progression but a cycle. In 1884 began a series of events and coincidences that rivaled any that Booth Tarkington later devised in *The Magnificent Ambersons*—the Baum family was soon to experience the downside of that cycle.

It is interesting to speculate about what Baum's life would have been like if it had continued in the charmed manner it had until 1884. His inventive and creative mind would still have needed an outlet. He might even have written children's books, but they would have been very different children's books from those he did write because Baum's imagination needed his struggles and experiences with America to spark the magic. However, the charmed life did not continue, and he was soon forced to begin a more intimate acquaintance with this country than he could ever have imagined possible.

When Frank had become involved in writing and acting for his theaters, his uncle John Wesley Baum had taken over the job of manager. In 1884 John became ill, and the bookkeeper took over his duties. The bookkeeper mismanaged the theaters and absconded with the money. Then, almost at the same time, the theater in Gilmore, Pennsylvania, burned and, with it, all the props and scenery for the plays, including *The Maid of Arran*. After all the debts had been settled, Baum had lost his real estate as well as the rights to *The Maid*.[24]

Along with losing a large part of his income, Baum lost his close connection with the greatest interest of his life, but he had a family to support, and there were the family businesses to fall back on. One can be certain that Baum was not without plans for the future, and most assuredly, those plans would have included writing more plays and perhaps managing a new theater company. He probably considered it only a short break in his theatrical career, but fortune had more shocks in store for him and it would be many years before he would return to the professional theater.

His most pressing problem at that time was the support of his wife and child; therefore, in early 1885 he became the superintendent of his elder brother's chemical-manufacturing company, Baum's Castorine Company, which was located at the retail oil outlet that Frank was in charge of in Syracuse. Despite the high-sounding title, Frank was the head salesman, and he had to go on the road.[25] That was the first of the jobs that took him away from his family, and he hated it. The many instances in his later stories of exiles longing for home surely stemmed from those traveling experiences.

Even if Baum had felt as though he was having to start all over, the family security of the Baums' wealth was still intact—but not for long. Later in 1885, his father had an accident, and when he did not recover as quickly as he should have, he went to Germany to consult with doctors there. While the elder Baum was away, there was a repetition of his son's experience: his business was mismanaged by dishonest employees, and when he returned home, it was too late. Frank's parents had to sell the farm and the Rose Lawn estate and move to a smaller house in Syracuse.[26]

After the birth of the Baums' second son in February 1886, Maud was seriously ill for several months. Because Frank had to be on the road so much of the time, he moved his small family into another house so that Maud would be near some of her relatives. To add to their troubles, only a few weeks after the baby was born, Frank's elder brother, Benjamin William, died, and his father's continuing bad health was a constant source of worry because the doctors in Germany had been able to do little good. The financial reverses that had met the elder Baum on his return had done more harm, and Frank's father died in early 1887.[27]

What a trauma that was for him when his lifelong source of support and strength was taken away. He must have felt as though his world was crumbling around him as event after event showed him the fragility of the American Dream. And still his troubles were not over. Going into the oil store early one morning in the spring of 1887, Frank discovered the dead body of the store's clerk. The clerk had shot himself, and soon after, it was discovered that he had gambled away most of the capital. So bad was the situation that the store had to be sold, and suddenly Frank was left without family resources and only a little money.[28] In less than four years, he had gone from an assured future of wealth and ease to an uncertain future with no financial resources. He still, however, possessed his most valuable personal possession—his imagination—and added to that was a belief in himself. He was a little old to be a Horatio Alger hero, but that did not deter him. He began again.

When L. Frank Baum had been growing up, he had been given every advantage, had been able to take security for granted, had been allowed almost free rein by his parents, and had been raised as a gentleman. He had had little preparation for a life of struggle and hardship, but along with all his advantages, he had had instilled in him the American virtue of hard work and the idea that a person should strive to improve the lot of mankind. It never occurred to him to give up. Years later in his book *Aunt Jane's Nieces and Uncle John* (1911), he made an interesting comparison between the English gentleman and the American version. His characters, a self-made millionaire and his nieces, are taking a motor trip through the still Wild West. The main problem that they encounter is not with Indians or with outlaws, but with a group of men called "Remittance

24

men," younger sons of wealthy English families or sons of noble English families who had gotten into trouble and had been sent to the American Southwest to keep them out of their families' way. While Baum admitted that some of the "Remittance men" had made something of themselves, many more merely existed any way they could on the small allowances they received from home. Baum's characters, Uncle John and his niece Patsy, have the following conversation with one of the younger men:

> "Your system of inheritance and entail may be somewhat to blame, [said Uncle John] but your worst fault is in rearing a class of mollycoddles and social drones who are never of benefit to themselves or the world at large. You, sir, I consider something less than a man."
>
> "I agree with you," replied Tim, readily. "I'm only good to cumber the earth, and if I get little pleasure out of life I must admit that it's all I'm entitled to."
>
> "And you can't break your bonds and escape?" asked Patsy.
>
> "I don't care to. People who are ambitious to do things merely bore me. I don't admire them or care to imitate them."
>
> From that moment they took no further interest in the handsome outcast. His world was not their world.[29]

Frank Baum *was* "ambitious to do things," but the decision that he and Maud made concerning the way to start over was a radical one. Maud's brother in the Dakota Territory had been writing to them about the great opportunities of the boom the territory was experiencing, and despite her earlier aversion to the West, Maud urged that they join her brother there. Frank's wife thus proved herself to be as adventurous as her husband because it was largely at her insistence that he made an exploratory journey to the Dakota Territory. He liked what he saw and returned home to help his family get ready for the move.[30]

On September 20, 1888, Frank, his wife, and their two sons

arrived in Aberdeen, Dakota Territory, and he soon opened a store called Baum's Bazaar, which sold a little bit of everything.[31] Aberdeen was a very young city, but it had grown rapidly with the influx of new settlers. Unfortunately for the Baums, their arrival coincided with the end of the boom and the beginning of a depression for that area. Frank was able to keep his store open only until the end of 1889. It closed soon after his third son was born in December 1889. Before the store closed, however, it had endeared itself to the local children as a place where they could be certain of hearing "Mr. Baum" tell a new and exciting story.

In 1890 Aberdeen supported a disproportionate number of newspapers—seven weeklies and two dailies—to publish the legal notices associated with the homesteading activity in the area.[32] Just about the time that Baum's store closed, one of those newspapers was put up for sale, and he bought it. Renamed the *Aberdeen Saturday Pioneer,* the first issue appeared on January 25, 1890.[33] Having his own newspaper gave Baum the opportunity to express his own views and opinions, and his editorials ranged over a wide variety of topics: from Theosophy to the rights of women to a comparison of Shakespeare's, Edward Bulwer-Lytton's and H. Rider Haggard's mysticism.[34]

The best of his columns for his paper is entitled "Our Landlady." It is reminiscent of Oliver Wendell Holmes's *The Autocrat of the Breakfast Table,* except that Baum's "autocrat" is the landlady of the boarding house, "a smart but uneducated woman who spoke in pungent vernacular."[35] One "Our Landlady" column, that of January 3, 1891, is particularly interesting because it may be the first time in print that Baum described "a much more wonderful place" than our everyday world.[36] The column deals, in a fantasy mode, with the future possibilities of electricity and details a series of inventions that would have given even Edison a few new ideas.

Baum tried very hard to make his newspaper a success, but the

---

W. W. Denslow's drawing of Baum for the Introduction to Father Goose, His Book *(1899).*

27

same depression that had caused the failure of his store made it impossible for Aberdeen to continue supporting so many newspapers. In the spring of 1891, he lost the paper, and around the same time, his fourth son was born. It was time to start over yet again, and this time he and Maud set their sights on Chicago. Once the Baums had made their decision to go west, they evidently never considered the possibility of living in the East again, but even they probably had no idea how far west they would eventually go.

It was an exciting time to be in Chicago; in a bare eighteen years, the city had literally risen from the ashes of the disastrous fire, and in 1891 was making preparations for one of the most spectacular of the great exhibitions: the World's Columbian Exposition. But this time Baum's entry into the city was less auspicious than it had been in 1882, when he was a successful playwright and actor. It was reported in Aberdeen that Baum moved to Chicago to accept a job on one of the major newspapers there,[37] and he did work as a reporter for a very short time. But with a wife and four children to support, he had to earn more money. He soon took a job with Siegel, Cooper and Company as a buyer, but later he accepted a position with Pitkin and Brooks (dealers in fine china and glassware).[38] The salary was better, but he was again a traveling salesman with much of the Midwest as his territory. Such a job was very hard on Baum, not only because his health was never robust or because he had to be away from his beloved family, but also because the average traveling salesman of that time was usually a very different type of person from him. He enjoyed the company of men of like interests, but he had nothing in common with the traveling fraternity. While they wiled away the tedious time on the train with card games and idle talk, he watched the landscape fly by and let his imagination wander freely; while they gathered around the stove in the hotel and told stories no lady could hear, he sat by himself and jotted down nonsense verse and stories with which to amuse his children when he returned home.[39]

That was probably the lowest point in Baum's life. There had been troubles enough in Syracuse, but they had been the result of chance and the dishonesty of others and had not shaken his confidence in himself. This time, he himself had failed; he had tried twice on the frontier and failed. There is no doubt that his mind still teemed with projects, but necessity now forced them to be of a more practical nature. They had to solve the problem of supporting his family in a comfortable style while allowing him to give up traveling and to be at home with them. He had not yet come up with the answer, and he had many more wearisome train rides and lonely nights in strange hotels before he did.

His imagination, though, would not always stay on practical matters, and if he could do nothing else, he could bring some joy and excitement into his children's lives with the stories he made up. Thinking only about pleasing his children with the story ideas he sketched out on pieces of paper, he had in his hands the key to his success. Maud's mother, Matilda Gage, who spent most winters with them in Chicago, often heard the stories Frank told his children and urged him repeatedly to write them down and publish them in a book because other children also would enjoy them. Matilda Gage was a "strong-minded" woman, and he finally began to listen to her.[40] On the day that L. Frank Baum began to take the advice of his mother-in-law seriously, even his vivid imagination could not have conceived that he was poised on the brink of a career that would make him one of the most beloved men in America or that he was about to discover a world that, to the children, would be as real and as important as America itself.

Chapter Two

The Discovery of the Other-World

1896–1900

We cannot measure a child by a standard of size or age. The big folk who are children will be our comrades; the others we need not consider at all, for they are self-exiled from our domain.

L. Frank Baum,
"To the Reader" in
A New Wonderland (1900)

L. Frank Baum began writing down some of his stories in 1895, but he was not yet convinced that his true vocation lay in writing for children. He also tried his hand at humorous poems and adult stories, which he published in newspapers. One story, "Yesterday at the Exposition," is a tale of futuristic inventions observed at the Chicago International Exposition in the year 2090.[1]

Once Baum was writing, he surely felt more comfortable on his visits to the Press Club and the Athletic Club, where he went to keep in contact with "the literary and business communities."[2] There he met most of Chicago's leading literary figures and publishers. On one of his visits to the Press Club in 1896, Baum mentioned to the popular novelist Opie Read that he had just copyrighted two books for children, *Adventures in Phunniland* and *Tales from Mother Goose*.[3] Read, in turn, brought Baum to the attention of Chauncey L. Williams of the Way & Williams publishing company.[4] After Williams had expressed an interest, Baum showed him *Tales from Mother Goose*, which Williams accepted for publication in 1897.

At last Baum was in the right place at the right time, and he fit perfectly in "the cultural ferment of the 'Chicago renaissance' of the 90's."[5]

With stories appearing in periodicals, with a book about to be published, and with the fellowship and encouragement of like-minded members of the clubs, Baum's confidence received a needed boost.

When Baum became excited about one project, other projects began popping into his mind, and he conceived an idea that would, he hoped, let him leave the road and return to his family. This had become an even more pressing need since his doctor had advised him to stop the constant traveling.[6] His idea was one that would call on knowledge acquired from many of his past endeavors: his experience with editing and design, with advertising, with working in dry-goods stores, and even with creating illusions in the theater. He wrote to his sister Mary Louise Brewster on October 3, 1897, just before the new project was to be launched: "I have wanted to quit traveling and find some employment that would enable me to stay at home, and I conceived the idea of a magazine devoted to window-trimming, which I know is greatly needed and would prosper if ever I could get it going."[7]

The magazine was called the *Show Window: A Monthly Journal of Practical Window Trimming,* and the first issue was published on November 1, 1897. It was a success and fulfilled Baum's hopes for it. In 1900 a collection of his articles from it was published in book form as *The Art of Decorating Dry Good Windows and Interiors* and appears rather oddly in his bibliography as the book published only a month after the publication of his fantasy classic, *The Wonderful Wizard of Oz!* Baum edited the magazine until 1902 when his success as a writer of children's books seemed assured and when his reawakened interest in the theater left him little time for it.[8]

After almost fourteen years of hardships, struggle, and failure, the Christmas of 1897 held for Baum and his family the hope of a better future; but for that future, he had, probably without realizing it, given up something important—his close contact with the countryside and vast spaces of America. Only once before, when he had been an actor for a short time in New York, had he lived in a very large city; it was to have an effect on him.

A NEW WONDERLAND
(THE MAGICAL MONARCH OF MO)

With only a few exceptions, the order of publication of Baum's stories is fairly close to the chronological order of their composition. One exception, however, appears right at the beginning of his career. *Mother Goose in Prose* (the final title of *Tales from Mother Goose*) was the first of Baum's books for children to be published, but it was not the first to be written. That was the book copyrighted under the title *Adventures in Phunniland* and finally published as *A New Wonderland* (with the spelling of the country changed to Phunnyland) in 1900, the month after *The Wonderful Wizard of Oz.*[9] In 1903 the book was reissued by the Bobbs-Merrill Company of Indianapolis under the new title *The Surprising Adventures of The Magical Monarch of Mo and His People.*[10] For the new edition, Baum revised the first chapter and substituted the new name of the country, Mo, for all references to Phunnyland. It is the text of the 1903 edition that will be used here because it was as Mo that this first of his imaginary countries later took its place in his fantasy continent.

The Magical Monarch of Mo, a collection of stories about the "Beautiful Valley" of Mo and the people who live there, effectively displays two of Baum's greatest talents: telling a good story and creating imaginative fantasy environments. He was a natural storyteller, and these stories are filled with fantastic characters, outrageous situations, absurd logic, and broad humor: the king escapes from a deep hole by turning the hole upside down; a donkey is one of the wisest beings in the kingdom because he has eaten and digested all the schoolbooks; the kingdom is saved from a cast-iron man by tickling him with a feather; a wicked wizard steals the toe of a princess; a prince goes through a giant's clothes wringer and is then blown up like a balloon; and a naughty dragon is destroyed by being stretched thin enough to be used for fiddle strings.[11]

Martin Gardner considered the humor to be "of the Carrollian variety,"[12] and Baum or the publisher must also have thought so to give the book on its first appearance the title of *A New Wonderland*. Certainly there are echoes of Lewis Carroll, but the stories are so robust, so abounding in exaggerated situations, and so filled, as Gardner noted, with "the kind of sadistic absurdities that later became so characteristic of the animated cartoons"[13] that they fit more comfortably into another tradition: that of the American tall tale, some characteristics of which are "heroic self-projection, comedy and exaggeration."[14] It is a type of story that is "indigenous to the American frontier,"[15] and Baum had begun telling his stories on the frontier. The tales about Davy Crockett, Mike Fink, and later Paul Bunyan contain outrageous situations and "sadistic absurdities" closer in spirit to Baum's stories than Baum's are to Carroll's.

That Baum made Mo a kingdom with a king, a queen, and several royal children does not make the stories any less American because tall tales are made up of bits and pieces of folktales from Europe that were adapted to the new environment.[16] The king of Mo certainly does not act like a European king; he acts like an American child's idea of a king. He may go to fight a dragon, but he also goes to pick blackberries wearing his second-best crown; and he is extremely fond of ice cream and birthday parties. Another aspect of the stories that brings the tall tale to mind is the improbable juxtapositions of traditional elements and the modern world: a prince exiled to an island for misdeeds uses the telephone to contact the palace; the throne room of a sorceress is lit by electric lights; another prince goes exploring on a bicycle; and the princess, on a quest to recover her toe, has among her magic weapons a mirror, a magic veil, *and* a package of chewing gum![17]

In *The Magical Monarch of Mo,* Baum was just beginning to find his own distinctive voice. In his later stories, he considerably toned down the tall-tale elements, although he continued to use broad humor and moderate exaggeration. Later he particularly worked to eliminate any violence from his plots, but it is undeniable that there are many violent episodes in the Mo stories: the king has his head bitten off by the Purple Dragon and must find a new one; a dog is kicked so high that it is flattened like a rug when it lands; a lion and a tiger devour each other; and a prince is cut into many pieces by a monster. These events would have been horrible even in Wonderland, but Baum told them in such an outrageous, exaggerated manner that they are not offensive because they are too incredible. And possible offense is further lessened by the fact that in Mo everything is always put right by the end of the story: the king regains his own head; the dog is restored to its original shape; the lion and the tiger were fated to be destroyed because they were evil; and the prince is put together again with the only ill-effect being that he is "very stiff in the joints for several days."[18]

The one thing that most neutralizes the violence in these stories, however, is that Baum made his people immortal—not fairies or magicians, but just people who live forever and who "are always young and beautiful." He specifically pointed out that "no inhabitant of the Valley of Mo can ever be killed by anything. If one is cut to pieces, the pieces still live." And the situation is made even more comforting by the knowledge that "wild and ferocious beasts [and monsters] may be killed in Mo as well as in other parts of the world."[19] However, beasts and birds that are not wild and ferocious enjoy the same privileges as the other inhabitants, and all the animals are able to talk intelligently. This philosophy that evil is more easily destroyed than good appears again and again in Baum's fantasies.

As the setting for his fantastic characters and outrageous adventures, Baum created an imaginary kingdom just as fantastic and outrageous. Mo itself is a young child's vision of paradise; it is literally made of good things to eat. The paths are taffy, and the stones are "jackson-balls and gum-drops"; the mud is jelly or chocolate. There is "a rough plain, composed entirely of loaf sugar covered with boulders of rock candy" and another "composed entirely of maple sugar." Rivers flow with milk, root beer, or maple syrup with the islands in them made of fruitcake or cheese, and there is a lake of sugar syrup that makes a perfect place to go skating after the sun has "candied the surface of the lake." There is also a "pond of custard" in the "back yard" of the palace on which is a "floating island of whipped cream."[20]

"All kinds of candies and bonbons grow thick on the low bushes," and the crops grown by the people are such confections as caramels, cream puffs, and plum puddings; everything else they need, from hats to bicycles, grows on trees. Probably the most necessary tree in a country such as this is the medicine tree, the blossoms of which cure stomachaches.[21]

The natural laws in Mo are also quite different from those in our world: there is no night, and the rays of the sun are perfumed. Snow, rain, and thunderstorms, which in our world can be inconvenient and even frightening, are in Mo quite pleasant events: the snow is popcorn, "nicely buttered and salted"; the rain is lemonade; "the lightning in the sky resembles the most beautiful fireworks; and the thunder is usually a chorus from the opera of Tannhäuser."[22]

Baum also set Mo within a geography of its own. It is a valley composed of agricultural and residential land, forests, and two great plains; it is traversed by several rivers and surrounded by mountains. In the southern part of the valley is a wilder region where a river that flows with needles, a deep gulf, and a thick forest protect the marble palace and beautiful gardens of the friendly sorceress Maëtta. The valley next to Mo is inhabited by a friendly giant couple, and in another direction, across the mountains, is a desert. This geography takes on special significance later after Oz is created because Oz is completely surrounded by deserts, the only ones in Baum's fairy continent. To the north of the valley is the land of King Scowleyow, "whose people lived in caves and mines and dug iron and tin out of the rocks and melted them into bars." Farther north, past the land of Scowleyow, is the sea—another significant point because Baum's future continent was to be bounded by the sea.[23]

When Baum rewrote the first chapter of *A New Wonderland* for the new edition, his revisions consisted mainly of additional passages describing the Magical Monarch in more detail to fit the new title. He eliminated only the opening paragraph from the original. That paragraph is not necessary to the book, but it is important in tracing Baum's development, since it contains in embryonic form his conception of an Otherworld and his attitudes toward it:

36

I dare say you have never heard of the Valley of Phunnyland;
and that is not surprising for when a person has succeeded in
crossing the deserts and mountains that surround it, and has
once enjoyed the delights of the beautiful Valley, he seldom
cares to return to this side of the world again. For my part,
after I got there I suddenly remembered I had forgotten some-
thing, and so came back after it. And while I am here I will
tell you all I know about Phunnyland, for when I go back the
next time I shall probably stay there.[24]

For Baum, the magical place is a part of the real world, though an un-discovered part that is protected by natural barriers. As fantastic as the valley is, nowhere in the book does Baum refer to it as a fairyland; it is only a country very different from ours that is hidden by deserts and mountains. It is also a beautiful and desirable place that, once experienced, draws the traveler back.

Baum enhanced the illusion of Mo's proximity to our world by having the giant in the valley next to Mo walk "over into Alaska" or South America to catch his dinner. He also has a yellow hen from Mo briefly visit our world and tells the reader that Mo is to the west of us.[25] As far back as the sixteenth century, there were legends and stories of wonderful places and cities of gold located somewhere in the western part of America, so Baum's imaginary country was not solely dependent on the European fairyland tradition. The hardships and struggles that Baum had experienced in Aberdeen and Chicago would naturally make his imagination turn to a place of ease where all the good things one could want were supplied without effort. If he was not able to give his children the luxuries of life, he could at least tell them stories about them.

Yet even with all of Mo's wonderful qualities, Baum realized that "there is no country so delightful but that it suffers some disadvantages, and so it was with the Valley of Mo." One of the disadvantages is the villains: the Purple Dragon, a monster called a Gigaboo, a wicked wizard, and the evil King Scowleyow, who "hated the Monarch of Mo and all his people, because they lived so happily and cared nothing for money." But these villains are nonthreatening because whatever they attempt, the people of Mo are unaffected since they cannot be hurt. A far more dangerous threat arises from the very qualities that make Mo a paradise. The lives of people who live forever in an unchanging world where all their wants are supplied can very easily be turned from pleasure to torture by dissatisfaction and boredom. Baum dealt with that dilemma in two of the Mo stories, and it recurs in his later fantasies.[26]

However attractive or unattractive this magic land of sweet things may be to us, it is undeniable that Baum, in his first attempt, created a coherent and consistent secondary world that matched his stories perfectly. But even with his hints about the closeness of Mo to our own world, his fantastic kingdom, strange people, and outrageous adventures are too alien to draw the reader far into the stories. When Baum next attempted to create an imaginary country, he made it much more like the real world and, therefore, more believable. And to inspire belief in a fantasy story is to succeed.

MOTHER GOOSE IN PROSE

In contrast to *Adventures in Phunniland,* Baum's first book to be published, *Mother Goose in Prose,* was less fantastic and less original. However, Way & Williams obviously had high hopes for it because the publisher was unusually lavish in the production of the book. Maxfield Parrish was contracted to do the illustrations; it was the first book illustrated by the artist, and he made fourteen exquisite drawings for it. When it was published in October 1897, it was a beautiful example of bookmaking. Peter E. Hanff observed, "*Mother Goose in Prose* was an impressive first-publishing venture for L. Frank Baum and one that signalled his connection with children's books of striking graphic design."[27]

In this book, Baum created stories to explain some of the familiar

Mother Goose rhymes, and he prefaced the collection with a detailed, almost scholarly, introduction that describes the possible origins and history of the rhymes. The stories are well told and often charming, but they are deficient in the sense of place. They contain fantasy, talking animals, and, sometimes, the broad humor of his first book, but the settings are vague and indistinct. Only once, in the story based on "Old King Cole," did Baum give a name to the setting, calling the country Whatland, but not giving any further description. Many of the stories can be said to have English settings because they mention squires, English money, and titled characters or because they refer to specific places such as London, Norwich, and Sussex. Others give so little background that it is impossible to say where they take place. Only one of the stories, "Little Bun Rabbit," can be said to have a definite American aura about it, and then only because Santa Claus, the American version of St. Nicholas, is mentioned. It is in this story that "little Dorothy" makes her appearance. *Mother Goose in Prose*, like *Adventures in Phunniland*, is a source for many of the themes and character types that Baum would use later. "Little Bun Rabbit" contains the seeds of two of Baum's later books: *The Wonderful Wizard of Oz* and *The Life and Adventures of Santa Claus*.

Perhaps Baum was constrained by having to fit the stories to the rhymes, but in doing so, he made the mistake of taking the magic out of the nonsense and images in the rhymes. This is the one instance when his inventiveness and wonderful sense of fantasy are only sporadically in evidence. Instead of using the rhymes as springboards for flights of fantasy and journeys to Other-worlds, he made many of the stories less interesting and more prosaic than the original rhymes. There is evidence that he himself was aware of this. He wrote in the Introduction: "The snatches sung in the nursery are never forgotten, nor are they ever recalled without bringing back with them myriads of slumbering feelings and half-forgotten images." And he admitted that "there are others [rhymes] which are but bare suggestions, leaving the imagination to weave in the details of the story. Perhaps therein may lie part of their charm."[28] It was a mistake he did not make again.

When *Mother Goose in Prose* was published, it was not a failure, but neither was it an overwhelming success, although the book was reprinted several times in the following years. The Parrish illustrations and the beauty of the book were much admired, and Baum said later that the success of the book was more artistic than financial.[29]

FATHER GOOSE, HIS BOOK

Adventures in Phunniland was to have been published in 1898, but Way & Williams went out of business that year, and Baum had to look for another publisher. He was also very busy with the *Show Window*, which was promising to be an adequate means of support for him and his family. But even with all the work the magazine demanded, he found the time to begin a project for his own pleasure.

In the winter of 1897/1898, he called on his past experiences with printing, borrowed a small press and some type, and began to print a book of his verse.[30] The book, *By the Candelabra's Glare*, was for distribution only among his relatives and friends, and, as he related in the Foreword, when his friends (those of the Press and Athletic clubs) found out his intention, they "insisted upon furnishing all the pictures and material, and I generously allowed them to do so."[31]

One artist who supplied two of the illustrations was William Wallace Denslow (1856–1915), whom Opie Read had introduced to Baum in 1896.[32] This was the first collaboration between the two men whose names would become as closely linked as those of Lewis Carroll and John Tenniel. Denslow was the same age as Baum, and in 1898 was becoming well known in Chicago for his innovative poster designs and book illustrations. They would do three books together, and so close was their working relationship that Denslow's pictures must be discussed along with Baum's stories.

Probably during the work on *By the Candelabra's Glare*, Baum

40

showed Denslow some of the verses that he had written for his children, and the two men began collaborating on a book of nonsense rhymes and pictures for young children. It was this book, *Father Goose, His Book,* published by the Chicago firm of George M. Hill in September 1899, that was the real turning point in Baum's life. At first, Baum and Denslow were going to pay the entire cost of publishing the book, but before it was released, Hill decided to shoulder some of the expense.[33] It was a wise decision because *Father Goose* became the best-selling children's book of the year, and more than 75,000 copies were in print by the end of 1899.[34]

It is a beautifully designed book; every page is a picture printed in flat poster colors of red, gray, and yellow (the lavish use of color was rare in American children's books of the time), and the verses were hand-lettered in large, easy-to-read print by another Chicago artist, Ralph Fletcher Seymour. In its totality, it is an example of innovative book design.[35] However, the reason for the phenomenal popularity of *Father Goose* was a combination of factors: Denslow's illustrations are simpler and more hu-morous than the ones Parrish did for *Mother Goose,* and Baum's verses are fun and full of fantastic imagery. From his mistake in *Mother Goose,* Baum had learned that most of the magic of such a nonsense collection lies in "the cadences of its rhymes" and in the very personal images and associa-tions that each child derives from those verses.[36] The next year, a selection of the verses was set to music by Alberta N. Hall and published by Hill, and that collection only increased the popularity of *Father Goose.*[37]

THE WONDERFUL WIZARD OF OZ

While *Father Goose* was in production and its success still in the future, Baum and Denslow began another project, this time a full-length fantasy. They offered it to George M. Hill, who was not enthusiastic, but who agreed to publish it under the same conditions as *Father Goose:* Baum and Denslow would supply all the printing plates, and Hill would print and distribute the book.[38] The story went through various title changes—*The City of Oz, The Great City of Oz, The Emerald City,* and *The Land of Oz*—before it was finally published in 1900 as *The Wonderful Wizard of Oz.*[39]

The design for *Father Goose* is innovative, but in comparison with it, the design for *The Wonderful Wizard of Oz* can only be described as *radically* innovative because there had never been anything like it, and few books since have equaled its amazing blend of story and pictures. Other artists have illustrated it in recent years, and the story itself has proved strong enough to exist apart from Denslow's pictures, but none of the other combinations of story and pictures can equal the impact of the Baum–Denslow collaboration.

The very close working relationship between Baum and Denslow on the creation of the book suggests a question: Did the design of the book in any way affect the creation of the story? In one major way it could have. In each section of the story there is a favorite, or appropriate, color mentioned, and the colors of the text illustrations follow that color scheme exactly. Either the color scheme of the story suggested the colorful design and merging of text and pictures in the book or, since it would be almost impossible to print black letters over black-and-white illustrations and still have the text readable, the design of the book suggested the addition of the color scheme to the story.

Douglas Greene and Michael Hearn speculate in their biography of Denslow that "the illustrator may have suggested a few of the plot elements and the development of the characters."[40] In two instances, Denslow's pictures make suggestions about the story that are not supported in the text. In Chapters 3 and 10, he drew a house and the gates of the Emerald City with faces. Baum never gave human qualities to the buildings of Oz, but John R. Neill, who illustrated the rest of Baum's Oz books, also drew the houses with faces (and in his own books gave them active parts in the stories). The second instance is even more intriguing: Denslow's illustrations for the dedication page and the Chapter 1 title page, which face each other, are, respectively, the Good Witch of the North swirling in a kind of dance and the cyclone sweeping Dorothy's house away. Both illustrations were printed against large blocks of brown. The swirls of the witch's dress resemble the swirls of the cyclone. The pictures being placed next to each other may have been pure chance, but, if not, the suggestion is that the witch caused the cyclone to bring Dorothy to Oz and that her effect on Oz was predestined. Baum's text gives no reason for the cyclone, but seemingly he did not object to the pictures as Denslow drew them.

I would also suggest that it is equally possible that the author may have suggested some of the design elements. Baum was an experienced printer who had learned the possibilities of the medium from actually handling the type,[41] and it should also be remembered that at the time *The Wizard* was being created, Baum was engaged full-time as the editor of a magazine devoted to design.

Whatever the possible contributions to the story by the artist or to the design by the writer, the first edition of *The Wonderful Wizard of Oz* presents story and pictures that blend to form a seamless whole.[42] The book is a riot of color, containing not a single purely black-and-white illustration. There are 24 inserted color plates, including the title page, in Denslow's poster-like style and about 130 text illustrations in two colors: black and either brown, blue, red, green, or yellow. The color plates were well executed and achieve an amazing variety of shades considering that they were printed (like color woodblock prints) using only the three primary colors of yellow, blue, and red. The outlines were printed in dark blue rather than the usual black. It is, however, in the text illustrations that the real magic lies. They range from vignettes and chapter headings to double-page pictures, and for them all the traditional boundaries between type page and margins and between text and illustrations were abolished. Pictures spill off the edge of the pages, flow from one page to the next, and invade the text. The text itself is often in odd shapes to allow

---

W. W. Denslow's illustrations for the dedication page and the Chapter 1 title from the first edition of The Wonderful Wizard of Oz. *The positioning of these drawings suggests a cause and effect not mentioned in Baum's text.*

This book is dedicated to my good friend & comrade. My Wife

L.F.B.

Chapter I.
The Cyclone.

Scarecrow, while Toto barked sharply and made a snap at the tin legs, which hurt his teeth.

"Did you groan?" asked Dorothy.

"Yes," answered the tin man; "I did. I've been groaning for more than a year, and no one has ever heard me before or come to help me."

"What can I do for you?" she enquired, softly, for she was moved by the sad voice in which the man spoke.

"Get an oil-can and oil my joints," he answered. "They are rusted so badly that I cannot move them at all; if I am well oiled I shall soon be all right again. You will find an oil-can on a shelf in my cottage."

Dorothy at once ran back to the cottage and found the oil-can, and then she returned and asked, anxiously, "Where are your joints?"

"Oil my neck, first," replied the Tin Woodman. So she oiled it, and as it was quite badly rusted the Scarecrow took hold of the tin head and moved it gently from side to side until it worked freely, and then the man could turn it himself.

for the flow of the pictures; sometimes it appears on small or large blocks of solid color; and often it is printed over the illustrations![43] This last, especially, results in the mind's receiving the picture that illustrates a portion of the text at exactly the same time as it is assimilating the meaning of the text.

Baum and Denslow had hoped to have the book ready to be published in 1899 (the illustrated copyright page reads 1899), but there were delays, and it was not until September 1900 that *The Wizard* was published.[44] By Christmas of that year, Baum knew that it was a success.[45] Initially, however, the book did not match the phenomenal sales that *Father Goose* had enjoyed; but in the following years, *The Wizard* easily surpassed it. And today, when the rhymes of *Father Goose* are all but forgotten, *The Wonderful Wizard of Oz* has taken its place as *the* classic American fairy tale.

It is, worldwide, one of the most familiar of American stories. It is also very frequently abridged and adapted to other media: films, stage versions, cartoons, comics, and picture books. Any abridgment or adaptation will, by its very nature, change the emphasis of the original story, and often whole sections of the plot are dropped and large and small details altered. Because the book is Baum's masterpiece and because it forms the real basis from which his fantasy continent was later developed, it is necessary to review the plot in some detail as it originally appears.

Dorothy, who lives with her Uncle Henry and Aunt Em on a farm on the bleak Kansas prairie, is swept, with her house and dog, Toto, to the eastern portion of the beautiful and magical land of Oz. There she is met by the Good Witch of the North, who welcomes her as a great sorceress because her house has fallen on and killed the Wicked Witch of the East, who had held that eastern part of the country in bondage. Dorothy is distressed by this, but her main concern is how to return home. By magic,

An example of the innovative way in which illustrations and text were merged in the first edition of The Wonderful Wizard of Oz. *In the original, the gray areas are light blue, making the black text quite legible.*

the Good Witch learns that Dorothy should follow the Road of Yellow Bricks to the City of Emeralds, which is ruled by the great Oz, a wizard who may be able to help Dorothy return to Kansas.

Dorothy puts on the Silver Slippers, which had belonged to the Wicked Witch, and she and Toto start on their journey to the city. While traveling through pleasant countryside, she finds a live scarecrow hanging in a cornfield. The Scarecrow tells her of his longing for brains so that he can be like other people. Dorothy suggests that he join her and see if the great Oz can help him.

From the settled area, the road leads into a great forest where Dorothy and the Scarecrow meet a strange man, a woodchopper made out of tin. The Tin Woodman tells them how, to prevent his marrying the servant girl of an evil old woman, the Wicked Witch enchanted his ax so that it began to cut off parts of his body. Each time that happened, a tinsmith replaced the missing part with metal until the woodchopper was made entirely of tin. The Tin Woodman's great sorrow is that he no longer has a heart, and he decides to join them to ask the Wizard for one.

Soon afterward, in a wilder part of the forest, they are attacked by a large lion but are unharmed because the Lion is a coward. When he learns where they are going, the Lion asks if he can accompany them to see if the Wizard can give him courage. After they emerge from the forest, they lose their way and are trapped in a large field of bright red poppies. The sleep-inducing aroma of the flowers overcomes Dorothy, Toto, and the Lion, but they are saved by the efforts of the Scarecrow, the Tin Woodman, and the Queen of the Field Mice and her subjects.

Finally they reach the City of Emeralds, and the Guardian of the Gates requires each of them to put on spectacles of green glass so the brilliance of the jeweled city will not blind them. The Wizard's servant informs them that the Wizard will see them separately, one each day. The great Wizard appears to Dorothy as a gigantic head, to the Scarecrow as a lovely lady with gorgeous wings, to the Tin Woodman as a terrible beast, and to the Lion as a ball of fire. To each of them, he promises to grant their requests if only they will kill the Wicked Witch of the West. That demand upsets Dorothy more than anything else that has happened to her, but the four friends have no choice but to begin the journey west.

The powerful witch sees them coming and sends wolves, crows, bees, and an army of her people, the Winkies, to try to destroy them, but each time Dorothy's companions protect her. Finally the witch uses the Golden Cap, which allows her to command the Winged Monkeys, and Dorothy, Toto, and the Lion are captured. The Scarecrow's stuffing is ripped out, and the Tin Woodman is thrown from a great height onto some rocks.

The Wicked Witch of the West cages the Lion and forces Dorothy to work for her. She covets the magical Silver Slippers, which the girl wears, but when she steals one of them, Dorothy becomes so angry that she dashes a bucket of water over her. The witch is old and dried up, and the water causes her to melt entirely away. This releases the Winkies from bondage, and they help Dorothy rescue and repair her friends.

Dorothy takes the Golden Cap, and the four companions begin the journey back to the City of Emeralds but become lost on the way. The Winged Monkeys, the servants of the Cap, rescue them and take them to the city. At first the Wizard is reluctant to see them, but after Dorothy threatens to call the monkeys, he agrees, and they enter the throne room together. This time the Wizard is invisible, only a voice booming around the room. The Wizard tries to delay, but they become angry, and the Lion roars. The roar frightens Toto, who tips over a screen. Behind the screen is a little old man who turns out to be "Oz, the Great and Terrible."

The man is an American from Omaha. Long before, he had been a balloonist with a circus, and his balloon had gotten out of control and brought him to Oz. The people thought that he was a great wizard, and he had them build the City of Emeralds for him. Inside the walls, the city is no different in color from other cities, but he requires everyone to wear green spectacles to create the illusion of a green city. The people have worn them for so long that they have forgotten that the city is not a real City of Emeralds. After the humbug Wizard failed to defeat the Wicked Witch of the West, he retreated to his city and refused to see anyone. His reputation as a powerful wizard grew, and while he has no real magical powers, he is clever with machines and illusions and fooled Dorothy and her friends with his mechanical devices.

Dorothy's companions still demand that he keep his promises, and the Wizard reluctantly agrees to do so. He fills the Scarecrow's head with bran and pins and needles; he puts a sawdust-stuffed heart into the Tin Woodman's chest; and he gives the Lion a drink of liquid that he says is courage. The three are well satisfied and think him a wonderful wizard. But time and time again on the journey, their actions had proved that they already possess the very things they believed they lacked.

To help Dorothy, the Wizard makes another balloon and is going to take her home himself. He has grown old in the City of Emeralds and has often longed for home. The balloon, however, leaves before Dorothy can get to it, and the Wizard floats away without her, leaving the Scarecrow to rule over the city.

There is nothing left for Dorothy to do but to make the journey to see Glinda, the Good Witch of the South, and ask her for help. Her friends decide to go with her. They first meet a line of fighting trees that guard a vast forest. Inside the forest, the Lion defeats a giant spider and is asked by the other animals to be their king. At the other edge of the forest, they find a wall made of porcelain that encloses a small country where everything and everybody is made of china. Once through that country, they encounter the Hammerheads, a strange race of people who have no arms but are able to butt people with their heads by stretching out their long necks. Dorothy calls the Winged Monkeys to carry them over the Hammerheads' country to Glinda's castle.

Glinda is guarded by an army of young women, but she receives the travelers graciously. She tells Dorothy that the Silver Slippers will carry her home and would have at any time since she began wearing them. Dorothy gives the Golden Cap to Glinda to use in order to send her friends back where they want to go, and she makes her wish to return home. The slippers carry her there, and Dorothy finds herself again on the

Kansas prairie near the new house her Uncle Henry has built. She is joyously greeted by her Aunt Em. The Silver Slippers, however, were lost in the desert that surrounds Oz.

The Wonderful Wizard of Oz has become part of American folklore; it is redolent with the spirit and space of America, but its themes are universal. There are experiences in the story that everyone can identify with: Dorothy's longing for home; the Scarecrow, Tin Woodman, and Lion's search for the things that will make them complete; the Wizard's fear and frustration that result from his pretending to be something he is not; and the universal need to believe in something or someone. The story, like all good stories, has many levels of meaning and can speak to different people in different ways according to their own personal needs and abilities to understand. As paradoxical as it may sound, good fantasy is most often about reality; it enables us to perceive the real world in a clearer way, and sometimes helps us go past surface illusions to the truth underneath. The power of illusion and the truth beneath the surface are two of the main themes of this story.

In *The Wonderful Wizard of Oz,* story and background are in balance; the story is a simple, yet powerful one, with depth and wisdom to it, and the background serves it well. To be able to trace the future development of Oz, Baum's most important imaginary world, it is first necessary to have an accurate picture of it as it was created in this book. Many of the studies of Baum treat Oz as a whole, as it evolved throughout his fourteen full-length Oz books, and correct and amplify what was written in *The Wizard* with information from the later books.[46]

In the Introduction to *The Wonderful Wizard of Oz,* Baum called the story a "modernized fairy tale," but nowhere in the text did he refer to Oz as a fairyland.[47] The only distinction he made was that Kansas is one of the civilized countries and Oz is not; therefore, witches and wizards, and, by extension, magical and wondrous things still exist there.[48] Baum was to make that distinction several times in his writings, and it is one indication that, for all his interest in the new inventions and ideas of his era, he was not a wholehearted enthusiast about modern civilization as he was experiencing it.

Baum definitely placed the Land of Oz in the real world, not in some alternative universe or in another dimension; nor did he make it, like many imaginary worlds, invisible to all but the initiated. It is not known and not civilized *only* because it is "cut off from all the rest of the world" by deserts that completely surround it. The exact location is vague: the cyclone carries Dorothy many miles from home, and the Wizard says that Oz is much farther from Kansas than is Omaha, Nebraska; the cyclone blows Dorothy there overnight, and the Wizard floated there in a balloon in less than two days. From these details, one is left with a nebulous idea that Oz could lie somewhere in the great deserts of the southwestern part of America, just as Mo could be located somewhere in the distant mountains.[49]

Although one receives from the story the sense of vast space, the exact size and shape of Oz are not given. It is stated that Oz is divided into four countries, which are referred to as the Countries or Lands of the East, North, West, and South; and in the exact center of Oz is the City of Emeralds, the only city mentioned.[50]

Oz is sparsely populated and contains large uninhabited areas. Dorothy and her friends encounter very few people on their journeys: Dorothy lands in a settled part, but then, except for meetings with the characters who will become her companions, she sees no other people until they reach the area around the Emerald City. On their journey west, the travelers meet no people, apart from the army of Winkies, until they arrive at the castle of the Wicked Witch of the West; on the journey south, they meet two strange races of people-like beings, but no real people until they reach the area of the castle of Glinda. In fact, the whole "feel" of Oz in this first book is that of large tracts of uninhabited land: forest, wilderness, and great open plains filled with sunshine.

The people who do live in Oz are small, not much larger than Dorothy herself, and theirs is predominantly an agricultural society. They live in round houses with domed roofs, and the size of the house depends on the wealth of its inhabitants, for it is a society based on money as a means of exchange. The people who live in the East are called Munchkins, and their favorite, or national, color is blue. The people who live in the West are called Winkies, and their color is yellow. Those who live in the South are Quadlings, and red is their favorite color. The favorite color of the Emerald City is, of course, green. But the name of the people and the color of the Land of the North are not given. Baum made it very clear that these favorite colors, with the exception of the Emerald City, apply only to man-made objects (clothes, houses, fences, and such) and, except for certain preferences in flowers and crops (daisies, buttercups, and grain in the West), do not apply to the terrain itself.[51]

The Emerald City is an exception to the general color scheme, just as the city itself is an exception to the rural nature of Oz and the humbug Wizard is an exception to the real workers of magic. The walls around the city are green, but on the interior, the green color is only another of the Wizard's illusions, created by the green spectacles that he makes the people wear.[52]

Baum's first two well-developed imaginary countries, Mo and Oz, share some attributes; for example, both are cut off from the rest of the world by natural barriers, and in both the animals are able to talk intelligently. There are also, in the first Oz book, certain borrowings and echoes of Mo: the sorceress Maëtta, who lives in the southern part of Mo, became Glinda the Good Witch, who rules the Land of the South in Oz; the description of Maëtta's throne room closely resembles the description of the Wizard's throne room in the Emerald City, but without the jarring mention of electric lights. The Tin Woodman's story of how his ax became enchanted echoes the absurd logic and cartoon humor of the Mo stories, as does the Tin Woodman himself echo the cast-iron man, but in a totally benign way.

Mo, however, is a magical country, while Oz is a country in which magical things happen—an important distinction. The most fantastic things happen in Mo and are accepted as normal because the country itself is fantastic. In Oz, fantastic things happen, but they are not accepted as normal because they go against the natural laws of that world: the Scarecrow comes to life, but he is the only scarecrow in Oz who does; the Lion becomes one of Dorothy's companions, but it is not normal in Oz for people to associate with wild animals.

Ultimately, however, Mo and Oz cannot be compared because they represent two very different aspects of Baum's imagination, both of which will play their parts in the development of his imaginary continent. Mo was Baum's first attempt to create a perfect place—a paradise—where all the things that could be desired are supplied; where all human worries about money, growing old, pain, and death are abolished; where people are always happy; and where only evil things can be destroyed, which, in effect, makes them not evil at all, but only irritants that add variety and interest to the endless days. It is a static world where nothing good can ever change. One day in Mo is all days in Mo.

Oz, though, as it is depicted in *The Wonderful Wizard of Oz,* was Baum's first attempt at creating a fantasy country that is a version of our own world—idealized, filtered through his own vision, and loaded with infinitely more possibilities, but a version of the real world nonetheless and, therefore, imperfect but with the possibilities of progression and change. The natural laws of Oz are those that are familiar to us: there is day and night; the sun rises in the east and sets in the west; the moon shines at night; the rain, the streams, and the rivers are only water and not exotic substances; the trees and flowers are fairly much like ours; and nothing grows on the trees and bushes but fruits, nuts and berries, just what we would expect. The people and the country are subject to time and death: the Yellow Brick Road falls into disrepair when it is not taken care of, and people grow old and die. Even the practitioners of magic are not exempt: the Wizard ages in the Emerald City, and the four witches are all quite old, although Glinda, the Good Witch of the South, is able to appear young through the use of her magic arts.

Because Oz is not a static world, it can have a history and the depth and richness that history gives. In the course of the story, Baum gives us two important interconnected glimpses of the past of this country. Long before Dorothy arrived there and before the Emerald City was built, there lived in the North "a beautiful princess who was also a powerful sorceress." Her name was Gayelette, "and she lived in a handsome palace built from blocks of ruby." Gayelette was to marry a man named Quelala, and became very angry when the mischievous Winged Monkeys who lived in the great forest played a trick on him. She made the monkeys slaves of the Golden Cap, which was her wedding present to Quelala. The monkeys were required to do the bidding three times for each owner of the cap. Gayelette and Quelala passed into history, and almost two generations later, a great "wizard" appeared out of the sky. He settled in Oz and caused a magnificent city to be built, the City of Emeralds. But before the city was finished, he went to war with the Wicked Witch of the West, and the Golden Cap and its slaves, the Winged Monkeys, played the decisive role in driving him from her land and back to his city. The past and present of Oz meet when the Golden Cap falls into Dorothy's hands, and at the end of her journey, the cap is given back to the Winged Monkeys, thus freeing them from their long bondage.[53]

Real evil and real danger can exist in Oz, and there can be real suspense in the conflicts. On the eve of Dorothy's arrival, an uneasy balance between good and evil existed in Oz: the Lands of the North and the South were ruled by Good Witches; the Lands of the East and the West were ruled by Wicked Witches who enslaved their peoples; and the Emerald City in the center of the country was ruled by the great Wizard, whom the witches believed to be more powerful than they were. That balance is upset and great changes are initiated the instant Dorothy arrives in Oz because her house falls on the Wicked Witch of the East and kills her. That balance of good and evil had had the same effect on Oz as an enchantment. While it existed, there could be no change or development. Dorothy's arrival, in true fairy-tale fashion, breaks the enchantment and brings the country to life again.

Just as the real magic workers live outside the City of Emeralds, the real magic of Oz is located outside the city in the landscape of the country itself. Baum's keen perception and love of nature first became apparent in this book. The single most magical moment in the story—and one of the most magical in all fantasy—is Dorothy's first view of Oz, and there the magic comes from nature, not marvels. Baum carefully built up the image of the bleak landscape of the Kansas prairie; he used the word "gray" nine times in his description of it.[54] Text and pictures have Dorothy surveying the dry, empty horizon from the door of the farmhouse. After the cyclone has swept the house away and dropped it in Oz, Dorothy again goes to the door. This is what she sees then:

> There were lovely patches of green sward all about, with stately trees bearing rich and luscious fruits. Banks of gorgeous flowers were on every hand, and birds with rare and brilliant plumage sang and fluttered in the trees and bushes. A little way off was a small brook, rushing and sparking along between green banks, and murmuring in a voice very grateful to a little girl who had lived so long on the dry, gray prairies.[55]

The transformation is as simple as stepping off of a dusty road into a garden; the effect is as powerful as an enchantment.

The Land of Oz itself is a celebration of the wonder inherent in nature, and as a reader travels with Dorothy and her companions on their explorations of this beautiful and wondrous land, there is a strange sense of familiarity about it. The friends travel through the settled area of the East, with its neat farms and houses, and through the old forests where people have yet to settle; they reach the broad, lush area of the great, new City of Emeralds; they wander, lost in the vast yellow grainfields of the West, and can, because of the absence of trees, see for miles to the horizon. The reader begins to suspect that Oz is more than just a version of our world, that Oz is "America"—an idealized and less overly civilized version maybe, but some form of America all the same. It is possibly

America as seen through Baum's eyes or as experienced by him. Baum himself had traveled from the East, with its forests and settled areas of neat farms; to the great new city of Chicago; to the vast grain-filled plains of the West; and to the warm and lush South. Thousands of people had traveled the same routes before Baum and had seen the same landscapes, but Baum looked at them with his own particular combination of vision and imagination and discovered a New World.

There is evidence that in the creation of the Emerald City, Baum was also transforming his own experience. Probably the most fantastic part of the description of that city is the Wizard's statement that this large, splendid place was built for him shortly after he arrived in Oz. Neither the Wizard nor his people possess any true magic, and the idea of such a magnificent city being built in such a short time seems like a lapse on Baum's part until we remember that he himself had seen a magnificent city covering more than six hundred acres built in less than a year—the great White City, as it was called, of the World's Columbian Exposition of 1893,[56] the architecture of which very much resembled Denslow's pictures of the Emerald City. The White City was a city of illusion (a point probably not lost on Baum) because much of it—buildings, statues, fountains—was built of staff, a substance composed mostly of plaster of Paris, with cement and a fiber such as hemp, jute, or sisal added.[57] It was a Hollywood film set before such things existed. That the Emerald City was also a city of illusion brings the parallel closer, and the early titles of the book suggest that the city, not the Wizard, was meant to be the central image of the story. Indeed, it is entirely possible to read the story as the surreal adventure of a child lost at the exposition. How like exhibits in a sideshow are "a live Scarecrow," "a man made out of tin," and "a cowardly lion," and the White City did contain a large midway with a variety of entertainments, including magicians, strange animals, rides, *and* a captive balloon.[58] Looking at the story from this angle also makes it more understandable that Dorothy would want to return to the gray Kansas prairie rather than remain in Oz. She preferred the reality to the illusion.

That gleaming White City must have been quite a contrast to the crowded, smoky, ever-expanding Chicago that surrounded it; and it must have been, after the close of the exposition, a depressing sight to see those buildings quickly deteriorate. The contrast between what could have been and what was may have contributed something to Baum's later cynicism about life in a large city.

It is important to note that *The Wonderful Wizard of Oz* is more than a celebration of the spirit and natural beauties of America; it also contains perceptive criticisms of certain traits in the national character. A prime example of these is Americans' strange attraction to humbugs: the confidence men, the crooked politicians, the purveyors of patent medicine selling snake oil guaranteed to cure all our ills no matter what they are if we only believe—and are willing to pay, of course. Baum himself was fascinated by humbugs; they appear often in his stories, but as the creator of the illusion, he knew the difference between the illusion and the reality. Even after the Scarecrow, the Tin Woodman, and the Lion discover that the Wizard is a humbug, they still seek his help. Because they have so little self-knowledge or self-confidence, they are able to believe the truth about themselves only after the Wizard has given them worthless tokens of the qualities they already possess. The Wizard speaks perhaps the most devastating criticism of this side of the American character when he asks, "How can I help being a humbug . . . when all these people make me do things that everybody knows can't be done?"[59] It may be that Baum meant the criticism in a humorous way; it may even be that Baum did not consciously intend the criticism; but it is there nevertheless. This cynical tone, which surfaces now and again in the book, combined with the fact that Oz as it exists in *The Wizard* is a more frightening, more disturbing, and less hospitable place than it was to become as the series developed, may partially explain why Baum's sunlit world has been the inspiration for a number of dark visions, such as *Zardoz, Was,* and the inner-city setting of *The Wiz.*[60]

To Baum, *The Wonderful Wizard of Oz* was only one of the five books he published in 1900, and he had little idea of which of them, if any, would succeed with the public.[61] He had many new stories to tell and no plans to write sequels to any of his stories. The children who read *The Wizard*, however, knew differently; they sensed immediately that Oz was a real, living place—a place they wanted to hear a great deal more about.

Chapter Three

Exploration of the Other-World

1901–1904

If fairies exist at all—and no one has yet been able to prove that they do *not* exist—then there is no good reason why they should not inhabit our favored land as well as the forest glades and flowery dales of the older world across the water. For fairies are not peculiar to any one locality, and every race has its own fairy legends.

L. Frank Baum,
"Author's Note" to
Baum's American Fairy Tales (1908)

L. FRANK BAUM HOPED FOR SUCCESS FOR THE FIVE BOOKS HE PUBLISHED IN 1900, but he did not have the advantage of hindsight to help him isolate the special elements that would make one succeed and another fail. One thing, though, that both he and W. W. Denslow realized was that the books they did together had captured the public's fancy, so they quickly began another project.

DOT AND TOT OF MERRYLAND

Dot and Tot of Merryland (1901) was Baum's third collaboration with Denslow. They hoped that it would continue their string of successes, but the book did not match *The Wonderful Wizard of Oz* in sales or appeal. It is, in fact, one of Baum's weakest books; yet Merryland is one of his most charming, serene, and finished imaginary countries. The problem is one of balance: the fantasy world is strong but the story is not, and both elements too often seem to exist independently of each other.

The story concerns Dot, the young daughter of a wealthy banker and an invalid mother, who is sent to a country estate, Roselawn, to grow healthy in the fresh air and sunshine. She makes a playmate of the gardener's son Tot, and they decide to have a picnic beside the river that flows past Roselawn. Discovering a boat, they have their lunch in it. The boat glides away from the bank and begins floating down the river, and when Dot tries to use an oar to steer it, she succeeds only in changing its direction and putting it into another current, which carries them toward the trees and cliffs on the opposite bank. Instead of stopping at the trees, they are carried by the current into a cave, and they emerge sometime later in the magical country of Merryland.

As their boat floats through Merryland, Dot and Tot see many interesting sights and many strange people. In the middle of the country, they meet the queen, who adopts them and makes Dot a princess and Tot a prince. With the queen, they float through the rest of Merryland, and when they are ready to go home, she sends them back out into the river opposite Roselawn.

Some of the problems with the story are apparent from this brief outline, including the major one that nothing particularly exciting happens in this imaginary country. Dot and Tot never feel the same pressing need to return home that Dorothy does. Also, no real obstacles are put in the way of their journey, and, except for their meeting with the queen, they do not become involved with any of the strange places and peoples of Merryland. The book has been described as a travelogue,[1] but it is also a stroll through a circus sideshow where the spectators move from one strange exhibit to another, looking, but never becoming personally involved.

In this, Baum's second full-length fantasy, place and mood are everything, and story does not rank even secondary importance. That Denslow failed to recognize this is apparent from his illustrations, which do not create a sense of place or define the different areas of Merryland. There is little action to illustrate, so he restricted himself in the main to picturing the many strange characters that are introduced and too often they seem to exist in a void. *Dot and Tot of Merryland* has been called Denslow's most "decorative" book,[2] as indeed it may be, but from the standpoint of design, it falls short in comparison with *The Wizard*. Denslow made no color plates for the book, but filled it with colorful text illustrations in black, reddish orange, and light brown. However, the use of the same three colors throughout the book tends to create a feeling of monotony. Like those in *The Wizard*, the illustrations often appear at odd places on the page, but unlike those in the earlier book, they seldom merge with the story, pictures and text usually retaining the traditional boundary between them.

This lack of harmony between story and pictures may also be indicative of the increasing discord in the relationship between Baum and Denslow. They were men of very different personalities and temperaments, and only their complementary talents had brought them together. With success came friction, as each began to feel that his own contribution had had the most to do with the success of their books. When they had worked on *Father Goose* and *The Wizard*, they had most often worked together in the evenings at Baum's home.[3] With success and more demands for the talents of both men, they more often worked separately, and during the time that Denslow was working on the pictures for *Dot and Tot*, he had a nervous breakdown and spent some time in a sanitarium.[4] This was the last book on which they collaborated; Baum never again had a personal, working relationship with any of his illustrators.

A children's book in which setting and mood completely overshadow the story is not apt to be a successful book, but it can have an important place in the development of the author's imagination. Baum told his children many of the Phunnyland stories and a version of *The Wizard* before he wrote them down,[5] and it is probable that he also told them most of the stories that appeared in *Mother Goose in Prose*, but it is unlikely that *Dot and Tot* was created in that way. The short period of time between his projects and the weakness of the story suggest that it was not. The tale is, in fact, more like a very personal story that Baum told himself because it is the one of his books that most clearly reflects his own childhood. The majority of his stories grew out of his experiences traveling through or living in various parts of America, but *Dot and Tot* reached all or guardians of the babies, and every now and then one of them would fill a bottle with sweet milk from the fountain, and place it beside a baby that acted as if it might be hungry. This fountain stood in about the center of the valley and sent many sprays of new milk into the air, from whence it fell in graceful curves into a big basin of pure white marble. The nursing bottles were kept on a wide shelf at the edge of the fountain, where they were handy for the Storks to use.

While Dot and

the way back to his own happy and protected childhood at Rose Lawn. The mood of the book reflects that secure and idyllic time, as does the story itself, which allows no dangers or hardships to menace its characters. No frontier privations such as Dorothy endured were allowed in this story. The little girl, Dot, is from a wealthy family, just as Baum was, and she lives on a beautiful, garden-filled estate that was Baum's own beloved Rose Lawn. Place has supreme importance in this book because it is the place of Baum's youth as filtered through his memories and his imagination.

Because place is the point of the story, Merryland is the easiest of all Baum's imaginary countries to extract from the story and present as a whole. It is also the one presented most completely and the one least affected by the mortal characters. Dorothy set changes in motion merely by her arrival in Oz, but Dot and Tot have no effect on Merryland, except on its accessibility to the outside world. They observe it and enjoy it, but leave it as they found it.

Merryland points back to Baum's previous creations *and* ahead to the fantasy countries to come. Its construction represents a development of the "journey to the South" section of *The Wizard*. On that journey, Dorothy and her companions encounter in quick succession a forest guarded by fighting trees, a country made entirely of china, and a land inhabited by strange beings, the Hammerheads. Those lands represent obstacles to their journey, but are also unlike anything else in the story because the sense of vast space is lost, and a series of strange countries adjoining one another is presented. The travelers experience the countries much like tourists. In Merryland, the danger and obstacles are discarded, but Dot and Tot experience one strange land after another in much the same way as Dorothy does in that part of *The Wizard*.

Merryland is unusual in that it has the most specific location in relation to the real world of any of Baum's countries, being located in the mountains on the opposite side of the river from Roselawn. Mountains

On this page from Baum and Denslow's Dot and Tot of Merryland, *the text and illustration are rigidly separated.*

are the only barriers that protect it from the outside world. Baum was usually so specific about the relative positions of places only inside his fantasy world, and one wonders whether, after all the changes in his life and all the years of struggle, the real Rose Lawn had not also reached the status of "Arcadia" or Other-world in his mind.

Merryland consists of eight bowl-shaped valleys that are connected by a branch of the river that flows past Roselawn; between each valley, it runs through a short tunnel. The valleys are set in a semicircle so that while Dot and Tot enter the country at one end and leave from the other, they emerge not far from where they began.[6]

After running through the long, dark tunnel that leads to Merryland, the branch of the river comes into the light again in a barren, boulder-strewn valley that is the threshold of Merryland and is not counted among its seven main valleys. It is guarded by a very old man who is called "the Watch-Dog of Merryland."[7] He is supposed to prevent strangers from entering the valleys, but can do nothing to stop them. The children feel sorry for him and give him a piece of jelly cake. With the dark tunnel, the man called a Watch-Dog, and the gift of food, it is impossible not to be reminded of the myth of Cerberus.

The first valley proper, the Valley of the Clowns, looks much like the outside world except that the houses are built so that the top of each is a padded platform on which the clowns perform. The houses are lit by electric lights. Only clowns live in this valley, which is the source for all the real clowns in the world.[8] Time and death act in the same manner as they do in the outside world (and this is true of all the flesh-and-blood inhabitants of Merryland).

The Valley of Bonbons—the second valley—is reminiscent of Mo because everything is made of candy, but in this valley the people are also made of candy. These candy people predictably eat candy, but in a rather bizarre flight of fancy, Baum tells the reader that if one of these candy people is broken beyond repair, he is eaten by the other inhabitants.[9]

Baum did not name the third valley, but it is the place where babies appear out of blossoms and are tended by storks who feed the babies milk from a beautiful fountain. The storks then take the babies out into the world and give them to parents.[10]

Baum also did not name the fourth and largest valley, but it is there in the center of Merryland that the queen lives. The queen herself is a large wax doll. She rules over all of Merryland, even though several of the valleys have their own prince or king; it is a form of government that Baum later introduced into Oz. In this fourth valley, the queen's subjects are other dolls who live in a toy city. Most of the time, the dolls are kept asleep (as they would be in the outside world). When awake, they are too mischievous and unruly, and the conclusion is that it is better for a child to exercise his or her imagination on a doll than to have a doll with too much life in it—a conclusion that modern toy manufacturers would do well to ponder.[11]

There are two components of this section of the book that are very important to Baum's future imaginary countries. The first occurs in the queen's reaction to Dot and Tot's presence in Merryland: "No one who enters my kingdom should ever be allowed to leave it again, for if they did the world would soon know all about me and my people. If that happened, all our comfort and fun would be spoiled, for strangers would be coming here every day."[12] The queen consults her "thinking machine"[13] and devises a way for the Watch-Dog to be able to bar the entrance to Merryland permanently if anyone else from the outside world should try to enter. After Dot and Tot leave, she closes the exit from the country.[14]

This problem of intrusion from the outside world seems to be an odd one for Baum to have raised in this story. He himself was its creator and could control who visited it, but the problem of encroaching civilization troubled him greatly. This theme appears again and again in the books Baum wrote during the next few years and even affected the kinds of stories he created. When, in some of the later books, he combined this theme with those of dissatisfaction with the life one has to lead and of longing for experiences and things one cannot have, the cumulative effect raises the question of how happy Baum was in Chicago. His whole life and character indicate that he was not a city person; his earliest stories grew out of the frontier and the countryside he traveled through when he was a salesman, but he had given up traveling. For the first time in his life, he was facing the prospect of living permanently in a large and rapidly expanding city.

It was not Chicago itself that was the problem; any large city probably would have made him feel the same because Baum had too great a love for the natural wonders of this country ever to be entirely comfortable in a city. In 1899 he and his family began to spend the summers in Macatawa, Michigan, an overnight journey north of Chicago on the shore of Lake Michigan.[15] Later, as finances permitted, he and Maud began to travel during the winters as well. Baum went out, south and west,[16] almost as though he were searching for something—possibly the lost paradise of the America of his youth.

Baum was well aware of the benefits of civilization, but he was also well aware of what was being lost in its relentless march west. He seems to have been concerned that the way in which civilization was developing in the United States was destroying the very elements of the country that enticed the people to move west: the pastoral nature of the landscape, the clean and well-ordered towns, and the simpler, slower life. It was a problem that he kept addressing in his stories until he finally removed his imaginary countries, which were not "civilized," from contact with the outside world.

The second element of importance to the development of Baum's future fantasies in *Dot and Tot* occurs in a conversation between Dot and the queen:

> *"Really," said Dot, with an admiring glance at her Majesty, "you must be a fairy."*
> *"To be sure I am!" laughed the pretty Queen.*
> *"Still, you are not like any fairy I have read about," continued the child, gravely.*

68

> *"No, I suppose not," returned the Wax Doll. "You must know that fairies are as different from one another as other people are."[17]*

Baum had not yet called any of his countries fairylands within the texts of the stories, nor had he designated any of his characters as fairies, but this passage in *Dot and Tot* bridges the gap between the popular nineteenth-century idea of fairies as tiny, winged creatures and Baum's conception that the term "fairy" denotes certain traits and magical abilities rather than a specific size or appearance. He stated much the same thing in an article:

> *I once asked a little fellow, a friend of mine, to tell me what a "fairy" is. He replied, quite promptly: "A fairy has wings, and is much like an angel, only smaller." Now that, I believe, is the general conception of fairies. . . . Yet we know the family of immortals generally termed "fairies" has many branches and includes fays, sprites, elves, nymphs, ryls, knooks, gnomes, brownies and many other subdivisions.[18]*

J. R. R. Tolkien would have agreed, as his essay "On Fairy Stories" suggests: "The diminutive being, elf or fairy, is (I guess) in England largely a sophisticated product of literary fancy." And he goes on to explain that "the trouble with the real folk of Faërie is that they do not always look like what they are; and they put on the pride and beauty that we would fain wear ourselves."[19]

This conception of fairies as including all kinds of immortal beings allowed Baum to begin categorizing his imaginary countries as fairylands and allowed his imagination greater scope. He also began to see himself as part of the great tradition of fairy-tale writers; by 1909, the date of the article, he was able to include two of his own creations, ryls and knooks, among the traditional fairy creatures.

In *Dot and Tot of Merryland,* after the children have spent some time with the queen in the fourth valley, they accompany her in their boat to see the rest of her realm. The Valley of Pussycats is the fifth valley, a country-like place inhabited solely by cats. It contains another echo of Mo in the stream that flows with milk and the bread that grows on trees.[20]

The sixth valley contains a forest that is filled with wind-up toys and a strange wooden man who keeps them all wound.[21] And the seventh, and last, valley is the Valley of Lost Things. It is very still, with no signs of life, only great piles of things that have been lost in the outside world. It is in this valley that the children decide to return home. After saying good-bye to the queen, they take their boat through the last tunnel and back into the outside world. While in the tunnel, they hear the sounds of falling rocks as the queen closes Merryland off from the rest of the world.[22] The Valley of Lost Things was a strange and sad image with which to end the book; one wonders if it might also be the place of Baum's own lost youth.

AMERICAN FAIRY TALES

Today we recognize that *The Wonderful Wizard of Oz* was the first real American fairy tale. That Baum also knew that he was creating an American tradition of fantasy is apparent in the other two books he published in 1901: *American Fairy Tales* and *The Master Key: An Electrical Fairy Tale.* Those books also illustrate Baum's new freedom in applying the classification "fairy tale," because, with the exception of one of the stories in *American Fairy Tales,* he did not create imaginary countries to set the stories in. The majority of them take place in our own world, but they do make some contributions to his developing imaginary world.

American Fairy Tales is a collection of stories that had first appeared in various newspapers between March and May 1901.[23] It is a pretty book, illustrated with full-page black-and-white drawings by N. P. Hall, Harry Kennedy, and Ike Morgan. Each page of text is surrounded by a pictorial border designed by Ralph Fletcher Seymour, who also designed the title page. Seymour had hand-lettered the text of *Father*

Goose, and he went on to become a noted book designer.[24] *American Fairy Tales* was the last of Baum's books to be published by the George M. Hill Company, which went out of business soon afterward.[25]

To study the ways Baum used and transformed traditional fairy-tale themes to fit America, none of his books would be a richer source than *American Fairy Tales,* which contains some of his best stories. These tales should be more widely known, not just by children but by adults as well, for accompanying the fairy-tale elements are humorous and perceptive comments about America that are as applicable now as the day they were written. Often the humor does not quite cover a cynicism about certain aspects of American society; for example, in the story "The Box of Robbers" the child Martha releases a trunkful of Italian bandits in the attic of her home in Chicago. The bandits are determined to continue their profession in America because they figure, "Even in Chicago there must be people to rob." But Martha, with wisdom beyond her years, answers, "I think they have all been robbed."[26] Baum realized that it was difficult for him to avoid cynicism when writing about the foibles of the real world. In a later collection of jokes and humorous verses, *Father Goose's Year Book* (1907), he, with tongue in cheek, claimed, "If anything at all cynical has crept into these verses he [the author] declares that he is innocent of intentional pessimism."[27]

Nine of the twelve stories in *American Fairy Tales* are set in the United States, some with very definite locations (New England, Boston, and Prairie Avenue in Chicago); two take place in the wilderness (the Congo and the Arctic); and one is in an imaginary country, Quok. The story "The Queen of Quok" concerns a bankrupt country where the king has died, leaving a ten-year-old heir. The new king's counselor decides that the only way to save the kingdom is to marry the young king to a rich woman. Thus the king is auctioned off and is, as Baum wrote, " 'sold to Mary Ann Brodjinsky de la Porkus for three million, nine hundred thousand, six hundred and twenty-four dollars and sixteen cents!' And the sour-looking old woman paid the money in cash and on the spot, which proves this is a fairy story."[28] It is an amusing tale that rather obviously refers to the tendency of certain American heiresses to marry impoverished foreign noblemen. However, no details of Quok are given, and, the point of the story being satire, it had no effect on the development of Baum's imaginary world.

Two stories that did play a part are "The Enchanted Types" and "The Dummy That Lived." These stories might almost be called fairy tales in reverse, because rather than being "the adventures of men in the Perilous Realm," they are the adventures of fairies in the perilous realm of modern American cities. They detail the unintentional and intentional mischief caused by two immortal beings when they are confronted with American society. Both are good stories—"The Dummy That Lived" is even reminiscent of the macabre humor of Poe's "Loss of Breath"—but their importance for Baum's future writing lay in the two new types of fairies he introduced: knooks and ryls.

In "The Enchanted Types," it is mentioned that "knooks have more wonderful powers than any other immortal folk—except, perhaps, the fairies and ryls"—and that they "are the especial guardians of birds."[29] A Yellow Ryl is introduced in "The Dummy That Lived," but nothing is told about him except that "in all Fairyland there is no more mischievous a person."[30] These two types of immortals, presented in only the sketchiest of outlines, are significant because they are the first two of Baum's fictional creations that he will reintroduce in other fantasies. It is the earliest indication that long before he became involved in writing series books, his characters and countries were loosely connected in his imagination.

In the story "The Runaway Shadows," there was to have been another mention of a ryl and another indication of things to come, but that story was dropped during the time the stories were appearing in newspapers and was not included in *American Fairy Tales.*[31] It is the story of the Prince of Thumbumbia and his playmate, the Lady Lindeva, who, by a trick of Jack Frost's, are separated from their shadows. When the king dies, the prince is rejected as the new king because he has no shadow. The shadows, which have been having adventures of their own, return just in time to ensure a happy ending.

Although, as in the story of Quok, no detailed picture of Thumbumbia is built up, the story is much more of a traditional fairy tale, with no intrusions from the modern world. When the shadows find themselves free, they run "in the direction of the Forest of Burzee"[32] where they meet the tiger Kahtah, who tries to attack them, and a ryl who urges them to return home. No information is given about the Forest of Burzee, not even if it borders on or is included in Thumbumbia, but it is obviously a magical place because it includes a tiger that talks and a ryl. Such is the almost casual introduction of Burzee, which would become one of the most important places in Baum's imaginary continent.

THE MASTER KEY: AN ELECTRICAL FAIRY TALE

After the great success of *Father Goose: His Book,* Baum received requests for manuscripts from many of the country's major publishers. He knew that the verses in *Father Goose* gave little indication of his real talent, and because his books for 1900 were already in production, he prudently decided to wait and see how they were received by the public.[33] When *The Wizard* confirmed that the success of *Father Goose* had not been a lucky accident, he accepted an offer for a book from the Indianapolis firm Bowen-Merrill. That book was *The Master Key: An Electrical Fairy Tale.*

Bowen-Merrill (which became Bobbs-Merrill in 1902) was a growing company that already had a national reputation. In 1883 the company, under the name Merrill & Meigs, had been a publisher of law books,[34] but with the publication that year of a book of poems by the Indiana poet James Whitcomb Riley, the direction of the company changed. The popularity of Riley's poems made the fortune of the firm and attracted other authors, and in the first decades of this century, the company published many of the nation's most popular authors, among them Owen Johnson, Meredith Nicholson, Emerson Hough, Mary Roberts Rinehart, and L. Frank Baum. The company was also known for producing beautiful, well-designed books.

The Master Key is an example of the broad application that Baum was making of the term "fairy tale"; today we would classify the story as science fiction. Its hero is Rob Joslyn, a boy who has a fanatical interest in electricity and electrical gadgets. (Baum's son Robert was the inspiration for this character.)[35] Purely by accident, Rob creates the electrical pattern that calls up the Demon of Electricity, "the Slave of the Master Key."[36] This Demon is required to do Rob's bidding, and each week for three weeks, he is to give Rob three marvelous gifts—mechanical devices that run by electricity. The first three gifts are meal tablets, each the equivalent of the daily three meals; a tube-like gadget that will stun an attacker and render him unconscious for an hour; and an antigravitational device that will allow Rob to travel through the air to any place in the world. The second set of three gifts are the Garment of Protection, which repels weapons; the Automatic Record of Events, which shows the events happening anywhere in the world; and the Character Marker, a pair of spectacles that shows the wearer the character of anyone he is viewing.

The main body of the story concerns the adventures and troubles that Rob experiences in the use of the gifts. In the end, Rob refuses the final three gifts and sends the Demon back to where he came from to await the person with the intelligence and experience to strike the Master Key.

The Demon himself is related to the conception of good and beautiful witches in *The Wizard,* and Baum has the Demon quote Hesiod and Shakespeare to prove that not all demons are evil. Baum makes it clear in his description of the Demon, who glows with light and color, that while the unknown can be frightening, it can also be beautiful.

Another link between the Demon and other of Baum's immortal beings is that once again, as he had implied in *The Magical Monarch of Mo* and stated in *Dot and Tot,* he points out the loneliness and boredom possible to an immortal. At the end of the story, the Demon says, "You've no idea how stupid it is for me to live invisible and unknown." And he laments, "I must wait—wait—wait—patiently and silently—until my bonds are loosed by intelligence rather than chance! It is a dreary fate."[37]

Even though some of the electrical gifts that the Demon gives to Rob turn up in Baum's later fantasies as magical devices, the real significance of *The Master Key* for Baum's development is the philosophy underlying the story itself. On the surface, it is a Jules Verne type of story, the adventures of a boy who is able to wield futuristic inventions; on a more personal level, its theme is the same as that of *The Wizard*, the gaining of wisdom through experience; but its deeper and more serious subject is Baum's concern about the effects of the expanding technological revolution on our humanity and his doubts that mankind has the ability to use the new inventions with wisdom and restraint. His doubts are evident at the very beginning of the book in the short, explanatory paragraph that concludes the title on the title page: *The Master Key: An Electrical Fairy Tale* "founded upon the mysteries of electricity and the optimism of its devotees. It was written for boys, but others may read it." The very phrasing "optimism of its devotees" seems to set Baum apart from that optimism. The special devotee whom Baum had in mind was his son Rob, and he may have intended the story as a cautionary tale for his son's instruction.

The doubts continue in the humorous description of the havoc that Rob's devices create in the lives of his family. They are also apparent in the Demon's regret that he was called by accident by a mere boy and not by an adult and a man of science; yet the scientist Rob encounters is an evil man and wants to use the inventions for evil purposes, and the businessman he meets tries to kill him so that he can patent the gadgets himself. (It should be mentioned that Rob comes across these evil men in large cities: Paris and Chicago.)

Baum's optimism was reserved for the children of America; he knew the adults of his generation too well, and his boy hero Rob has the wisdom to realize that he does not want to use the Character Marker to learn the true characters of himself and his family—it is better to know some things in the heart. He knows, too, that man "has no right to take away what he can not bestow; to destroy what he can not create."[38] And he is able to learn enough from his mistakes to acknowledge, when he refuses the Demon's last three gifts, "I'm *not* wise enough. Nor is the majority of mankind wise enough to use such inventions as yours unselfishly and for the good of the world. If people were better, and every one had an equal show, it would be different."[39] Baum most succinctly stated his concerns about the relationship between humans and their inventions when he had Rob say to the representative of those machines, the Demon, "I've no fault to find with you except that you forgot you were a slave and tried to be a master."[40]

While it was quite different from Baum's other full-length fantasies, this book was also not a radical departure; rather, it was the fully realized working out of the theme of the future possibilities of electricity that had appeared in his early "Our Landlady" column and in his story "Yesterday at the Exposition." All of Rob's adventures occur in our world. Baum did not create any new magical countries for the story, but the themes and attitudes in *The Master Key* do play their parts in his great fairy world that was already in the first stages of development.

THE WIZARD OF OZ: MUSICAL EXTRAVAGANZA

The year 1901 was a busy one for Baum. Besides his publishing activities, he was again seriously engaged in projects for the theater. With success and recognition, Baum felt freer to indulge again his great passion. He planned and possibly wrote large portions of two comic operas—*King Midas* and *The Octopus; or, The Title Trust*—and he completed the script of a musical version of *The Wonderful Wizard of Oz.*[41]

The theater projects took up a large amount of Baum's time, and he published only one book in 1902. In spite of this, he probably would have considered that year the most successful one of his life. It was the year that he and Maud bought their own summer house at Macatawa Park on Lake Michigan. The money from *Father Goose* enabled them to do this, and they named the house "The Sign of the Goose."[42] It was also the year that Baum felt financially secure enough to sell his magazine, the *Show*

Window, and devote himself full-time to his other interests. And it was the year that his most cherished dream came true: his script for the musical-comedy version of *The Wizard,* with music by his friend Paul Tietjens, had been accepted for production by Frederick R. Hamlin, the manager of the Grand Opera House in Chicago.[43]

Hamlin contracted Julian Mitchell, a noted director of stage extravaganzas who later worked on the Ziegfield Follies, to direct and the young comedy team of Fred A. Stone and David C. Montgomery to appear in it.[44] Mitchell, however, rejected Baum's script, which closely followed the plot of the book, and insisted on changes to make it more stage worthy.[45] His "changes" left little of the plot apart from the main characters and added several subplots and new characters, such as Cynthia Cynch, the lady lunatic; Sir Dashemoff Daily, the poet laureate; Pastoria II, the former king of the Emerald City and a streetcar conductor from Topeka; Tryxie Tryfle, a waitress; Sir Wiley Gyle, a conspirator; and Imogene, Dorothy's pet cow! The simple story of Dorothy and her companions journeying to the great Wizard to have their wishes granted was almost lost in the added elements of love interests, Pastoria's attempt to regain the throne of Oz, and the armies of young and pretty chorus girls in tights. One of the advertisements for the show stated that it had "more pretty girls than any other show in town."[46] All but four of Baum and Tietjens's songs were dropped, and others were substituted.[47] In fact, songs and routines were added and dropped according to what was topical, and what little was left of the original plot became like a thin thread holding various disparate and shifting elements together.

Baum stated publicly that he was neither "heartbroken" nor "ashamed" of the production as Mitchell had changed it. The public statement was, however, in response to newspaper stories that he *was* much disturbed by what had been done to his story. He added, probably with a touch of cynicism, "The people will have what pleases them and not what the author happens to favor, and I believe that one of the reasons Julian Mitchell is recognized as a great producer is that he faithfully tries to serve the great mass of play goers—and usually succeeds."[48] It is no wonder that Baum, in the years following, came more and more to trust the taste of children rather than that of adults.

The amazing thing about this seeming hodgepodge was that it was the most spectacularly successful musical extravaganza of the first decade of the twentieth century! It opened in Chicago on June 16, 1902, to great success and played there until it went to New York in January 1903 for a two-week run. Instead, it stayed in New York for many months, and continued to play in various parts of the country until 1911.[49] The show was imitated in the United States and England, and one of those imitations, Victor Herbert's *Babes in Toyland*, is still sometimes revived. The country was to experience no similar furor over a stage production until Franz Lehar's operetta *The Merry Widow* was brought to America. The show made stars of Montgomery and Stone, who played the Tin Woodman and the Scarecrow, and when they broke their contract after nine hundred performances, Victor Herbert signed them for his musical *The Red Mill*.[50]

Putting aside the question of fidelity to the book, *The Wizard* was probably good, light entertainment. Daniel P. Mannix wrote that "it became a national institution, somewhat like a circus."[51] Fred Stone, when writing his autobiography in the 1940s, could speak of characters such as Cynthia Cynch, the lady lunatic, with the assurance that his readers would still remember them.[52] Perhaps if the music had been of the same quality as that for *Babes in Toyland*, the stage *Wizard* would still be known.

THE LIFE AND ADVENTURES OF SANTA CLAUS

It was good that Baum had the theater project to occupy much of his time because in early 1902 his income from his books was threatened when the George M. Hill Company went bankrupt. His book for 1902 had already been announced by Hill, but Bobbs-Merrill stepped in and published it as well as acquiring the rights to his other Hill books and *A New Wonderland*. Bobbs-Merrill had bought a gold mine; the firm's records show that between 1903 and 1956, when it went into public domain, it "published or licensed for publication" 4,195,667 copies of *The Wonderful Wizard of Oz* alone.[53]

The book for 1902 was *The Life and Adventures of Santa Claus,* which is one of Baum's most unusual and enchanting fantasies. It is also the most lyrical of his books. Many of the American traditions about Santa Claus grew up in the nineteenth century and were literary in origin,[54] but none of the stories or poems gave much detail about how Santa Claus came to be. Baum set out to remedy that situation by writing a biography of the American Santa Claus. He already had had the experience of expanding traditional nursery rhymes into stories in *Mother Goose in Prose,* and a very conventionally pictured Santa Claus appears in the final story in that volume, "Little Bun Rabbit." But many of those stories are not successful because Baum's treatment lessened rather than enhanced the magic of the original rhymes. No such problem affects *The Life and Adventures of Santa Claus* because Baum created such a mystical and radiant background against which to set the story of Santa Claus that even the magic of the Santa Claus story cannot overshadow it. In addition to the imaginary place, Baum created a whole history and mythology of the immortals out of which Santa Claus grew to become a link between them and mortals. Thus Baum's version of why Santa makes toys for children, why he comes down the chimney, and how he acquired the reindeer to pull his sledge is presented against a larger, more magical and mystical background than stories about Santa usually are. Santa is the main character in the book, but he is only a small part of the mythology, and it is this background that later becomes the mythology for Baum's entire Other-world.

Baum's immortals were created with the world by Nature to be its keepers, and they were created fully grown. He mentions the Water Sprites; the Sleep Fays; the Gnomes, who "guard the precious metals and the jewel stones that lie buried in rock and ore"; the Sound Imps, who carry sounds; the Wind Demons; and the Light Elves. But the four principal bands of immortals are the wood nymphs, who "guard the forests and . . . minister to the wants of the young trees"; their first cousins, the ryls, who "watch over the flowers and plants" and give the flowers their colors; the knooks, who "watch over the beasts of the world, both gentle and wild" and "look old and worn and crooked"; and "the Fairies, the guardians of mankind."[55]

Over all these are the three greatest immortals on earth: "Ak, the Master Woodsman of the World, who rules the forests and the orchards and the groves; and Kern, the Master Husbandman of the World, who rules the grain fields and the meadows and the gardens; and Bo, the Master Mariner of the World, who rules the seas and all the craft that float thereon."[56] And above all of them and everything is the Supreme Master.[57] It is entirely consistent with Baum's character that he should have chosen the word "master" to refer to God and the three rulers of the earth because in addition to meaning a person (or being) that others are subject to, "master" refers to a craftsman, maker, or creator.

Baum probably wrote the stories for *American Fairy Tales* and *The Life and Adventures of Santa Claus* fairly close together in time, but proximity does not explain why, for the first time in his writings, he made use of characters and places in one story that had been created for another story. The answer certainly is not lack of invention; his facility for the invention of magical characters and places was sometimes almost too fertile, as in *Dot and Tot,* where the places and odd characters become the main point of the story, or in some of his later books that include what amount to tours of imaginary places that have little or nothing to do with the story. The answer lies, I believe, in the nature of his imagination. He had created magical countries such as Mo, Oz, and Merryland and characters that are immortal, like the inhabitants of Mo and the toy and the candy people of Merryland, but, with the exception of the queen of Merryland, he had not yet created nonhuman immortals who have magical abilities and powers over the world or places that are sources of magic for the world. Once he began to create such immortals and such places, their particular attributes and powers came to transcend the stories for which they were created and became in Baum's imagination part of the citizenry of fairyland to be used whenever a story called for the magic or services they performed. For example, the knooks have a definite and important part to play in the story of Santa Claus because they are the guardians of the animals, but that same guardianship forms the premise of the very different story "The Enchanted Types"; thus the two stories, one taking place in an imaginary world and the other in our own world, are subtly linked.

The same is true of places. When Baum explained why Santa Claus brings children good things to eat as well as toys, it was natural for him to have the candies and bonbons come from the Valley of Phunnyland,[58] for it is one of the attributes of that country that such things grow in abundance on bushes there, but such a reference also draws the two magical places closer together. In *The Life and Adventures of Santa Claus*, Baum again used the Forest of Burzee, and whether he originally created Burzee for his story "The Runaway Shadows" or for this book is not important. What is significant is that once it was created and given the status, by the presence of the Queen of the Wood Nymphs and the Queen of the Fairies, of the most important of the many residences of the immortals, it became the principal source of magic in Baum's imagination and was used as such in his later books. He would create other sources of power, but because of the underlying consistency of his imagination, they would complement and supplement Burzee, not displace it.

Burzee is the core of *The Life and Adventures of Santa Claus*, and none of Baum's other books is so filled with his love of—one could almost say reverence for—nature. Wonderful plants and places exist in Burzee: casa plants, which give strength; grawle plants, which confer speed; marbon plants, which offer longevity; and the pool of Nares, which bestows beauty.[59] However, the real enchantment of this world comes from the magic of nature itself, from the beauty and variety of its yearly cycle, and from the mystery of growing and living things. In the opening of the book, Baum immediately takes the reader into this enchanted world, with prose that has the comfort and wonder of a lullaby:

Have you heard of the great Forest of Burzee? Nurse used to sing of it when I was a child. She sang of the big tree-trunks, standing close together, with their roots intertwining below the earth and their branches intertwining above it; of their rough coating of bark and queer, gnarled limbs; of the bushy foliage that roofed the entire forest, save where the sunbeams found a path through which to touch the ground in little spots and to cast weird and curious shadows over the mosses, the lichens and the drifts of dried leaves.

The Forest of Burzee is mighty and grand and awesome to those who steal beneath its shade. Coming from the sunlit meadows into its mazes it seems at first gloomy, then pleasant, and afterwards filled with never-ending delights.[60]

Baum was very close to the spirit of J. R. R. Tolkien in this book. Both men had a particular love of trees and forests, and Tolkien would have appreciated Baum's ancient Forest of Burzee. He also would have appreciated the tone of the story, which so often calls up a distant, mythical past. Baum's description of the beginning of one of the incidents in his book—"Thus arose that terrible war between the immortals and the spirits of evil which is sung of in Fairyland to this very day"[61]—anticipates Tolkien's subject and style in *The Lord of the Rings*. And Tolkien would later use two other themes that also occur in Baum's book: the coming of the civilization of men into the world of the immortals and the very different destinies of men and immortals.

In *The Life and Adventures of Santa Claus*, Baum once again expressed his concern about the advance of civilization. At the end of his first description of Burzee, he wrote: "Civilization has never yet reached Burzee. Will it ever, I wonder?"[62] And in the story, after many years have passed and people have begun to spread throughout the world, cutting down forests as they go, the great Ak, the Master Woodsman of the World, says with "far-seeing" wisdom, "The world was made for men . . .

and I have but guarded the forests until men needed them for their use." Yet he adds a plaintive plea, "But I hope they will not cut down all the trees, for mankind needs the shelter of the woods in summer as much as the warmth of blazing logs in winter."[63] In Tolkien's mythology, too, the age of the immortals gives way to the age of men, and in the process, many unbearably beautiful things are lost.

Through the theme of the different destinies, Baum wove the story of Santa Claus into his rich mythology and placed his story in the distant past. The forests have grown "old and sturdy" since the beginning of the world,[64] and the enemies of the trees have been kept in abeyance by the wood nymphs. With much of the work done, the never-ending years become burdensome to Necile, one of the nymphs of Burzee; she has become restless and longs for experiences beyond those allotted to her kind. Again Baum has introduced one of his favorite themes—the problems inherent in immortality.

When a mortal baby is discovered on the edge of the forest, it is Necile who breaks a law of the immortals and brings the baby into the forest. Using the great Ak's own arguments against him, she obtains permission to keep and care for the baby. She gives him the name Claus, which in the language of the wood nymphs means "little one." She has also opened herself to the experiences of human love and human grief. Claus grows up loved and protected by all the immortals of the forest; he is happy and has no idea that there are others like him in the great world outside.

When Claus has grown so much that he and Necile look more like brother and sister than son and foster mother, the wise Ak decides that Claus must see the world and his own kind. Claus then observes all types of people—rich and poor, good and bad, wise and foolish—and he is saddened by the constant struggle and the brief existences of mortals. He is especially drawn to the children, who at that time were not treated well by adults. When he and Ak return to Burzee, Claus knows that he must leave that paradise and accept "the endless struggle to which humanity is doomed,"[65] but in gratitude to Necile for caring for him, he vows, "I must devote myself to the care of the children of mankind and try to make them happy."[66]

Claus, however, is set apart from the rest of mankind because he is a friend of the immortals; therefore, he chooses the Laughing Valley in which to live. Claus is the only mortal inhabitant of that valley, which embodies all the joy of nature. Burzee borders the valley on one end, and on the other, the valley opens out onto a great plain where men live.

He begins to make friends with the children in the towns of men and by accident makes the first toy the world has ever seen. As his fame grows as a friend of the children and a giver of toys, he attracts the attention of the Awgwas, creatures who "were neither mortals nor immortals, but stood midway between those classes of beings,"[67] and who encouraged and inspired wicked behavior. They first try to kidnap Claus and then to kill him, but Claus's friends the immortals fight "The Great Battle Between Good and Evil" and vanquish the Awgwas.[68]

Claus continues his work for the children, going farther and farther out into the world each year, and he gains those attributes, such as his red suit and reindeer, that are familiar to us as belonging to Santa Claus. Years pass, and he grows very old. It seems, though, only an instant to his foster mother, Necile, who remains as young and as beautiful as the day she found the baby Claus. But finally comes the day that Claus is forced to lay down his tools; he is dying.

All the world of men and nature is sad. The great Ak, after much thought, comes to a momentous decision. He calls a meeting in Burzee of all the rulers of all the immortals in the world at which it is decided that the one and only Cloak of Immortality, which was made at the beginning of time and which, like the Holy Grail, exists between heaven and earth, will be bestowed on Claus so that he can continue ever after to make the children of men happy.

Baum's version of Santa Claus has not become part of the general tradition, but it is a beautiful story and one of his most enchanting books. And he had finally provided himself with a real fairyland—that is, an enchanted land that is inhabited by fairies, and with a background and source of magic for much of his later fantasy.

Just as in *Dot and Tot of Merryland,* there is a lot of Baum himself in this book, but it goes beyond the idyllic childhood of the earlier fantasy and deals with the child's acceptance of the struggles and trials of mankind. Baum had realized, as Claus did, that "every man has his mission, which is to leave the world better, in some way, than he found it." He and Claus chose the same mission, "the care of the children of mankind."[69]

Baum's own personal philosophy also comes through strongly: his love of nature and his belief in the sacredness of every living thing. When Claus moves to the Laughing Valley, he uses only fallen trees to build his house; he will not cut into a living one. He also cannot bring himself to till the land because to do so would be to destroy the flowers. The immortals are part of nature, and Baum implies that the best of men are also. He also reiterates his view that in his imaginary worlds evil can be destroyed but good cannot: "it is the Law that while Evil, unopposed, may accomplish terrible deeds, the powers of Good can never be overthrown when opposed to Evil."[70]

Baum's Santa Claus is a creator who finds it impossible to be idle. Claus makes the first toy because the cold winter and deep snow make it impossible for him to follow his normal pursuits. In that instance, Baum was directly transferring one of his own characteristics to his fictional character. At this time in his life, Baum was stricken with Bell's palsy, which temporarily paralyzed part of the left side of his face.[71] The doctor ordered him to stop writing for a while and rest his mind. What Baum did to "rest" was to create a stenciled frieze of geese for the living room of the lake cottage and to build a grandfather clock. And, finally, as Paul Tietjens' wife, Eunice, remembered, "he had made an elaborate piano arrangement of Paul's music for *The Wizard of Oz*—though he was no musician it was pretty good—had then figured out the system by which pianola records were made and had cut a full length record of this arrangement out of wrapping paper. This seems to have done the trick, and he was presently back at work."[72]

THE ENCHANTED ISLAND OF YEW

In 1903 Bobbs-Merrill reissued many of the Baum titles that it had acquired from Hill. The firm also published the revised version of *A New Wonderland* as *The Magical Monarch of Mo*, but Baum's only new book to appear that year was *The Enchanted Island of Yew*, also published by Bobbs-Merrill and illustrated by Fanny Y. Cory. For it, Baum created another imaginary land that consists of several individual countries, with the whole cut off from the rest of the world by the sea. Yew is a large round island "divided into four quarters . . . except that there was a big place in the center where the fifth kingdom, called Spor, lay in the midst of the mountains."[73] The four quarters correspond to the four directions: in the east is the Kingdom of Dawna; in the west, Auriel; in the north, Heg; and in the south, Plenta. Besides these five important kingdoms of Yew, there is a small, hidden land between Spor and Auriel called Twi.

Countries that correspond to the directions of the compass are reminiscent of those in Oz, but in *The Wonderful Wizard of Oz*, Baum gave no indication of the shape of Oz itself; it could be round, square, rectangular, or irregular. Also, he gave no indication of how or where the countries are divided from one another. Thus Yew may have influenced his thinking about Oz when later he was more specific about the geography of that land, making it a large rectangle that is divided into four quarters with the area of the Emerald City in the center.

Baum specifically pointed out that the kingdoms of Yew are ruled by mortals and that their subjects are mortals. What makes the island enchanted is that at the time the story takes place, immortals are still living there. Although the immortals are rarely seen, they have taught some men how to be magicians and sorcerers. The island itself is a beautiful, pastoral setting of meadows, fields, forests, and orchards with mountains in the middle. The only unusual topographical features occur in the small Land of Twi, where there is twilight instead of bright sunshine and where everything animate and inanimate is double.

The Life and Adventures of Santa Claus and *The Enchanted Island of Yew* are the only two of Baum's full-length fantasies that are specifically set in the distant past. To explain the origin of the immortals in *Santa Claus,* he went back to the beginning of the world, and to weave the story of Santa Claus into that mythology, he placed the main events of his story at a time before men had explored much of the world. However, in the last chapters of that book, he brought the story of Santa Claus down to the present and, in effect, brought his immortals and the ancient Forest of Burzee into the present also. In contrast, the story in *The Enchanted Island of Yew* takes place entirely in the past, "years and years and years ago."[74] Baum's explanation of why this and so many other stories take place "once on a time" is worth quoting for what it shows of his attitudes toward city life and civilization when it was written:

> *In the old days, when the world was young, there were no automobiles nor flying-machines to make one wonder; nor were there railway trains, nor telephones, nor mechanical inventions of any sort to keep people keyed up to a high pitch of excitement. Men and women lived simply and quietly. They were Nature's children, and breathed fresh air into their lungs instead of smoke and coal gas; and tramped through green meadows and deep forests instead of riding in street cars; and went to bed when it grew dark and rose with the sun—which is vastly different from the present custom. . . .*
>
> *So people knew fairies in those days . . . and loved them, together with all the ryls and knooks and pixies and nymphs and other beings that belong to the hordes of immortals. . . .*
>
> *To-day the fairies are shy . . . [and] perform their tasks unseen and unknown, and live mostly in their own beautiful realms, where they are almost unthought of by our bustling world.*

> *Yet when we come to story-telling the marvels of our*
> *own age shrink into insignificance beside the brave deeds and*
> *absorbing experiences of the days when fairies were better*
> *known.* [75]

The explanation seems to begin with a contrast in favor of the wonders of the modern world, but that impression is quickly dispelled. It is not possible to doubt Baum's meaning when he talks of having to breathe smoke and coal gas instead of fresh air, of riding streetcars rather than enjoying healthy exercise, or of our "bustling world" keeping people too occupied to appreciate the natural wonders of this world. His concerns are even more applicable today when cities have grown ever larger and uncontrolled suburban development has carried air and noise pollution out into the countryside and the forests. In 1903, though, the small towns and countryside were largely free of the evils he wrote of; it was only in the large cities that such conditions existed. Baum, however, was living and supporting his family in a large city, and his reaction to life there is another strong indication of his longing for a lost paradise of unspoiled natural beauty.

The Enchanted Island of Yew was of great significance for the development of Baum's imagination because, more than just making references to places or characters that had appeared in other stories, he utilized in it the whole mythology he had created for *The Life and Adventures of Santa Claus*. This mythology was so well fixed in his mind as the background that he did not bother to describe again the various characteristics and attributes of the immortals. He mentioned some of them in the explanation just quoted; and the Prince of the Knooks (from Burzee), the King of the Ryls, the Sound Elves, and the Governor of the Goblins, a new character, play parts in the story.

Illusion—whether interior (as in the self-deceptions of the Scarecrow, the Tin Woodman, and the Lion) or exterior (as in the tricks of the Wizard)—plays a part in all of Baum's fantasies. This story contains his most generous user of it since *The Wizard;* almost no character is what he appears to be or what he thinks himself to be.

The story is about one of those rare instances, mentioned in *Santa Claus*, when a fairy allows herself to be seen by mortals.[76] In Baum's chronology, the story takes place after Santa Claus has been granted immortality.[77] In *Santa Claus*, we learned that Burzee is the most important and inviolate residence of the fairies, but that they also live in other places. One such place is the Forest of Lurla in the Kingdom of Heg on the island of Yew.

Lady Seseley, the daughter of the most powerful baron in the kingdom, and two companions meet an unhappy fairy in that forest. The fairy tells them that she has existed from even before the island of Yew rose out of the sea and that she has "grown tired of remembering—and of being a fairy continually, without any change."[78] She explains her discontent and her longing to have new experiences and to be something different, even if for only a little while. With the help of the three mortal girls, the fairy's shape is changed for one year. On the inside she is still a fairy, but on the outside she has the appearance of a fifteen-year-old knight in shining armor whom the girls name Prince Marvel. Girls, as Baum explained, were not able to go out and have adventures at that time.

During Prince Marvel's year of existence, he has a number of adventures and turns many enemies into friends and companions, including Nerle, a noble's son; a band of fifty-nine thieves; the awful King Terribus of Spor; and the High Ki, the double girl ruler of Twi. He needs these friends on his last adventure when he must rescue the three girls who helped him become Prince Marvel. They are prisoners in one of the two magic mirrors of the Red Rogue of Dawna. All of Marvel's friends are also captured by the mirror before the prince frees them by shattering it and capturing the Red Rogue in the second mirror.

The year ends soon afterward, and Prince Marvel sorrowfully takes his leave of his friends to return to his eternal existence as a fairy. Baum, however, does not end the book there, and the sense of sadness and nostalgia are only increased in the last chapter, where he describes the island a hundred years later. The mirror containing the image of the Red Rogue falls off the wall of the deserted castle and breaks, freeing him. He is dazed at the changes in the island and confused because he is no longer feared but is regarded as a freak. All the knightly adventures have passed away, and, as Baum put it, "civilization had won."[79] The enchantment had left the land.

Because Baum ended the enchantment of this imaginary country and brought it into the real world, Yew is the only one of Baum's major imaginary countries that he did not later incorporate into the area of his fantasy continent. But Yew does have its place in his imaginary chronology, where it performs the same function that the legends of King Arthur and the vanished Camelot do in ours: it becomes the medieval epic of his imaginary world.

In *The Enchanted Island of Yew,* Baum ended up with too much country for his story, which may indicate that the place was created before the plot was completely worked out. The largest part of the book is taken up by the adventures in Heg (six chapters), Spor (six chapters), and Twi (seven chapters), which is not even mentioned in his initial description of Yew. In comparison, the adventures in Auriel (two chapters), Plenta (one short chapter), and Dawna (three chapters) seem perfunctory and hurried, and those kingdoms are barely described. Thus the promise inherent in the first alluring description of the imaginary world of Yew is not fulfilled. That imbalance between story and place causes a decline in interest and a sense of dissatisfaction about three-quarters of the way through the book that mar what is otherwise one of Baum's most unusual fantasies. The ending revives the reader's interest in the story, but the sense of dissatisfaction with place remains.

QUEEN ZIXI OF IX

Baum's fantasy publications for 1902 and 1903 include only *The Life and Adventures of Santa Claus* and *The Enchanted Island of Yew* and two short stories that contribute nothing to his developing Other-world. His illness had been one reason for the small number of publications, but a far greater reason was his heavy involvement in more projects for the theater. After the success of the stage version of *The Wonderful Wizard of Oz*, he was in great demand as a playwright, and among the projects he worked on either alone or in collaboration were *The Maid of Athens, King Jonah XIII,* and *The Whatnexters.*[80] None of those plays was produced, and some of them were never carried past the planning stage. However, one that was finished and almost produced was Baum's adaptation for the stage of the book *Prince Silverwings and Other Fairy Tales* by Edith Ogden Harrison, the wife of the mayor of Chicago. Michael Patrick Hearn, David L. Greene, and Peter E. Hanff show in their article "The Faltering Flight of Prince Silverwings" that Baum was solely responsible for the scenario and the play script based on the book. Because the stories were unrelated, Baum had to develop a consistent plot out of disparate elements.[81]

The play was scheduled for production, but a disastrous theater fire caused its cancellation. Even though *Prince Silverwings* was never produced, the play was very important for Baum's subsequent development because a case can be made for its being the source for several important incidents and characters in Baum's later books. The manuscript has survived and Hearn, Greene, and Hanff assert that "it shows how Baum assimilated details, motifs, and themes from various sources and how carefully and tastefully he reworked them in new and larger works for children."[82]

In his fantasies, Baum had been moving away from American subjects. Santa Claus is an American character, but Baum's mythological treatment of the tradition and his setting of the story in an age that vaguely resembles the Middle Ages give the story a European ambience. Prince Marvel's adventures as a knight in armor certainly is not an American subject, although in both books there are incidents, viewpoints, and characteristics that indicate that the stories could have been written only by an American.

The themes of discontent, longing, and nostalgia for what has been lost are more evident in these books than they are in either the earlier or the later books. The cause was probably a combination of reasons:

Baum's increasing dislike of civilization as it was developing in a large, fast-growing city; the energy and concentration that his many theatrical projects required; and his illness and enforced creative inactivity. But more than any of these, or because of all of them, Baum seems to have lost touch with the America he loved—the nation of vast spaces, smaller towns, and breathtaking scenery. He seems to have felt that he had lost something important and necessary.

That Baum's fantasy had definitely taken a new direction and was coming more and more to deal with the traditional fairy-tale themes—the long ago and far away of European fairy tales—is evident from his next book, *Queen Zixi of Ix*. Many critics consider it his best story. It is also his most traditional fairy tale, and the logical continuation of the trio of books that include *The Life and Adventures of Santa Claus* and *The Enchanted Island of Yew*, rather than a development of the type of American fantasy he had created in *The Wonderful Wizard of Oz*. It is probable that he would have continued in this direction if something had not happened to reacquaint him with America and revive his ideal of an American paradise.

The close relationship between *Queen Zixi of Ix* and the two books preceding it is obscured because it was not Baum's next full-length fantasy to be published. That was *The Marvelous Land of Oz*, which appeared in the summer of 1904 and signaled the rejuvenation of Baum's more obviously American fantasies. To get away from the cold weather in Chicago, Baum and his wife had spent the winter of 1903/1904 in the West. In a letter to the novelist Emerson Hough, Baum stated that between early January and the date of the letter, March 15, 1904, he had "written the new book for this year [*The Marvelous Land of Oz*] and got it into the pub's hands. It was sketched before. And I have revised and prepared for *St. Nicholas* a serial called 'The Magic Cloak,' which I send to Mrs. [Mary Mapes] Dodge today."[83] Baum's wording would seem to indicate that the first draft of "The Magic Cloak" had been finished before he left Chicago. *St. Nicholas*, the best known and most respected of the magazines for children of that time, planned the contents of the issues far in advance of publication, so "The Magic Cloak," retitled *Queen Zixi*

92

of Ix; or, The Story of the Magic Cloak, did not begin appearing until the November 1904 issue; the book version was not published until late 1905.

Queen Zixi is the story of a magic cloak woven by the fairies to aid helpless mortals. It takes place in Baum's most conventional imaginary world; in fact, the sense of place in this tale is the weakest in all his full-length fantasies. Noland and Ix are adjoining kingdoms, separated by mountains, a river, and a forest, but they are not given any specific geographical location except the mention that the river eventually flows into the sea. Very little of the topography of Noland is described, and almost none of Ix. Much of the action takes place in the city of Nole, which is ruled by the boy Bud because he was the forty-seventh person to enter the city gate after the old king died. His sister, Fluff, is the owner of the magic cloak. Nole is only the second large city to appear in Baum's major fantasies; the city, like the countries, is given very little individual character in the written descriptions.

Ix is ruled by the witch-queen Zixi, who is 683 years old but, by magic, appears to be a beautiful girl of 16. She is a wise and just ruler, but her secret sorrow is that she cannot see the beautiful, young image of herself that others see, for her mirrors reflect only her true hag-like appearance. When Zixi hears about the magic cloak from a wandering minstrel, she becomes obsessed with the idea of possessing it, but during her attempts, the cloak is damaged.

The two kingdoms become allies and friends when Noland is attacked by a race of strange creatures, the Roly-Rogues from high in the mountains. It is Zixi's magic that saves Noland. At the end of the story, the Queen of the Fairies appears and is angry because the cloak, which was made to assist mortals, has been used for so many foolish wishes. She revokes the unwise wishes but lets the cloak grant one last wish, which is Bud's to "become the best king that Noland has ever had."[84] Zixi's wish, however, she refuses to grant because "fairies do not approve of witchcraft,"[85] and Zixi is forced to become reconciled to her destiny.

Both the background and the story are reminiscent of traditional European fairy tales. The Roly-Rogues are the only really nontraditional creations in the book. The time in which the story is set is also more vague than that in other of Baum's books; the story seems to be set in the present, but the only clue is the fairies' mention of America in the first chapter.

Yet the fantasy does work because of the associations it evokes and because of the story. Noland and Ix, being conventional fairy-tale countries, call to mind all the reader's past associations with the whole body of traditional folk- and fairy tales, from Charles Perrault and the Brothers Grimm to Andrew Lang. The illustrations greatly support this feel of tradition because the artist, Frederick Richardson, drew pictures that—with the many towered palaces, nobles in rich silks and velvets, and common people in traditional European garb—call to mind many earlier illustrated editions of fairy tales. Only Richardson's representation of Zixi was in any way contemporary, and he made her very much the Art Nouveau ideal of woman.

An even stronger association for readers familiar with Baum is the opening of the book. It begins—as does *The Life and Adventures of Santa Claus,* the action in *The Enchanted Island of Yew,* and the play *Prince Silverwings*—in an enchanted forest. It is, also just as in *Santa Claus,* the wonderful Forest of Burzee where Lulea, Queen of the Fairies, and her band conceive the idea of weaving the magic cloak.[86] And even though the fairies have little else to do with the story until the very end, Baum gave his story the background of his whole mythology of the immortals.

The story—the other ingredient of the book's success—is one of Baum's strongest, certainly the strongest since *The Wonderful Wizard of Oz* and stronger than many of those to follow. All the adventures are integrated into the plot; there are no visits to exotic countries or encounters with strange characters that have no relation to the story. Even Baum's recurring themes are well integrated: the fairies wove the cloak because they were bored and dissatisfied with their usual, never-ending occupations, and Queen Zixi's longing for what she cannot have precipitates the working out of the plot. Zixi herself is Baum's most nearly tragic character; she must learn to live with the knowledge that what she is inside is very different from what she appears to be. She has to learn to be reconciled—contentment is ever beyond her.

Despite the strengths of *Queen Zixi of Ix*, it is not an American fairy tale and, from that standpoint, represents a step backward and a retreat for Baum. His imaginary worlds had been inspired by his own exploration of new places, but after seven years of living in Chicago, it seemed that the store of his inspiration derived from the American landscape was dwindling. His evocations of nature are more perfunctory and less detailed in this book—even the description of the Forest Burzee lacks enchantment. Not being able to turn the modern city as he saw it into a fantasy setting, he retreated to the traditional type of fairy-tale city, from which all references to modern life could be eliminated.

But even as he revised *Queen Zixi* in the winter of 1903/1904, Baum's situation had changed. He and Maud were spending that winter in southern California, their first visit there. In an interview in February 1904, he said that "those who do not find Coronado a paradise have doubtless brought with them the same conditions that would render heaven unpleasant to them did they chance to gain admittance."[87] Baum felt that he had discovered a real American fairyland.

Chapter Four

Further Exploration
1904–1907

Imagination transforms the commonplace into the great and creates the new out of the old. . . .

In fact, man is the only commonplace being in the world. Nature is not commonplace. Man's familiarity with the objects around him reduces him to the commonplace. Imagination and faith alone can keep him above it. . . . [W]e must be kept above the commonplace. Our success, our progress and achievements depend upon that.

"Interview with Mr. Frank G. [*sic*] Baum" (1909) in *The Advance*

THE SHEER VARIETY OF STORIES THAT L. FRANK BAUM TURNED OUT IN
THE FIRST YEARS OF HIS WRITING CAREER IS AMAZING, and it seemed as
though he could continue forever without once repeating himself. Nevertheless, in 1904 special circumstances caused him to turn back to one of
his earlier books and write a sequel to it.

THE MARVELOUS LAND OF OZ

The Marvelous Land of Oz, L. Frank Baum's fantasy for 1904, signaled his
return to his more American-style fairy tales; it would also appear to
signal the beginning of the Oz series, but there are strong indications that
Baum himself did not view it in that light—no more so than Lewis Carroll
viewed *Through the Looking-Glass* as the beginning of a series. There is a
finality about the conclusion of the book that indicates that Baum considered it to be exactly what he called it, "a sequel to *The Wizard of Oz,*" and
no more. Even though, since the publication of *The Wonderful Wizard of
Oz,* he had been receiving letters from children asking for more stories

about Oz, there is evidence that the demands of his reading public played the lesser part in his decision to write a second book about Oz.

In the "Author's Note" to *The Marvelous Land of Oz,* Baum stated the "public reason" for writing a sequel. He said that he had promised a little girl named Dorothy "that when a thousand little girls had written . . . a thousand little letters asking for another story of the Scarecrow and the Tin Woodman . . . [he] would write the book."[1] The ostensible reason, however, was not the major reason; it was not the popularity of *The Wonderful Wizard of Oz* that Baum was most desirous of repeating, but the popularity of *The Wizard of Oz* musical extravaganza.

That the theater was the greatest passion of Baum's life has to be kept in mind to understand many of the odd twists and turns of his writing career. That love, which began when he was eighteen, never lessened, although too often it was a one-sided adoration. To Baum, the phenomenal success of the stage version of *The Wonderful Wizard of Oz* was the high point of his life. It was also its tragedy because the kind of circus-like extravaganza that his story had been turned into was alien to his talents. He wasted much of his time and creative energies—sometimes to the detriment of his books—trying to duplicate a type of musical theater that was already old-fashioned and that the very success of *The Wizard* and its host of imitators quickly made obsolete.

As the "author" of the most successful stage musical of the era, he had become frustrated by his inability to get any of his other theatrical projects into production. He probably also knew that David Montgomery and Fred Stone were tiring of *The Wizard,* and he wanted to provide another vehicle for them. Their characterizations of the Tin Woodman and the Scarecrow had been the single most important element in the show's success; the character of Dorothy, having been turned into a young lady and given a love interest, had declined in importance in the production.

When Baum's explanation given in his "Author's Note" is examined more carefully, it becomes clear that he was thinking more of the stage play than of the original book. Dorothy is the raison d'être of the

98

first story, but she is not a character in *The Marvelous Land of Oz*. For the readers of the original book, the Cowardly Lion, Toto, and even the Wizard had shared popularity with the Scarecrow and the Tin Woodman; yet Baum was specific about the sequel being "another story of the Scarecrow and the Tin Woodman," and the other popular characters do not appear. Only in the stage production had those two characters so far outshone the rest, and the original title of the book was *The Further Adventures of the Scarecrow and the Tin Woodman*.[2] That Baum was thinking in terms of a play for Montgomery and Stone is further supported by his dedication of *The Marvelous Land of Oz* to them and by his inclusion in the first edition of photographs of the two in costume.

The strongest evidence that the story was written with the intention of turning it into a stage play is in the style and the plot of the book. Despite Baum's public statement that Julian Mitchell's changes and additions to his original script for *The Wizard* had not angered him and that the success of the play had proved Mitchell right, it *had* bothered Baum that the stage script had strayed so far from his original story, even though he was forced to admit that Mitchell understood the taste of the adult audience better than he. To solve the dilemma of catering to the taste of the public and still being faithful to his story in the stage adaptation, Baum had to work into the story those elements that had been a success on stage. Therefore, in *The Marvelous Land of Oz*, the Scarecrow and the Tin Woodman have prominent, comic parts; one of the major threads of the plot involves an army of beautiful girls; a magical illusion of sunflowers with girls' faces in the center resembles the successful scene of girls dressed as poppies in *The Wizard;* many more comic dialogues are included than had appeared in his earlier books; and his story ends with a theatrical fairy-tale transformation.

The plot reflects his preoccupation with the stage because, as will be seen, it is a development and continuation more of the stage play than of the original book. Yet all this does not mean that Baum did not care about what his child readers thought or wanted, but he seems to have believed that the popularity of the play had been solely responsible for the

To those excellent good fellows and eminent comedians David C. Montgomery and Fred A Stone whose clever personations of the Tin Woodman and the Scarecrow have delighted thousands of children throughout the land, this book is gratefully dedicated by THE AUTHOR

ever-increasing popularity of the book. Naturally, then, he felt that the children wanted a continuation of the successful elements of the play. He was very careful, however, to keep out of his book the sexuality inherent in rows of chorus girls in tights and the sometimes vulgar topical humor of the stage.

There were also other concerns, apart from the stage, that led Baum back to Oz. None of his Bobbs-Merrill books had had a success to match that of *Father Goose* or *The Wizard*. He needed another best-seller, and he felt that the Indianapolis firm did not market his books aggressively enough. His dissatisfaction with Bobbs-Merrill made him ready to listen to two old friends, Frank K. Reilly and Sumner S. Britton, who had been secretary and head salesman for the George M. Hill Company.[3] They were about to start their own publishing company in Chicago, and they wanted a strong book for their first-year list. Writing a book for them appealed to Baum, not least of all because he missed the personalized treatment he had enjoyed at Hill.

Even with all the disparate elements that went into persuading Baum to write a second Oz book, *The Marvelous Land of Oz* is a good story and has always been one of the most popular of the Oz books— Gore Vidal called it "one of the most unusual and interesting books of the series."[4]

The plot revolves around the adventures of a young boy named Tippetarius (usually called Tip) and begins in the north part of Oz, which is the Country of the Gillikins where the favorite color is purple. Tip has been raised by Mombi, a wicked old woman who is also a witch, even though the practice of witchcraft has been forbidden to anyone else by the Good Witch of the North. While Mombi is away buying groceries and trading magic secrets with a crooked wizard, Tip amuses himself by making a figure out of branches and tree bark to frighten Mombi on her

The dedication page from the first edition of The Marvelous Land of Oz. *Baum hoped that David Montgomery and Fred Stone would star in his stage version of this story.*

return. Tip dresses the figure in old clothes and carves a pumpkin into a face for the head. When Mombi encounters the dummy, she decides to try out the magic Powder of Life, which she got from the crooked wizard, and she brings the pumpkin-headed man to life. Mombi does not punish Tip for his prank immediately because she has other plans for him; with the live dummy to do his work, she is going to turn Tip into a marble statue by using another of the new potions. The brew must cool overnight, and while Mombi sleeps, Tip takes the Powder of Life and the live dummy, whom he names Jack Pumpkinhead, and runs away.

They travel all night, but Jack is awkward and their progress is slow. Thus when they come across a wooden sawhorse that looks some-what like a real horse, Tip brings it to life for Jack to ride. Tip mistakenly tells the Sawhorse to go as fast as it can, and the horse, with Jack on its back, leaves Tip far behind. The Sawhorse does not stop until it reaches the Emerald City, where it and Jack Pumpkinhead are taken to His Majesty the Scarecrow.

Tip, on his slower journey, meets a pretty girl who calls herself General Jinjur. She is leading an army of revolt, composed entirely of young women, against the Emerald City. Their goal is to seize the throne, end the rule of men, and take all the jewels in the jeweled city for them-selves. They are armed with sharp knitting needles and easily conquer the city because no one can bear to hurt such young and pretty girls. Tip, how-ever, manages to reach the palace and help barricade it against the army.

The Scarecrow decides to seek help from the Tin Woodman, who is now Emperor of the Winkies, and he, Jack, and Tip make a dash for freedom on the back of the swift Sawhorse. The Tin Woodman readily agrees to help them, but their return to the Emerald City is made difficult because Mombi is now helping Jinjur, and she conjures up various illu-sions to confuse them. While trying to find their way, they meet Mr. H. M. Woggle-Bug, T.E., a very strange creature that is an insect the size of a man. He had once been a normal-size insect that lived in a school-house. By listening to the teacher, he became "thoroughly educated" (T.E.), and when he was discovered and magnified onto a screen as an

102

illustration for the students, he escaped in his "highly magnified" (H.M.) state. The Woggle-Bug joins the party and is a good companion, except for his tendency to tell very old jokes and make very bad puns.

The companions, with the help of field mice, manage to recapture the palace, but they end up barricaded there again and surrounded by the army. The Scarecrow decides that they must build a flying machine and seek the help of Glinda the Good, the ruler of the Country of the Quadlings. They tie two sofas together, add palm leaves for wings, and place the stuffed head of a Gump (an elk-like creature) on one end, and Tip uses the last of the Powder of Life to bring the object to life. They fly all night, but in the morning discover that they have flown over the desert and out of the Land of Oz. After more adventures—one in which the Scarecrow's straw stuffing is replaced by banknotes—they finally reach Glinda's palace.

Glinda has unexpected news. She tells them that the Scarecrow has no more right to rule the Emerald City than has Jinjur and that the rightful ruler is the daughter of Pastoria, the former king of the Emerald City. The girl, whose name is Ozma, had been hidden somewhere by the Wizard when she was a baby, and Glinda has not been able to learn her whereabouts. The sorceress kept an account of all the Wizard's activities when he ruled the city, and among the suspicious ones had been several visits to Mombi.

The Scarecrow does not want the throne if he has no right to it, so he and his companions join forces with Glinda and her army of women to recapture the Emerald City for Ozma and to force Mombi to tell them what she knows of the girl. They are successful in winning back the city, and after a duel of magic between Glinda and Mombi, the witch is captured and forced to tell the truth. Mombi shocks all of them when she reveals that to hide the baby girl she turned her into a boy. Tip is Ozma.

Tip is upset by the news, but reluctantly agrees to let Mombi return him to his original form. After the transformation, Ozma takes her place as the rightful ruler, "the loveliest Queen the Emerald City had ever known."[5] The Woggle-Bug becomes her adviser, and the Scarecrow goes to live with the Tin Woodman and be the emperor's Royal Treasury now that he is stuffed with money. Jack Pumpkinhead "remained with Ozma to the end of his days; and he did not spoil as soon as he had feared."[6]

It was not easy for Baum to return to a world that he had created almost five years earlier for a very different story; it was also against his inclinations. *The Marvelous Land of Oz* was his first attempt to fit a full-length story into a preexisting background, and the first time he had to adapt and develop a background to accommodate a major new plot. Baum himself appears to have been uncertain just how to do this. The result is that in regard to the details of the imaginary world of Oz, *The Marvelous Land* is one of the more inconsistent books in the series, and the discrepancies make it difficult to sort out which alterations were the result of a change in his conception of Oz and which were the result of carelessness and hasty writing.

The "feel" of Oz remains the same; it is still a land of vast open spaces, divided into four separate kingdoms with the Emerald City in the center. Baum completed its geography by giving the area of the north a name, the Country of the Gillikins, and a color, purple. Oz is still sparsely populated and rural, but not to the extent that it was in *The Wizard*. Now the Emerald City is not the only city, but only "the biggest town in all the country"[7]; there is also a City of the Winkies[8] around the castle of the Tin Woodman, and there are villages. The people of Oz are no longer referred to as small, and there is no indication in the text that they are anything but normal-size, mortal people.

Another, obviously conscious, alteration Baum made was to refer to Glinda only as Glinda the Good, not as a Good Witch. She is still the ruler of the Country of the South, but she is now "a mighty Sorceress" who understands "magic better than any other person in the Land of Oz."[9] Baum had changed his opinion of witchcraft in *Queen Zixi of Ix;* Zixi is not portrayed as an evil woman, but as a witch she is shunned by the fairies. Glinda and Zixi are similar because both are very old but appear young and lovely. Baum may have decided that a sorceress is more easily thought of as good than is a witch.

Baum still had not decided on a definite shape for Oz; the country

104

seems to expand and contract to fit the story: "It's a long way to Glinda's palace,"[10] Tip learns when he and his friends leave the Emerald City to go south. But when, during the duel of magic in the Emerald City, Glinda pursues Mombi in another direction from the city, they reach the desert in a little over an hour. Also, when the travelers fly out of the Land of Oz in the Gump, they go south, but when they return the same way, they come first to the Country of the Munchkins (east) and then to the Country of the Quadlings. Baum does slyly insinuate that the Scarecrow's directions may have been at fault, but even so, no idea of the exact shapes of the whole country and the kingdoms inside it can be drawn from the information in the text.

None of the alterations mentioned thus far have been of much consequence, but there are three areas of change that do major damage to Baum's original conception of Oz; these pertain to the color scheme of the country, the origin of the Emerald City, and the character of the Wizard.

Working without W. W. Denslow, Baum seemed unsure about what to do with the color scheme of Oz. In *The Wizard*, it is very precisely delineated, providing a deliberate contrast to the false color of the Emerald City. In *The Marvelous Land*, it is confused and contradictory. These are the most glaring examples: the pumpkins in the Country of the Gillikins are described as "golden red" and the corn as being in "rows of green stalks," but only two chapters later, it is stated that "everything in this Country of the Gillikins is of a purple color." That is, "the grass is purple, and the trees are purple, and the houses and fences are purple. . . . Even the mud in the roads is purple." This is a radical change from *The Wizard*, where only man-made objects display the favorite color of the country. Baum emphasized this change a little farther on; when Tip approached the Emerald City, he "noticed that the purple tint of the grass and trees had now faded to a dull lavender, and before long this lavender appeared to take on a greenish tinge that gradually brightened as they drew nearer to the great City." But when the travelers fly back into Oz and look down on the Country of the Munchkins, they see that "the houses and fences are blue," which accords with *The Wizard*. Only two pages later, however, when they enter the Country of the Quadlings, they see "the red houses and fences and trees." *And* only two paragraphs after that, the Gump lands in Glinda's palace garden "upon a velvety green lawn."[11]

The *illusion* of green in the Emerald City is an important part of the first story, but Baum also changed that in the second book. When the Sawhorse and Jack first enter the city, the Guardian of the Gates puts the green spectacles on them to keep them "from being blinded by the glitter and glare of the gorgeous Emerald City"[12]; this is the same explanation from *The Wizard* that disguises the fact that the interior of the Emerald City is no different in color from that of any other city. But from the moment Jinjur and her army invade the city, there is no more mention of green spectacles and of anyone being blinded by the brightness of the city. No one wears the green spectacles after that, yet everything in the city is *still* described as green.

Baum was never able to work out a completely consistent color scheme of Oz in his later books. Color had played such a unique part in both the story and the book design of *The Wizard* that to find other plots in which it would be as necessary an element proved impossible. The nearest he came was to use the favored color of a country as an indication of which part of Oz his characters were in, and often, when that fact was established, he seems to have forgotten about it. In later books, Baum went into more detail about the other colors in the Emerald City, but in *The Marvelous Land*, inadvertently or not, he changed his city of illusion into a real, green-colored city.

Color, however, is not the most confusing contradiction about the Emerald City in *The Marvelous Land*. Early in the book, Tip tells Jack its history, how "it was built by a mighty and wonderful Wizard named Oz." But later the Scarecrow says, "The former King of this City, who was named Pastoria, lost the crown to the Wonderful Wizard, who passed it on to me."[13] That statement completely contradicts the story of the origin of the city in *The Wizard*. Pastoria, a former king of the city, which already had been built before the Wizard arrived in Oz, comes directly from the stage play, and it is that version that continues to be developed in the remainder of the book. Glinda then tells Tip and the others that Pastoria is dead, but that he had a daughter, Ozma, whom the Wizard had hidden away somewhere. Baum, by this contradiction, has maligned the character of the gentle little humbug and negated a carefully constructed contrast in *The Wizard:* in that book, everyone thinks that he is a great Wizard but does not know if he is a man, but in reality, he is "a very good man; but . . . a very bad Wizard."[14] In the stage play, though, the Wizard is a sinister character, more consistent with someone who would commit evil acts to gain power.

Some of the discrepancies suggest that Baum made changes in his plot somewhere in mid-writing; it is known that he added the character of the Woggle-Bug when the book was already well under way.[15] But outside of saying that Baum needed a good editor, no explanation that would bring some kind of accord to these contradictions can be given. However, among those who love Baum's books, the inconsistencies have not always been considered faults. Instead, they have given rise to fanciful and ingenious solutions to the Oz mysteries, using the same Sherlockian kind of logic with which devotees of Sherlock Holmes explain the problems and inconsistencies in those stories. But putting such pleasant speculations aside, it is clear that Baum left his imaginary world in a very confused state at the end of *The Marvelous Land of Oz*, and though Reilly & Britton may not have supplied him with an alert editor, the contradictions did not get past his readers, the children, who were writing him fan letters in increasing numbers.

The Marvelous Land of Oz, the first publication of the new Reilly & Britton Company,[16] was a beautifully produced book, profusely illustrated with sixteen color plates, twenty-four full-page black-and-white pictures, and almost a hundred smaller drawings. The illustrator was John Rea Neill (1877–1943), a Philadelphia artist who would become Baum's principal illustrator. Neill must have worked at an incredible speed to complete the large number of beautifully detailed drawings in such a short time. Baum had witten to Emerson Hough on March 15, 1904, that he had just finished the manuscript and sent it to the publisher,[17] and the book was published in July. It was Baum's most successful book since *The Wonderful Wizard of Oz*. Almost all of the many reviews were favorable, although the perceptive reviewer for the *Cleveland Leader* spotted Baum's real reason for writing the story:

> *Mr. Baum, we have said, has the child heart. But he has the business head as well. Part of the book, and that the least enjoyable, has been written with a view to the stage. General Jinjur and her soldiers are only shapely chorus girls. The observant reader can see their tights and their ogling glances even in the pages of the book. This is a minor blemish, though. Otherwise,* The Marvelous Land of Oz *is innocent, spontaneous, jolly. It's as good as* The Wizard of Oz, *which is the highest compliment we can pay it.[18]*

THE WOGGLE-BUG

The Marvelous Land of Oz spawned two ephemeral publications: a series of twenty-six short stories (plus a Prologue) entitled "Queer Visitors from the Marvelous Land of Oz," which ran in several newspapers from August 28, 1904, to February 26, 1905; and a short book, *The Woggle-Bug Book,* published in the summer of 1905. The newspaper series was probably intended to sustain interest in the new Oz book and keep interest alive for the inevitable stage version, although as Douglas G. Greene points out, "Baum must have hoped that it would succeed on its own."[19] *The Woggle-Bug Book* was released to coincide with the play of the same name, which was Baum's adaptation of *The Marvelous Land.* Both newspaper stories and book are negligible as anything but curiosities, and both are very far from the spirit of Oz, concerning as they do the adventures of the

---

John R. Neill's illustration for page 172 of the first edition of The Marvelous Land of Oz.

"IT'S TOO EASY, ALTOGETHER."

Scarecrow, the Tin Woodman, Jack Pumpkinhead, the Woggle-Bug, the Sawhorse, and the Gump on a visit to America. Warren Hollister best stated the problem: "The Scarecrow and Tin Woodman are not merely characters—abstract personalities. They are inseparable from their environment; they are inhabitants of Oz. Bring them to America . . . and they lose their magic. In Oz place and people become one, in a way that critics have no means of describing."[20] The format of these stories is the kind of reverse fairy tale that Baum used in several of his *American Fairy Tales,* where the United States is the land of wonder and magic to characters from a fairyland. On the whole, America comes across as a much less pleasant and innocent place than Oz.

With one major exception, the newspaper stories had almost no effect on the future development of Oz. The exception occurs in the Prologue, at the end of the "Proclamation Extraordinary," in which Ozma gives the characters permission to visit America. There she is referred to as "Ozma, Reigning Princess of the Fairyland of Oz."[21] Baum had changed Ozma from Queen of the Emerald City to Princess Ozma, Ruler of all Oz—a change that is continued without comment in the next Oz book and that allowed him to reorganize the government of Oz in later books. This is also the first time that Baum referred to Oz as a fairyland within the text of a story. The "Proclamation Extraordinary" would also seem to indicate that Baum had located Oz on another planet, but the promotional material for the series is confusing regarding this and open to more than one interpretation. It may be that Baum merely meant that his characters were touring the planets before visiting the United States.[22] In any case, the idea of Oz being on another planet was not developed in any later stories, and what is of real significance is the indication that Baum was beginning to think of Oz as distinct from America.

The Woggle-Bug Book is an extended tale along the same lines as the newspaper stories, and it relates the Woggle-Bug's adventures in America when he becomes separated from his companions. One of the adventures concerns his efforts to earn money for use in America because "in the Land of Oz they use no money at all."[23] This was a strange

110

statement for Baum to make since money plays so large a part in *The Marvelous Land of Oz*, but it points ahead to a change that Baum would later make to Oz.

At this time, it seemed as though Baum's dream of continuing and lasting success in his beloved theater was about to come true. The contracts for the stage adaptation of the second Oz book that Baum signed with producers included provisions for a new musical each year from him for the next several years.[24] *The Woggle-Bug* opened in June 1905 without, however, Montgomery and Stone, who early in 1905 broke their contract for *The Wizard of Oz* because they were afraid of becoming typecast.[25] The play was a dismal failure. It had all the ingredients that had made *The Wizard* a huge success, but that was a large part of the problem—they were the same ingredients. One critic called it "only a shabby and dull repetition of a cheapened 'Wizard of Oz.'"[26] Because the theater was Baum's ultimate goal, the failure was a crushing defeat for him; it would be almost eight years before he would be able to get another of his plays produced.

ANIMAL FAIRY TALES
AND OTHER STORIES

Apart from the disaster of *The Woggle-Bug*, Baum's life was going well: *The Wizard of Oz* was still playing around the country; *The Marvelous Land of Oz* was a success; *Queen Zixi of Ix* was appearing monthly in *St. Nicholas*, soon to be followed by the book issue; and the series "Animal Fairy Tales" was appearing in another well-known magazine, the *Delineator*.

This was the period of much of Baum's best work, and the variety of fantasies that he published validates his claim that he had a lot of other good stories to tell besides those about Oz. The Prologue and nine stories known as *Animal Fairy Tales* are among his most unusual and interesting,[27] and it is a puzzle why they were not published in book form during his lifetime. They are fables based on the question: "Why should not the animals have their Fairies, as well as mortals?"[28] These stories show a very different side of Baum, for they are not the pretty stories of animals acting like humans, but incorporate the sometimes savage laws of the jungle into their structure. Baum always recognized that animals have different natures from humans, and he did not try to disguise the fact even with his more "civilized" animals, such as the Cowardly Lion and the Hungry Tiger.

Baum's second encounter with Oz had not caused him to abandon his fairy mythology and the more traditional fairy tales he had been publishing since 1902. In December 1904, the *Delineator* published his story "A Kidnapped Santa Claus"; in June 1905, his story "Nelebel's Fairyland" was published;[29] and sometime in 1905, he wrote another full-length traditional fantasy, *King Rinkitink*.

"A Kidnapped Santa Claus" adds more information about the geography of the Laughing Valley when it reveals that on the opposite side of the valley from the Forest of Burzee "stands the huge mountain that contains the Caves of the Daemons."[30] The Daemons of Selfishness, Envy, Hatred, and Malice kidnap Santa Claus because he makes children happy, but he is released by the Daemon of Repentance just as a vast army of the immortals comes to rescue him. In his previous stories about these immortals, Baum had made the knooks the guardians of the trees, a duty that had belonged to the nymphs. He repeats this change in "Nelebel's Fairyland" and in a later Oz book in which the knooks make an appearance. Nymphs, which are mentioned only once in this story, virtually disappear from Baum's writings after it. Perhaps he felt that these figures from Greek and Roman mythology did not fit in well with his more northern European fairy mythology. The Fairy Queen and her band take over the central position in Burzee. "A Kidnapped Santa Claus" is one of Baum's most beautiful stories.

The Marvelous Land of Oz may very well show the influence of Baum's stay in California in a sunnier and happier ambience than is apparent in his previous two or three books, but "Nelebel's Fairyland" is the first of his published fantasies to show that influence directly. The

112

story of the hundred-year exile of the fairy Nelebel, it utilizes one of the most common devices of the tall tale, to invent fanciful explanations of how the natural wonders of America were formed—in this case, the San Bernardino Mountains, the Bay of San Diego, and Coronado (which was Nelebel's fairyland). Queen Lulea sends knooks, ryls, and gigans (gigantic, but stupid immortals) with Nelebel, and they create the paradise of southern California to ease the exiled fairy's sorrow.

"Nelebel's Fairyland," an occasional piece, is not one of Baum's best stories, but the central idea of turning a favored area of the real world into a fairyland is one that Baum would use again to much greater effect in his last four fantasies.[31] Both "A Kidnapped Santa Claus" and "Nelebel's Fairyland" are also memorable because they are the last close-up views of the Laughing Valley and the Forest of Burzee he gave us before they, too, were drawn into the might and power of Oz.

KING RINKITINK

The influence of California is also evident in *King Rinkitink,* the full-length fantasy that Baum wrote sometime in 1905;[32] Baum's winter trips to Coronado, on the edge of the Pacific Ocean, may have inspired this story of the adventures of young Prince Inga of the island kingdom of Pingaree. Baum had already created one island country: Yew; however, in that book, the characters never come within sight of the sea, but the ocean is very present in the tale of Pingaree.

The story resembles *Queen Zixi of Ix:* both are traditional tales, and both involve gifts from the fairies—the magic cloak in *Queen Zixi* and three magic pearls from the fairy mermaids in *King Rinkitink.* Unfortunately, this book was never published in its original form, and the manuscript is not known to exist. But it was revised and published as an Oz book in 1916 under the title *Rinkitink in Oz.* The later revisions, however, do not appear to be extensive. Most of the original course of the plot can be followed, although there is an element of speculation about certain of the details and especially about the ending, where most of the revision occurred.

Pingaree is a peaceful island inhabited by pearl fishers who trade their pearls for the things they need with the mainland kingdom of Rinkitink. The island is wisely ruled by King Kitticut and Queen Garee, who have a young son, Prince Inga. The story opens with the king showing his son their family's greatest treasure, three magic pearls, which long before had enabled Inga's grandfather to repel an invasion from the islands of Regos and Coregos to the north. The pearls had been a gift from the Mermaid Queen; the blue pearl gives its owner unlimited strength, the pink pearl keeps any danger from touching him, and the white pearl gives wise advice.

The one fear the islanders have is that there will be another attack from the other, war-like islands. They are alarmed when a ship is sighted, but it turns out to be that of the jolly king from Rinkitink and his ill-tempered, talking goat, Bilbil. King Rinkitink has fled his subjects and the dreary duties of kingship. Soon after, however, the dreaded attack does come, and King Kitticut is captured so suddenly that he is unable to retrieve the pearls from their hiding place. He and all his people are taken to Regos and Coregos—all, that is, except Prince Inga, King Rinkitink, and Bilbil.

Prince Inga takes the pearls, and the odd trio sets out to rescue the people of Pingaree. After exciting adventures, including the temporary loss of two of the pearls, they conquer Regos and Coregos and free all the people except Inga's father and mother, who have been taken by the evil rulers to the Kingdom of the Gnomes on the mainland where they are held captive by the monarch of the underworld.

Prince Inga, Rinkitink, and Bilbil follow, and after overcoming a series of dangerous obstacles set by the Gnome King, Inga manages to free his parents. Also, Bilbil is disenchanted and found to be the prince of Boboland, a kingdom near Rinkitink. They all return to Pingaree, which has been restored to its former beauty. But after the celebration, more boats are sighted. They are from Rinkitink, and they have come to retrieve their beloved but wayward king. Rinkitink must reconcile himself to devoting three hours a day to being king.

The characters in *King Rinkitink* inhabit the same kind of traditional fairy-tale world that Baum used for *Queen Zixi*. It has a vaguely medieval feel to it, with no references to the modern world. It is the kind of place in which magic is not common, but in which magic and magical beings exist, such as the three pearls and the gnomes. In contrast to Mo and Oz, but like Ix and Noland, animals do not talk, and Bilbil the goat is regarded as quite out of the ordinary. Yet the world of *King Rinkitink* is a stronger imaginary world than that of *Queen Zixi*. The geographical features and the locations of the islands are described in detail. The plot grows very naturally out of the place, and story and background fit together and interact in a much more satisfactory manner than they do in the earlier book.

It is a bit of a mystery why Baum did not publish this excellent story when it was written, but two factors make it possible to give a speculative answer. Baum had learned early in his writing career that it was best to publish only one full-length fantasy a year, because otherwise he would be competing against himself. In 1905 he had a backlog of manuscripts: the book edition of *Queen Zixi* was to be his fantasy for that year, and another manuscript about a live gingerbread man was scheduled to be published in 1906. Thus the earliest that *King Rinkitink* could have been published was 1907, but by then he had found it necessary to return to the Oz stories. In that book for 1907, *Ozma of Oz*, he incorporated incidents from the Gnome King section of *King Rinkitink*. In both stories, the Gnome King holds royal prisoners, and the rescuers have to undergo a series of trials to free them.[33] Because that was the section most heavily revised in *Rinkitink in Oz*, it is impossible to estimate how much of *Ozma* was taken directly from the earlier story, but a comparison of an incident common to both will illustrate that they had the same origin. The Gnome King is showing the would-be rescuers his army:

[The king] took a gold whistle from his pocket and blew a shrill note that echoed through every part of the cave. Instantly nomes began to pour in through the side arches in great numbers, until the immense space was packed with them as far as the eye could reach. All were armed with glittering weapons of polished silver and gold, and Inga was amazed that any King could command so great an army. . . .

"I have shown you," said he to Inga, "a part of my bodyguard."[34] *(From* Rinkitink in Oz*)*

When the little maid from Oz gazed wonderingly upon this scene the Nome King uttered a shrill whistle, and at once all the silver and gold doors flew open and solid ranks of Nome soldiers marched out from every one. So great were their numbers that they quickly filled the immense underground cavern and forced the busy workmen to abandon their tasks. . . .

"This," said the Nome King, "is but a small part of my army."[35] *(From* Ozma of Oz*)*

(It should be noted that in *Ozma*, Baum changed the spelling of "gnome" by dropping the first letter; the ostensible reason was to make it easier for children to pronounce, but the effect is to make these traditional, immortal creatures more truly his own.) Having used part of the story in another book, Baum probably put the manuscript of *King Rinkitink* aside until such time as he had the time or the need to revise it.

"PREMIERE JUVENILE AUTHOR"

The contracts that Baum had signed with the producers of his play had offered him the hope of financial security with the provisions for a new play to be staged each year. The failure of *The Woggle-Bug* destroyed those hopes, and Baum had to look elsewhere for the security that, at fifty and in fragile health, he so desperately needed. Thus in October 1905, he signed a contract with the Reilly & Britton Company that called for an ambitious schedule of publications.

By 1905 Baum had built up impressive credentials as a writer, but he had not been lucky with his publishers. Both Way & Williams and the George M. Hill Company had gone out of business, and he had become dissatisfied with Bobbs-Merrill because he felt that he was just one among the many authors on its list. The Century Company was publishing *Queen Zixi of Ix,* but that firm also had a long list of established authors. What he needed was a publisher with which he could make long-term plans rather than dealing manuscript by manuscript. The new Reilly & Britton Company fit his needs exactly; its first book had been *The Marvelous Land of Oz,* and the firm had publicized it extensively. In 1905 the company published *The Woggle-Bug Book* and the first book that Baum published under a pseudonym, the adult novel *The Fate of a Crown* by "Schuyler Staunton," and it had already contracted to publish his next full-length fantasy. Being a new company, its author list was short, and Baum was by far the most important name on it. In the new contract he signed with Reilly & Britton, he agreed virtually to create the publisher's juvenile list, committing to write five juveniles and one adult novel (excluding the fantasy already agreed on). Of the six books, only one was published under Baum's name.

The contract is a curious document.[36] The humor of some of the wording indicates that it was written by Baum, but the light tone does not conceal the realities underneath: he was committing himself to an exhausting schedule of writing, but he was also assuring himself of the position of premiere juvenile author with the company. By the terms of the contract, Reilly & Britton agreed not to publish any juveniles in 1906 except those by Baum. That year, the company actually published six full-length books and six shorter booklets by him, and Baum's productivity was all the more amazing when one takes into account that he and Maud spent the winter of 1906 on a tour of the Middle East and Europe!

The contract marked the real beginning of Baum's career as a writer of series books. Two of the books for 1906, *Sam Steele's Adventures on Land and Sea* by "Captain Hugh Fitzgerald" and *Aunt Jane's Nieces* by "Edith Van Dyne" became the bases for series. It was the beginning of the golden age of juvenile serials, and Reilly & Britton quickly became known as the publisher of series books for children and teen-agers. The quality of such serials varied widely, but even today, those books by Baum are interesting and very readable and easily outclass the numerous other serials of the time. It should be noted, though, that Baum still considered his individual full-length fantasies published under his own name to be his primary and most important works.

JOHN DOUGH AND THE CHERUB

The Baums had again spent the winter of 1905 in southern California, and Baum's happiness there and delight in the natural beauties of the region are evident in his fantasy for 1906, *John Dough and the Cherub*. Unfortunately, so is his tendency to try to shape some of his stories in a way that would fit them for stage adaptation.[37]

John Dough and the Cherub contains some of Baum's most imaginative characters and countries, but it is also one of his most uneven books; the fault lies both with the plot and with the background. John Dough is a man made out of gingerbread who is brought to life on July Fourth when a vial of the Elixir of Life belonging to a mysterious Arab is inadvertently mixed with the dough. The very thin thread that holds the plot together is the Arab's pursuit of the gingerbread man. John leaves our part of the world by clinging to a very large sky rocket that is set off in celebration of Independence Day; he is probably the first fairy-tale character to enter an imaginary world by rocket! He lands first on the Isle of Phreex, where he meets the child Chick, the first incubator baby. When the Arab arrives, John and Chick leave Phreex in a flying machine and, after a brief stop at the Palace of Romance, crash the air ship on another

118

island, this one inhabited by unpleasant creatures called Mifkets. There they meet Para Bruin, a bear made of rubber, and a young human girl, sarcastically called "Princess" by the Mifkets. When the Arab arrives on the island also, the Fairy Beavers offer John and his companions protection and arrange for the Princess to be reunited with her parents and the rest of them to be carried away from the island by a flock of flamingos. After another brief stop on an island inhabited by retired pirates, bandits, and a strange creature made of sporting equipment, John, Chick, and Para Bruin arrive in the divided kingdom of Hiland and Loland, where John is proclaimed king.

This type of plot was unusual for Baum. Normally his narratives are more positive: reaching a goal, going on a quest, solving a mystery, or even the more passive one of observing strange peoples and places. This negative plot of fleeing danger with no specific place of safety in view is one that he did not handle well. The thin thread of the story snaps almost six chapters from the end when John, Chick, and the Princess gain the protection of the Fairy Beavers, and the Arab is rendered helpless to pursue them further. After that danger has ended, their actions are random and aimless. The Princess's wish to rejoin her parents gives indications of picking up the thread of the plot, but she disappears from the story when the reunion is accomplished five chapters from the end. The actual ending is abrupt and anticlimactic; it has the air of an afterthought, since nothing in the story up to that point has prepared the way for John's acquisition of a kingdom.

John Dough and the Cherub is not Baum's only book with a weak story line; *Dot and Tot of Merryland, The Enchanted Island of Yew,* and some of the Oz books also have thin plots, but they are supported and given unity by the strength and coherence of the "places" that Baum invented for them. This is not true in *John Dough,* although Baum's inventiveness cannot be faulted because there are enough fanciful, imaginary countries in it to fill three books. After John leaves America, he visits five fantasy countries, each very different from the others. The trouble is that the countries are visited at random and are not linked together in any way; thus the book falls apart into episodes, and it feels as though one is reading three different books, none of them with a satisfactory ending.

Baum had given Oz, Merryland, and Yew very precise geographies; the organization of the five areas of Oz, the seven valleys of Merryland, and the five kingdoms of Yew are carefully described. Baum had placed the countries around Mo in such a way that the reader can picture them, and had clearly established the proximity of the Forest of Burzee and the Laughing Valley and of Noland and Ix; but he did not give the reader the geographical relationships among the island countries in *John Dough* the way he did in *King Rinkitink*. Not even the direction the characters take when leaving one island for another is mentioned. The randomness and purposelessness of the journey is summed up when the flamingos ask, "Where do you wish to be taken"? And John answers, "We don't much care."[38]

The first version of *John Dough* was most likely written before the failure of *The Woggle-Bug* put a temporary end to Baum's theatrical career, and the absence of the geographical details that Baum was usually careful to give to his imaginary countries may be one of the indications that it was written with a stage adaptation in mind. Such details would not matter in the theater, but a variety of novel and surprising adventures would be necessary to the type of musical extravaganza that Baum favored.

An additional reason for the episodic nature of the plot may be that Baum also originally wrote *John Dough* (without the later central character of Chick the Cherub) with the hope that it would be serialized in the *Ladies' Home Journal,* with each installment of the serial somewhat self-contained.[39] The variety of episodes, however, works against the unity of this book; the five imaginary countries are so different from one another that without strong links of plot, theme, or geographical location, they do not seem to exist in the same fictional world.

In most respects, the Isle of Phreex is no different from islands in our own world. What makes it unusual is that the inhabitants form a regular circus sideshow of freaks, including a two-headed dog, a two-legged horse, a live wooden Indian, a fat lady, and an artificial general who lost most of his real parts in various battles.[40] There is, though, another category of freaks on the island, and with that category, Baum took the opportunity of poking fun at certain modern types of individuals: inventors whose inventions either do not work or, if they do, are not accepted by the world; the Brotherhood of Failings (the Blunderer, the Thoughtless One, the Disagreeable, the Unlucky, the Sorrowful, and the Ugly); a musician who wants to compose music that no one will understand; and the "Fresh-Air Fiend." Baum was probably interjecting some of his own philosophy when he had Chick say, "Oh, the Isle is all right. . . . It's the people here that are all wrong."[41]

Chick the Cherub is also an inhabitant of the Isle of Phreex by virtue of being the first incubator baby. Baum's past experiences with raising chickens made him interested in the new incubators that, as Chick tells John, were displayed at the Pan-American Exposition and the Louisiana Purchase Exposition.[42] Chick is about eight years old, but Baum never tells the sex of the child. In fact, much of the early publicity for the book revolved around having the readers give reasons why they thought Chick is either a boy or a girl.

The marvels of the isle are the freaks and the inventions. There seems to be no magic of the fairy variety, but it is an interesting place all the same that Baum developed in a detailed enough way to gain the reader's interest. The development, however, leads nowhere since to escape the Arab, Chick and John leave the island abruptly, and it plays no further part in the story.

In contrast to the fairly extensive development of the Isle of Phreex, the Palace of Romance is allotted less than two chapters, which is frustrating to the reader because the magnificent gold palace, inhabited by a hundred ladies and gentlemen who, in a variation on the Scheherazade motif, allow strangers to live as long as they have more stories to tell, is one of Baum's most intriguing creations. The reader wants to know more of the history of such a dream-like place and is disappointed when the episode passes so quickly.

The island of the Mifkits is the only other of the five countries to be fairly extensively developed. It is an exotic place with unusual topographic features. The usual relationship between trees and plants is reversed, as is that between foliage and flowers. The trees on the island are no more than two inches high and form the grassy ground cover; the plants, conversely, grow enormously large and form the forests. The colors of the foliage and flowers of the enormous plants are the opposite of what would be expected, the flowers being various shades of green and the leaves and stems being all the colors of the rainbow, forming a "wilderness of color."[43]

The native inhabitants of the island, the Mifkets, are an aborigine-like race with pear-shaped bodies, round heads, long arms, and short legs. Their chief characteristics are laziness and ill-temper. They are mortal and seem to possess no particular magic powers. Except for Para Bruin, the rubber bear, the animals on the island are normal, but Baum treats communication with these animals, and all the others encountered in the story, in an unusual way for him. The animals do not have the power of human speech, but each species has its own language, which John is able to understand because the Elixir of Life also gives him great knowledge.

There is fairy magic on the island, however, for it is the residence of the King of the Fairy Beavers, and this animal fairy lives in a richly appointed underwater palace. There are marvelous inventions there—a television, a submarine, and a musical instrument played by water—but unlike the inventions of Phreex, these work because they are magical.

In sharp contrast to the island of the Mifkits, the last two countries in the book receive almost no development. The island of the pirates occupies only one chapter, and no reason is given why the strange, disagreeable creature made of sporting equipment, the pirates, and the bandits should all exist on the same island. The final two chapters, which describe the kingdoms of Hiland and Loland, are probably the most unsatisfying in the book. Hiland and Loland are two adjoining kingdoms separated by a high wall. In the center of the principal city, a large and beautiful palace straddles the wall. From this palace, a king rules both kingdoms. The inhabitants of Hiland are tall and thin, and those of Loland are short and fat. The people on either side of the wall consider those on the other side as inferior and disagreeable, but the prejudice is based on the lack of knowledge that each side has of the other.

When John, Chick, and Para Bruin arrive on the island, the old king has been dead for some time, and both kingdoms have a prophecy that the next king will be someone "who is wise and just, but not made of flesh and blood."[44] John Dough, of course, fits that description and is crowned king. Baum's premise for Hiland and Loland is potentially the most interesting one in the story, but he does absolutely nothing with it. The book, like the various adventures in it, ends abruptly and unsatisfactorily.

Another minor reason for the absence of unity in *John Dough and the Cherub* is that it contains the fewest references of any of the non-Oz fantasies of this period to Baum's other stories. There are only two: the Fairy Beavers continue the premise of *Animal Fairy Tales*. Chick asks, "Can a beaver be a fairy?" and the answer is, "All the animals have their fairies, just as you human folks do."[45] The second reference occurs when John says to an irritating macaw, "You're a rampsy, that's what you are!"[46] He is referring to the name given to the gigans in "Nelebel's Fairyland" after Queen Lulea has changed those gigantic, stupid creatures into the smallest of all immortals.[47] Neither of these references would have been familiar to any but Baum's most avid readers, since *Animal Fairy Tales* had not yet been published in book form and "Nelebel's Fairyland" had appeared only in a small, local magazine in southern California.

Later, when Baum finally drew all his imaginary countries together into one fantasy Other-world, Oz was, in general, the benefactor, gaining depth and reality. However, *John Dough and the Cherub* is the one non-Oz fantasy in which the benefits go the other way. When Baum later placed some of the countries from *John Dough* into a geographical relationship with Oz, he added a retroactive coherence to the book that was lacking in the story itself. Thus *John Dough* gains by being read after one is already familiar with Baum's total Other-world.

"LAURA BANCROFT"

Except for the six stories in *The Twinkle Tales* (1906) and the full-length sequel, *Policeman Bluejay* (1907), published under the name Laura Bancroft, Baum used pseudonyms only for his nonfantasy books.[48] His Bancroft books proved to be quite popular, and they were the first books illustrated by Maginel Wright Enright, one of Frank Lloyd Wright's sisters. In these books Baum could not, of course, develop or mention his other characters and imaginary countries; therefore, these nature fairy tales did not directly play a part in his developing Other-world. Indirectly, however, they do shed light on the ways in which the United States served as the source for Baum's fantasies.

The stories are more properly American fairy tales than are those in the volume that bears that title because they take place on the Dakota prairie and in the Ozark Mountains of Arkansas, and they deal with the natural landscape and the animals and birds of America. One of the main themes of the stories is a plea for people to live in harmony and understanding with the wild creatures of this country.

In several previous tales, Baum had made the distinction that civilization was the only difference between his fairylands and the real world. The little girl Twinkle lives in Edgeley, Dakota, called that "because it is on the edge of civilization"[49]; beyond the town is the great prairie, the place where wonders occur. Baum continued the idea of a dividing line between this world and the other in "Twinkle's Enchantment" when Twinkle, while out playing in a big gulch, steps across a "line of enchantment," which is "an invisible line that divided the common, real world from an enchanted country" and "whoever steps over it is sure to see strange things and have strange adventures."[50]

Sometimes it is more than a dividing line: in "Prince Mud-Turtle," a fairy prince takes Twinkle to the Black Mountains (the Black Hills?) where "she stood on the side of a beautiful mountain, and spread before her were the loveliest green valleys she had ever beheld."[51] But when she rubs her eyelids with a magic plant, her eyes are truly opened and she sees the beautiful valleys filled with fairy palaces. And in "Sugar-Loaf Mountain," Twinkle and her friend Chubbins find a fairy city made of sugar inside one of the mountains in the Ozarks.

In these stories, almost more clearly than in Baum's other fantasies, it is possible to form an idea of the inspirations for his imaginary worlds. He had lived on that great westward advancing edge of civilization,[52] and his imagination had allowed him to wander in the great unknown on the other side of it. He alone of the people pushing the edge farther and farther west had the vision to see the fairy palaces sitting on the broad prairie or the knowledge to know where the fairy cities were hidden. His countries lay on the other side of that prairie or were concealed in mountains like the Ozarks, and it may be more than coincidence that the word "Ozark" begins with "Oz."

It was that edge—the "line of enchantment"—that Baum lacked in Chicago, surrounded as he was by civilization. The summer months spent out of the city and the trips during the winter are indications of his need for more open spaces. The appeal of California to him and the effects it had on his imagination become easier to understand when viewed from that standpoint. He was drawn back there again and again to that most natural of all dividing lines between the known and the unknown—the seashore. The sea was another great, mysterious, and unknown prairie.

Policeman Bluejay is the sequel to "Bandit Jim Crow," one of the stories in *The Twinkle Tales*. In it, Twinkle and her friend Chubbins are enchanted and given the bodies of birds while retaining their own faces. In that condition, they are befriended by the Bluejay and taken to live in the trees with the other birds and animals. Strictly speaking, they are not in a fairyland because Baum tried to depict bird life "in strict accordance with

125

natural history teachings."[53] He did not completely succeed in this aim, but the part of the story that takes place among the normal birds is more naturalistic than any of his other fantasies, with the exception of some in *Animal Fairy Tales*. He shows the constant dangers the birds are exposed to from their own kind and from the other animals of the forest, but he points out that that is the law of the forest and therefore natural. What is unnatural is man, and one can detect real anger when Baum has the Robin say, "Mankind . . . is the most destructive and bloodthirsty of all the brute creation. They not only kill for food, but through vanity and a desire for personal adornment. I have even heard it said that they kill for amusement, being unable to restrain their murderous desires. In this they are more cruel than the serpents."[54] And Baum illustrates the nature of humans in the most savage and heartrending episode in all his fantasies when hunters, whom he refers to as "The Destroyers," come into the forest and needlessly slaughter all the other residents of the tree in which Twinkle and Chubbins live—a female possum and her four babies, a friendly owl, and a shy squirrel.

That forest is definitely not a fairyland, but a real fairyland does exist in its center, one that emits a rosy glow all around and that is protected from intrusion by strong winds blowing outward from it. It is called both the Land of Paradise and the Bird's Paradise, and humans are excluded. In it are beauty, plenty of food, and absolutely no danger. Birds live in the Land of Paradise, but it is not open to the normal birds of the forest; its only reason for being seems to be as a contrast to the real world.

Some critics have felt that the Land of Paradise is an unnecessary addition that weakens the story, and considering the story only from the standpoint of structure and not from the standpoint of Baum's changing ideas regarding his fantasy world, it probably does. However, in the context of the development of that world, the description of the Land of Paradise is a very necessary counterbalance and contrast to the episode of savagery that precedes it, and that juxtaposition, I believe, unconsciously reflects the theories of fiction of the English author Sir Edward Bulwer-Lytton. Baum probably was not familiar with Bulwer-Lytton's actual theoretical writings—though many of his ideas were set forth in the prefaces to his novels—but Baum was familiar with the three mystical novels, *Zanoni* (1842), *A Strange Story* (1862), and *The Coming Race* (1871), in which his theories are exemplified.[55] It is easy today, when Bulwer-Lytton's popularity has faded, to overlook the fact that his novels would have been as familiar to someone of Baum's generation as were those of Dickens. Years before, Baum had written an editorial for his newspaper in Aberdeen in which he discussed the mysticism of Bulwer-Lytton. One of his primary aims in his novels was to present the world as it is, and then turn it around and present it as it could be. As Edwin Eigner put it, "[E]xperience is presented first in purely materialistic or associational or positivistic terms, which are then contradicted from the idealist point of view so that experience is mystically transformed and a new reality is established."[56] That is what Baum did in *Policeman Bluejay:* the Land of Paradise needs no reason for being; that it exists as a refutation of the savagery of the real world is enough. And in that sense, Oz, as it develops, becomes more like the Land of Paradise in *Policeman Bluejay*—more cut off from the real world and more a vision of what could be.

Chapter Five

Concentration on Oz
1907–1910

To have pleased you, to have interested you, to have won your friendship, and perhaps your love, through my stories, is to my mind as great an achievement as to become President of the United States. Indeed, I would much rather be your story-teller, under these conditions, than to be the President. So you have helped me to fulfill my life's ambition, and I am more grateful to you, my dears, than I can express in words.

It's no use; no use at all. The children won't let me stop telling tales of the Land of Oz. I know lots of other stories, and I hope to tell them, some time or another; but just now my loving tyrants won't allow me. They cry: "Oz—Oz! more about Oz, Mr. Baum!" and what can I do but obey their commands?

L. Frank Baum,
"To My Readers" in
Dorothy and the Wizard in Oz (1908)

J. R. R. TOLKIEN HAS BEEN MENTIONED IN THIS STUDY IN ASSOCIATION WITH BAUM not because Baum had any direct influence on the British writer, but because they had some basic things in common: a similar way of looking at fantasy, an instinctive understanding of the genre, and an ability to create an Other-world so real that their readers suspend disbelief almost without being aware of it. One great difference between them as creators of fantasy is that Baum's imagination was not naturally inclined, as Tolkien's was, toward the greater elaboration and development of a single Other-world.

Between 1896 and 1907 Baum created a large and varied repertory of independent imaginary countries and types of fantasies. Tolkien would later write: "Stories that are actually concerned primarily with 'fairies' . . . are relatively rare, and as a rule not very interesting. Most good 'fairy-stories' are about the *adventures* of men in the Perilous Realm or upon its shadowy marches."[1] Baum had reached the same conclusion through experience with roughly six different forms of fantasy. He never theorized about it in print, as Tolkien did, but it is apparent from his published works. Before approaching the change in direction that his writing took in 1907, these six forms need to be briefly summarized, in order of appearance.

1. Stories that deal with marvelous machines and inventions of the future. These stories today would be classified under the heading of science fiction, but to Baum the inventions of his own day and the imagined possibilities of the future were too much like magic to be considered anything but fairy tales. His first uses of this form were not in stories for children, but in the "Our Landlady" column of 1891, which deals with future, household laborsaving inventions, and in his story "Yesterday at the Exposition," which describes the exhibits at a world's fair in A.D. 2090. Machines make appearances in many of his children's stories, too, and this form reaches its fullest development in *The Master Key: An Electrical Fairy Tale* (1901), in which Baum worked out the consequences, as well as the benefits, of unleashing limitless power onto mankind, and in which his attitude changed from one of optimism to one of caution. After *The Master Key,* this form of fantasy as a pure form disappeared from Baum's publications, although machines, as magical appliances, continued to appear in his stories.

2. Stories that take place completely in the imaginary world without the appearance of any character from our own world. Baum generally sidestepped Tolkien's conclusion that this kind of story is "as a rule not very interesting" by making children, citizens of that Other-world, the heroes. However, even that solution leaves a gap in the link of identification because only a character who is an outsider can fully appreciate the total otherness of the imaginary world. Baum's *Adventures in Phunniland* (1896) and *The Enchanted Island of Yew* (1903) are examples of this type of fantasy, and *Queen Zixi of Ix* (1905) was his last major use of this form.[2] Only one of his Oz books, *The Marvelous Land of Oz* (1904), falls into this category.

3. Stories that explain origins. The stories in *Mother Goose in Prose* (1897) fit under this heading because they attempt to provide backgrounds and explanations for the nursery rhymes. Baum's more mythical stories are also included in this category, and *The Life and Adventures of Santa Claus* (1902) is his finest example of this form. In that book, Baum

gave his own, fairy-tale version of the origin of Santa Claus, as well as hints about the mythical beginnings of the imaginary world described in that book—hints that grew in importance as his imaginary worlds were drawn together into one, great Other-world. This form of fantasy continued to play a secondary role in most of his later fantasies, especially in those about Oz, which as it developed needed more explanation about its history and beginnings.

4. The adventures of American characters "in the Perilous Realm or upon its shadowy marches." Baum quickly found this to be the most popular form for his stories. His masterpiece, *The Wonderful Wizard of Oz* (1900), utilizes it, and all of Baum's full-length Oz stories—with the exception of *The Marvelous Land of Oz*—contain characters from America.

5. The adventures of fairies in our world. This form is a reversal of type 4. In it, fairies or other beings from an imaginary world are the main characters, and the stories relate their adventures in America, which appears to them just as strange, confusing, and wondrous as the imaginary worlds do to mortal characters. The form could be put to good use for satire, but seems to appeal more to adults than to children. Baum utilized it in some of his short stories, in the series of newspaper stories "Queer Visitors from the Marvelous Land of Oz" (1904–1905), and in *The Woggle-Bug Book* (1905), but he did not use it in any of his major fantasies. It disappeared in his later writings, where the only hint of it is a fairy-land character's occasional reaction of surprise or wonder to mention of life in America.

6. The animal fairy story. In these tales, animals obey their own natural laws and do not act like humans, yet they have their own fairylands and fairies. Some of Baum's best stories, those in *Animal Fairy Tales*, make use of this form, but perhaps negative reaction to the strong morals and realistic portrayals of animal life discouraged him from developing it further. *The Twinkle Tales* (1906) and *Policeman Bluejay* (1907) are toned-down versions of this form, mixing human characters and animal fairylands.

The boundaries among these various types of stories are not always rigid, but elements from one type appearing in stories of another type still do not lessen the individuality of each one, nor does Baum's inventive and original device of loosely linking some of his stories together by means of the same hierarchy of immortals. Having the Forest of Burzee the source of magic in both *The Life and Adventures of Santa Claus* and *Queen Zixi of Ix* in no way makes the stories similar or detracts from their individuality. Baum would also make use of elements from all these forms in his later books, but the boundaries among them almost ceased to exist as Oz emerged as his most important imaginary world.

TURNING POINT

After his "Laura Bancroft" books, Baum would publish fourteen more full-length fantasies, but David L. Greene quite rightly observed that with *Policeman Bluejay* Baum "concluded his experiments in writing fantasy for children."[3] That is, of course, hindsight, and it is certain that Baum felt that he was only temporarily bowing to his readers' demands by returning to Oz for a few more books, beginning with *Ozma of Oz* in 1907. He hoped that they would soon tire of that fairyland, but we know, also from hindsight, that Baum's readers have never tired of Oz and that for the rest of his life he was unable to break free from that most wonderful of fairylands. Thus although Baum himself did not know it, 1907 was the turning point for his Other-world.

Money was largely the reason that Baum returned to Oz with a third book. The failure of *The Woggle-Bug* had made it impossible for him to secure backing for any of the play projects he had worked on since then, and he needed capital because he had conceived an idea for a unique type of entertainment that he would have to finance himself. It was an economic fact that *The Marvelous Land of Oz* had sold better than any of his books since *The Wizard*. It is also highly likely that Baum's publishers, Reilly and Britton, had a great deal to do with his decision to write more Oz books. Because theirs was a new company, they were as desirous as Baum for more financially successful books from their principal author.

Baum knew from the letters from his readers that there was a large market for more Oz books. And although at first he did not quite comprehend the magic that the Land of Oz itself held for his readers, he was aware, also from their letters, that they considered Dorothy an integral part of an Oz story and that they also had great affection for the other original characters from *The Wizard* who had been absent from the second book. Some of the children even suggested plots, such as "Why don't you make Ozma and Dorothy meet, and have a good time together?"[4] Thus his plan, as it evolved over the course of four books, was to reintroduce these popular characters, settle their fates satisfactorily, and make a definite end to Oz as a source for new stories.

Not surprisingly, the development of Baum's great Other-world was not smooth and logical; very often, the changes created glaring inconsistencies from book to book, but that is because Oz did not grow organically from a central idea. Rather, it developed in successive versions, each enlarging while superseding the one before and each reflecting Baum's current idea of what constituted the most magnificent and alluring fairyland in the world. That Baum's Oz does not exist continuously makes it impossible to speak of only one Oz—the version in *The Marvelous Land* (1904) is as different from the version in *The Road to Oz* (1909) as that is from the one in *Glinda of Oz* (1920).

One of the frequent complaints about series books is that the characters are usually two-dimensional and exhibit little complexity or development, but to look to Baum's Oz characters for three-dimensionality is to look in the wrong place. Fantasy has different rules from realistic stories; in fantasy, not only the characters, but also the backgrounds can be movable, changeable, and capable of growth. In the Oz books, it is Oz that is the real three-dimensional, developing main character.

It has been noted that Baum sometimes wrote too hastily and that he lacked the services of a vigilant editor. But, with the exception of *The Marvelous Land*, which had a different origin from the other books in the series, it is usually clear which changes from book to book were conscious and intentional and which were the result of carelessness. Part of the reason for the haste was Baum's very heavy writing schedule, but then, he depended on his writing for his income. Even if he had wanted to, he could not have written his saga of Oz in private; he could not have rewritten it in reverse, as Tolkien did *The Lord of the Rings*, to remove the inconsistencies before presenting it to the public in its perfected form.[5] The stages of Oz's development are set out for all to see, but no matter how many discrepancies exist among the books, the Oz presented in each of them "works," for even in the weakest there is still a very real sense of entering an authentic Other-world.

Baum's return to Oz was certainly not caused by any lessening of his creative powers; he still had many interesting countries and characters to create, but the emphasis changed, and almost all the new countries would be either borderlands of Oz or small lands inside Oz. Although he did not know it, he had created his last, important, independent imaginary country; therefore, before proceeding with the discussions of the books, it may be helpful to mention briefly the three primary methods Baum used to develop Oz: (1) the addition of information and details, as when Baum added the name and color of the northern Country of the Gillikins in *The Marvelous Land of Oz;* (2) the alteration of previously given facts, as when Glinda became a Sorceress instead of a Good Witch; and (3) the reinterpretations of the nature of Oz itself. This last, of course, had the most far-reaching effects. In addition, it should be mentioned that in the following years, Baum would also rob his earlier creations of their autonomy to enrich "the most attractive and delightful fairyland in all the world,"[6] and, in the process, he would create his and America's great fairy continent.

OZMA OF OZ

Baum was forced by external pressures to develop Oz (unlike Tolkien, whose Other-world grew naturally of its own accord in his mind), which made for a dilemma because Baum's imagination was more geared toward creating new imaginary countries than elaborating previously invented ones. In his book for 1907, *Ozma of Oz,* Baum attempted to satisfy both his readers and himself by combining his Oz characters with a story that takes place outside Oz in a new fantasy country. By this device, he was able to construct a story and a background for it without having to take the "givens" of Oz into consideration; he was also largely able to avoid dealing with the confused state in which he had left that country in *The Marvelous Land.* The only part of the book that takes place in Oz is the final two chapters (out of twenty-one), which are in the nature of the celebration after the completion of a difficult adventure.

Yet even with so little of the story set in Oz, the development had begun, and *Ozma* is a milestone in Baum's writing career. In it, he began the process that would lead to his single Other-world, and in it he totally reversed the meaning and significance of Oz as it had first been created in *The Wizard.* It can be said that *Ozma of Oz* is the real beginning of the Oz series.

The main plot line of *Ozma of Oz* concerns the rescue of the queen of the seaside kingdom of Ev and her ten children from the Nome King, an underground monarch who is a combination of the benign Gnome King of *The Life and Adventures of Santa Claus* and the wicked King Scowleyow of *The Magical Monarch of Mo.*[7] The cruel king of Ev had sold his wife and children to the Nome King in exchange for a long life, but later, overcome with remorse, he had drowned himself in the sea. The Nome King has transformed his new slaves into ornaments for his magnificent palace. Although he and his subjects are immortals, his special magic comes from a magical jeweled belt he wears.

The ruler of a neighboring kingdom, hearing of the plight of the royal family of Ev, brings her army and closest advisers to Ev with the intention of rescuing the slaves. There they meet an American child and a yellow hen, Billina, who had been washed up on the shore, and a copper clockwork man, Tik-Tok, who had been discovered by the child. They all join forces in the rescue attempt.

135

In a show of good nature, the Nome King agrees to let the rescuers enter his palace one by one and try to guess which ornaments are the people from Ev. If a guess is correct, the person's true form will be restored; if no guess is correct, the rescuer will also be transformed into an ornament. The catch is that there are thousands upon thousands of ornaments in the palace, and one by one the rescuers fail and are turned into ornaments until Billina learns the secret and restores them and the royal family to their proper forms. The Nome King's true evil nature then emerges, and he assembles his army to prevent the people of the upper world from leaving. They defeat the king by cleverness and capture his magic belt, after which, they restore the royal family of Ev to their rightful position.

Ozma of Oz has one of Baum's most interesting and tightly constructed plots. He was careful to include enough necessary information early in the narrative to give the successive stages of the story a logic and inevitability that are lacking in the more arbitrary adventures in *John Dough and the Cherub*. He also delayed the full resolution of the plot until close to the end of the book to keep the return journey from the Nome King's domain from being anticlimactic. Throughout, the plot shows evidence of unusually careful thought and planning, and it probably contains less irrelevant material than any of his other books. I have, though, deliberately summarized the plot without mention of Oz to demonstrate how little the special attributes of that country have to do with it.

The Oz elements can be summarized briefly and separately: Dorothy and her Uncle Henry are on their way to Australia to visit relatives when Dorothy is swept off the deck of a ship by the strong winds of a storm. She manages to save herself by clinging to a large, wooden chicken coop that had been washed from the ship. The coop, with Dorothy and one of the hens, drifts to the shore of the Land of Ev, where the girl finds Tik-Tok and meets with Ozma and her old friends the Scarecrow, the Tin Woodman, and the Cowardly Lion from the Land of Oz. She also meets a new friend from Oz, the Hungry Tiger. They have come to Ev with Ozma's comic-operetta army to try to restore the royal family. Dorothy joins the expedition, and, after interesting and exciting adventures, they

136

achieve their goal. Dorothy then goes to Oz with her friends and finally returns to her Uncle Henry in Australia by means of the magic belt captured from the Nome King.

Ev is one of Baum's more interesting creations; it contains unusual and clever characters, and its geography is more fully detailed than that of Ix, Noland, or any of the countries in *John Dough;* yet with the addition of the Oz elements, Ev becomes of only secondary importance. Although it appears in only two chapters, Oz dominates the book, and the primary interest of Ev shifts from its uniqueness to its position in relation to Oz. Whether or not Baum fully realized it at the time, he was conceding to the view held by his readers that Oz was the most important of his imaginary creations. Oz was emerging as the most powerful nation in his imaginary world, just as the United States was, during Baum's lifetime, emerging as one of the most powerful nations in this world.

In *The Wizard* the strange and beautiful, but illusory, Land of Oz is the place of danger and trial, the ordeal through which Dorothy has to go to reach her goal of home. Baum subtly changed all that in *Ozma:* the illusion is made reality, and Oz becomes not the ordeal but the goal, the place of the heart's desire and, in a very real sense, Dorothy's true home because Ozma crowns her a princess of Oz, thus making her a part of that land.

Baum's reversal of the nature of Oz is evident in the plot. If Baum had retained the structure of this book, but had made it a non-Oz fantasy, the final two chapters, which recount events that take place after the mission is accomplished, would have been anticlimactic, just as the Hiland/Loland section of *John Dough* is. But the significance of the final section in Oz is much greater than its role of concluding the story, because underneath all the exciting and interesting adventures encountered during the rescue, there has been the feeling that Oz is the real and ultimate goal. Once in Oz, Dorothy returns to the everyday world only with reluctance and only because a "magic picture" that Ozma owns shows her that her Uncle Henry's health has worsened because of his worry about her. And even though Dorothy returns to the real world, she does so only because of her love for her Uncle Henry and Aunt Em. Ozma even promises to look at Dorothy in the Magic Picture at certain intervals in the event that she should ever want to return to Oz.

Once Baum had changed Oz from a place to escape from into a great and good place to be sought, he opened the way for a whole new kind of development, and Oz became the haven and the goal for almost all his American characters—in much the same way as America was viewed at that time as a place of haven and freedom by the downtrodden of Europe. The problem became not how to leave Oz, but how to reach it, and a new type of plot entered his fantasies—the quest for Oz.

BEGINNING OF THE CONTINENT

Ev is the first of the fantasy countries Baum created that border Oz. He would continue to invent countries to surround Oz, but their contributions would be, like those of the countries that adjoin Mo, to enhance and make more real the geography of Oz itself. In *The Marvelous Land of Oz,* the Gump and its passengers reach "the terrible outside world"[8]; while it is clear in that instance that Baum meant our world, even after Oz becomes surrounded by other fairylands, anything beyond the desert is sometimes referred to as the outside world. In *Ozma* he made it clear that the "line of enchantment," or whatever separates our world from that one, is a good distance outside Oz. When Dorothy and Billina the hen are floating on the sea, Dorothy is surprised that the hen can talk—an indication, she realizes, that she is not in the everyday world. She remarks, "If we were in the Land of Oz, I wouldn't think it so queer, because many of the animals can talk in that fairy country. But out here in the ocean must be a good long way from Oz."[9] It is also significant that this is the first time that Baum referred to Oz as a "fairy country" within the text of one of his full-length stories.

Baum also made his usual comparison between civilized and uncivilized countries: Dorothy says about Ev that "this is a new, wild country, without even trolley-cars or tel'phones. The people here havn't been discovered yet, I'm sure."[10] Ev, though, is described as so beautiful and pleasant that there is little doubt about which Baum preferred. Ev may have lacked modern conveniences, but civilization lacked magic and wonder as Baum pointed out when he had Dorothy say to Billina, "[Y]ou wouldn't be able to talk in any civ'lized country, like Kansas, where no fairies live at all."[11]

Ev is a kingdom that bears many resemblances to southern California; the first trees Dorothy sees are punita, cottonwood, and eucalyptus.[12] On one side, Ev is bordered by the sea; on the other side is the desert that separates it from the Munchkin Country of Oz; and in the north, it contains rocky valleys and mountains, under which are the domains of the Nome King.

It was to the desert that forms the boundary between Ev and Oz that Baum made the first modification to his previous descriptions of Oz. Ozma and her followers cross it on a magic carpet that unrolls in front of them and that protects them from "the deadly, life-destroying sands."[13] Before this, there had been no indication that the desert is unusual. A normal desert is enough of a barrier to prevent Dorothy from leaving Oz on her first visit there, and in *The Marvelous Land,* Glinda actually chases the witch Mombi onto the sands of that desert. By this change in the nature of the desert (which is permanent), Baum made Oz even less accessible to the rest of the world and preserved its uniqueness by limiting contacts with the countries he was beginning to place around it. One wonders also if that desert is symbolic of some barrier that Baum would have liked to place around his own personal paradise—that of his lost childhood or of California—to protect it from insensitive and jaded intrusions from the real world.

The next modification that Baum made to Oz is clear when Ozma arrives in Ev and announces, "I am Ruler of the Land of Oz."[14] Baum had made that change in the newspaper stories "Queer Visitors from the Marvelous Land of Oz," and repeated it in *Ozma of Oz* without explanation. Later in the book, he went into more detail about the government of Oz:

For Ozma of Oz ruled the King of the Munchkins, the King of the Winkies, the King of the Quadlings and the King of the Gillikins just as those kings ruled their own people; and this supreme ruler of the Land of Oz lived in a great town of her own, called the Emerald City, which was in the exact center of the four kingdoms of the Land of Oz.[15]

The change in the structure of the government was an inspired one, being a type that was more familiar to his American readers. Ozma, however, is the absolute ruler and no elected leader; Oz is not a democracy. (The description of Oz's government, though, contains the only example of carelessness or lapse of memory, as opposed to conscious modifications, that appears in this book. Baum seems to have forgotten that the Tin Woodman rules the Winkies; Glinda the Good, the Quadlings; and the Good Witch of the North, the Gillikins.)

Baum, of course, had to have Dorothy brought up to date on what had happened in Oz during her absence, and it is interesting to note the ways Baum manipulated this information to correct and eliminate some of the confusion in *The Marvelous Land*. He wrote that Dorothy "was much interested in the story of Ozma, who had been, when a baby, stolen by a wicked old witch and transformed into a boy. . . . Then it was found that she was the only child of the former Ruler of Oz, and was entitled to rule in his place."[16] Baum conveniently dropped the role that he had given the Wizard in Ozma's abduction in *The Marvelous Land;* his readers had let him know that the Wizard was a more popular character than he had suspected. He also altered Ozma's father from ruler of the Emerald City to ruler of all Oz, making his position consistent with hers, and he said nothing about the Emerald City having existed before the Wizard's arrival.

By setting the majority of the story outside Oz, Baum was able to avoid making a decision about the color scheme of Oz or the exact shape of the country. He did mention "the green slopes" of "the Munchkin territory,"[17] but said nothing else about color, not even concerning the Emerald City.

Baum's new characters—the Hungry Tiger, Tik-Tok, and Billina—were happy inspirations, fitting in well as new residents of Oz and becoming popular with his readers. He also reintroduced some of his characters from *The Marvelous Land:* the Sawhorse, which the Scarecrow rides to Ev; Jinjur, now married and ruling her husband as she had tried to rule the Emerald City; the Woggle-Bug, now president of the new College of Art and Athletic Perfection; and Jack Pumpkinhead, "a little over-ripe but still active."[18]

Ozma of Oz is a transitional book. The story can stand alone without the section in Oz; the action is complete, and the place of safety and repose is reached in Ev. However, the visit to Oz at the end is the reward for both Dorothy and Baum's readers to whom the main point of the story is Dorothy's eventual return to Oz, but that return is not the main point of the plot. Only the readers' prior knowledge of Dorothy and of Oz as a desirable place gives Oz its dominant role and superimposes the larger, overarching goal onto the plot of the rescue of the royal family of Ev.

DOROTHY AND THE WIZARD IN OZ

Baum repeated the structure of having the dangerous or difficult adventures take place outside Oz and introducing Oz as the place of celebration at the end of the journey in his next two books, *Dorothy and the Wizard in Oz* and *The Road to Oz,* but with a difference. The attainment of Oz becomes more obviously the goal of the journey; Oz becomes the place of sanctuary as well as the place of celebration; and getting Dorothy to Oz *is* the plot of both books. From a structural standpoint, this makes both books far weaker than *Ozma of Oz* because the connecting link among the various, and sometimes unrelated, adventures of the journeys is solely the reason given in each story for the journey to Oz.

The "reason" given in *Dorothy and the Wizard in Oz,* Baum's book for 1908, is a vital one—safety. Dorothy and her Uncle Henry have stopped in San Francisco on their way back from Australia. Uncle Henry

141

has gone on ahead to Los Angeles to visit relatives, and Dorothy and her new pet, a kitten named Eureka, are taking an evening train to join him. The train has made very slow progress because there have been frequent earthquakes during the night,[19] and it arrives only shortly before dawn. Dorothy and Eureka are met by her cousin Zeb, a boy near her own age, and his buggy and horse named Jim. As they start off in the ominous half-light, the earth continues to shake. Suddenly it splits into a large crack right under the horse, who falls in, drawing the buggy after him. Like Alice down the rabbit hole, Dorothy and her companions fall swiftly at first and then more slowly. Dorothy becomes calmer when she realizes "that she had merely started upon another adventure, which promised to be just as queer and unusual as were those she had before encountered."[20] The impression of being in another fairy adventure is strengthened when they see different-colored globes of light below them and when Jim is suddenly able to speak.

The landscape toward which they are falling resembles that on the surface of the earth, but because of the colored "suns," it looks as though it were lit by light coming through a stained-glass window. The country they come to rest in is the Land of the Mangaboos, which is inhabited by a race of beautiful people who are vegetable rather than flesh and blood and, therefore, have no hearts or human kindness. This underground world probably owes some of its inspiration to the underground world created by Edward Bulwer-Lytton in his novel *The Coming Race.* Bulwer's race of people are so far advanced in logic as to be heartless where human emotions are concerned.

Dorothy and her companions are not the only mortals who are trapped underground by the earthquake. Her old friend Oz the Wizard arrives shortly after she does. After leaving Oz, he had again become a circus balloonist, and his balloon also descended through one of the great cracks in the earth. He has with him nine tiny piglets with which he does fake magic tricks, and one of the running jokes of the story is Eureka's desire to eat them.

The Mangaboos decree that the intruders must be killed, and

even though Dorothy and the Wizard pick a new princess from the royal bush, the fresh ruler upholds her subjects' decision. Thus begins the flight of Dorothy and her friends from one danger to another in their effort to reach the surface of the earth. Through an upward-inclining tunnel, they reach the beautiful Valley of Voe, which contains vicious, invisible bears; by a stairway in Pyramid Mountain in Voe, they arrive in the Land of Naught where the dreaded, wooden Gargoyles live; escaping the Gargoyles, they continue their ascent in a dark tunnel where they encounter a "Den of Dragonnettes"; and finally, they end up trapped in an enormous, dark cavern where, far out of reach above them, they can see a single ray of real sunlight coming through a crack in the ceiling. Only then—when everything seems lost—does Dorothy remember that Ozma has promised to look at her periodically in the Magic Picture and to bring her to Oz if she makes a certain secret sign. Dorothy makes the sign, and she, and then her friends, are magically transported to the Emerald City.

During the festivities to celebrate the return of Dorothy and the Wizard, one of the piglets disappears, and Eureka is tried for murder. The piglet is found unharmed, but Eureka remains in disgrace because she had intended to eat it. She begs Dorothy to send her home; Zeb and Jim also feel that they do not belong in Oz; and Dorothy knows that she must return to her Uncle Henry and Aunt Em, who again believe that she is dead. With the Magic Belt, Ozma sends Zeb and Jim back to California, and Dorothy and Eureka to Kansas, where Uncle Henry had returned. The elderly Wizard is given a home in Oz.

The only point in this story where both the plot and the imaginary world falter is in the transition from the underground world to Oz. Dorothy's too convenient recollection of Ozma's promise to look at her in the Magic Picture is not believable. Why did not Ozma do something to help them earlier? Baum created this problem himself: in *Ozma of Oz*, he stated that Ozma will look at Dorothy only "every Saturday morning," but in *Dorothy and the Wizard*, he needlessly changed this to "every day at four o'clock."[21]

The problem with the imaginary world is that after precisely detailing the geographical relationships among the underground countries, Baum gave no clue to the geographical relationship of Oz to them. For all the reader knows, Oz could be directly above or half a world away, and this failure to link the imaginary countries together damages the reality of the secondary world. However, Baum lessened the seriousness of the damage by continuing the themes introduced in the underground world in Oz: danger still threatens there in the possibility that Eureka may be executed, and Zeb and Jim's dissatisfaction with Oz make that country only another short stopping place in their struggle to reach home.

Very little of the story is set in Oz (six out of twenty chapters) and that part only in the Emerald City, but those final chapters are not anticlimactic because the reader's knowledge of Oz is not expected to be restricted to the information offered in that short section. Baum made no major changes to Oz, but there are some significant additions and alterations.

Baum made two noteworthy additions. First, Oz has definitely acquired the status of fairyland and is repeatedly referred to as a "fairy country" or a "fairyland." And second, for the first time, Baum gave some indication of its shape and of the way the countries within it are arranged. He states that the Emerald City was built "just where the four countries cornered together,"[22] which, since the four countries correspond to the four directions, can only mean that they are roughly triangular, like the four main kingdoms of Yew. He also described the royal flag of Oz as "divided into four quarters, one being colored sky-blue, another pink, a third lavender and a fourth white. In the center was a large emerald-green star. . . . The colors represented the four countries of Oz, and the green star the Emerald City."[23] It is not stated, but the assumption is that the flag is the same rectangular shape as the American flag since Baum, in the same paragraph, named the Oz national anthem "The Oz Spangled Banner." He was careless in his choice of colors: pink and lavender are shades of the red and purple that should refer to the countries of the Quadlings and Gillikins, but white does not work for the yellow Winkie Country. It is not a serious lapse, and it should be remembered that it had been four years since Baum had last mentioned the countries having special colors.

What is not carelessness is his mention of the characters wearing clothing of colors other than green in the Emerald City.[24] He was establishing a pattern that he would follow throughout the rest of the series whereby green predominates in the outward appearance of the city, but other colors appear in costumes and interiors. He also seems to have been in the process of toning down some of the more magical aspects of the city that he had introduced in *The Marvelous Land.* When the Wizard and Zeb arrive in the city, it is described as "bathed in a grateful green light"[25]—not green sunlight, as he had said before, but merely "green light," which would be expected in a city built of polished green marble and adorned with sparking emeralds.

The alterations that Baum made are in the histories of both Ozma and the Wizard, making them more consistent with *The Wizard* and farther from the confused version given in *The Marvelous Land.* In the process, he added to the prediscovery history of Oz.

The Wizard explains that the reason the people accepted him so quickly as their ruler was because his first two initials, which had been painted on his circus balloon, are O. Z. And he goes on to say:

> "At that time . . . there were four separate countries in this Land, each one of the four being ruled by a Witch. But the people thought my power was greater than that of the Witches; and perhaps the Witches thought so too, for they never dared oppose me. I ordered the Emerald City to be built just where the four countries cornered together, and when it was completed I announced myself the Ruler of the Land of Oz, which included all the four countries of the Munchkins, the Gillikins, the Winkies and the Quadlings. Over this Land I ruled in peace for many years, until I grew old and longed to see my native city once again."[26]

Baum thus made it definite that the Wizard was ruler of all Oz, which had been only implied in *The Wizard.* And in *Dorothy and the Wizard,* he has presented the Wizard as the unopposed ruler, not as the loser of a war with the Wicked Witch of the West who was afraid or unable to leave his own city, as he was depicted in *The Wizard*. Baum also refuted his statement in *The Marvelous Land* that the Emerald City had been in existence before the Wizard's arrival by having the Wizard himself state that he built it. Baum further emphasized this point by mentioning three other times within the course of the story that the Wizard built the Emerald City.[27]

In turn, Ozma tells the Wizard her own history:

> *"Many years before you came here this Land was united under one Ruler as it is now, and the Ruler's name was always 'Oz,' which means in our language 'Great and Good'; or, if the Ruler happened to be a woman, her name was always 'Ozma.' But once upon a time four Witches leagued together to depose the king and rule the four parts of the kingdom themselves; so when the Ruler, my grandfather, was hunting one day, one Wicked Witch named Mombi stole him and carried him away, keeping him a close prisoner."*[28]

When the Wizard reminds Ozma that there were two Good Witches in Oz when he arrived, she replies that "a good Witch had conquered Mombi in the North and Glinda the Good had conquered the evil Witch in the South. But Mombi was still my grandfather's jailor, and afterward my father's jailor. When I was born she transformed me into a boy."[29] It will be noticed that the former ruler of Oz who was deposed is now her grandfather, thus making it even more impossible that the Wizard had a hand in kidnapping the rightful ruler.

The Wizard says that he grew old in the Emerald City—something he also said in *The Wizard*—and Baum has Ozma kindly say to him, "So, as you are now too old to wander abroad and work in a circus, I offer you a home here as long as you live."[30] With this incident, and the mention of the deaths of Ozma's grandfather and father, Baum again emphasized that the people of Oz are not immortal and that time acts there just as it does in our world. There is still another suggestion of mortality in something he did not mention in this story. All the companions from *The*

Marvelous Land, including the Gump, are reintroduced except for Jack Pumpkinhead, who is not mentioned at all. He had been described as "a little overripe" in *Ozma,* and the impression left in this story is that he finally spoiled. However, the illustrator, John R. Neill, confused the issue by picturing him twice, once on the "List of Chapters" page and again on the last color plate.[31]

Dorothy and the Wizard in Oz is literally and figuratively one of Baum's darkest fantasies. Even the transition to the brilliant sunshine of Oz does not completely dispel the gloom, for in Oz he introduced the themes of murder and judgment. That darkness and those themes place this book among those of Baum's writings that seem to demand interpretation on more than one level of meaning. *The Wonderful Wizard of Oz* and the mystical *Life and Adventures of Santa Claus* are other full-length stories that come most readily to mind, but there are elements and episodes in just about every fantasy he wrote that transcend the stories and suggest richer levels of meaning that, as Tolkien noted, reach ahead toward the supernatural or back toward the world of men. In *Dorothy and the Wizard in Oz,* Dorothy makes her third violent and life-threatening entrance into fairyland, and for the third time, her aunt and uncle assume that she is dead. This suggests that Oz is something more than a fairyland, and critics have speculated that it may even be a version of heaven.[32] Of course, the idea of Oz as heaven throws an entirely different light on Baum's uses of "the journey to Oz" as plots for some of the stories, because the journey would then be more than an adventurous sightseeing trip: it would be the progress of the soul to heaven. Such a reading is almost impossible to avoid in *Dorothy and the Wizard,* which is in some respects Baum's *Divine Comedy.* And the surprising thing that supports such an interpretation is that the transition to Oz, which at first seems to be a flaw in the plot structure, becomes, instead, absolutely necessary and right. The reinterpretation of Oz in the following books make it very clear that *if* Baum did not come to view Oz as heaven, he did come to consider it an Earthly Paradise.

Baum would have been familiar with Dante's masterpiece. There was already the classic translation by H. F. Cary, which he could have read as a child, and in 1867, the most popular American poet of the time, Henry Wadsworth Longfellow, published his own translation. Also in the 1860s, Gustave Doré's enormously popular illustrations for *The Divine Comedy* made it one of the premiere "coffee-table books" of the era. No household with any pretense of culture could avoid some familiarity with Dante's poem.[33]

Edward Bulwer-Lytton's *The Coming Race* (1871) has already been mentioned as a possible source for this Oz book, and Jules Verne's *A Journey to the Centre of the Earth* (1864) is another probable influence. However, Dante's story provides the closest correlation to Baum's and makes *Dorothy and the Wizard in Oz* a particularly good example of "how Baum assimilated details, motifs, and themes from various sources . . . and reworked them."[34] The story opens in darkness with cataclysmic upheavals of the earth; the dawn does not come because "the sky had grown darker again and the wind made queer sobbing sounds as it swept over the valley."[35] Dorothy and her companions descend into an underground world where the cold, heartless vegetable people bring to mind Dante's frozen, lowest circle of hell. There they find a magician, the Wizard, to act as their guide and protector, and they begin their ascent through mountains, just as Dante and Virgil ascend the Mountain of Purgatory. They strive upward just as far as their human ability and their human guide can take them, but are finally left in a dark cavern gazing at a ray of sunlight still far above. It is then that Ozma (acting like a personification of Grace) lifts them the rest of the way to Oz. Once there, they are judged; the trial of Eureka is only the most obvious example. Jim and Zeb, to a certain extent, clearly do not belong in Oz, and they, like Eureka, are sent home. The Wizard is judged worthy and allowed to stay. Dorothy, of course, already belongs to Oz and could remain, but her love and sense of duty make her decide to return home. These differing judgments

---

John R. Neill's illustration for the chapter "Into the Black Pit and Out Again" from Dorothy and the Wizard in Oz.

THROUGH THE BLACK PIT.

are Baum's first indication that Oz is not open to everyone; that to be a welcome visitor there, one must have special qualities of goodness and innocence. Oz is not for the masses.

THE FAIRYLOGUE AND RADIO-PLAYS

While *Dorothy and the Wizard in Oz* was in production, Baum had again been involved with the theater, this time in his most unusual theatrical experiment. His stage extravaganzas had been somewhat old-fashioned, but this new venture took advantage of the most advanced technology of the day; it was a two-hour combination of narration, original music, live actors, colored slides, and color motion pictures. The grandiose title of this unique form of entertainment was *The Fairylogue and Radio-Plays,* and it presented the stories *The Wonderful Wizard of Oz, The Land of Oz,* and *John Dough and the Cherub,* with some scenes from *Dorothy and the Wizard.* It must have been a sumptuous production: Baum, dressed in a white formal suit and backed by an orchestra, provided the narration, and the stories were presented by live actors, 114 glass slides, and 23 motion-picture clips.[36] It had been only several years since motion pictures had first been used to tell a story, and D. W. Griffith would not direct his first film until 1909, but Baum already was presenting story films in color to his audiences. The films were made by the new Chicago studio of Selig Polyscope, and they had been hand-colored, frame by frame, in Paris by Duval Frères. Baum explained that the term "Radio" referred to Michel Radio, the inventor of the colored film process.[37]

Baum's adaptations were faithful to his original stories, emphasizing again his belief that his stories would make good theatrical entertainments in their unaltered forms. The only major significance that *The Fairylogue and Radio-Plays* had for his imaginary world is that one of the glass slides represented the first map of Oz; it pictured a square land, surrounded by desert on all sides. Inside the country were the four triangular kingdoms corresponding to the four directions and colored their appropriate colors, with the Emerald City in the center.[38]

    The Fairylogue and Radio-Plays opened in Grand Rapids, Michigan, on September 24, 1908, and toured the Midwest and New York until the middle of December.[39] The venture was a success with audiences, but it was a financial disaster. The costs of paying a full orchestra and a cast of actors and of transporting them and the equipment from town to town made the entertainment lose money even while playing to full houses. And added to that deficit was the great initial cost of producing the films and slides. Unfortunately, the majority of the debt fell on Baum and wiped out any financial security he had been able to achieve. The complete extent of the disaster was not immediately apparent, but his writing became even more important to him because it was the only sure means he had to pay off the debts.

THE ROAD TO OZ

What is surprising is that none of the stress caused by Baum's financial difficulties is apparent in his next fantasy, *The Road to Oz* (1909), which was probably being written during this time. The story opens with a "shaggy" man asking Dorothy the way to Butterfield, Kansas. Deciding that it would be easier to show him than to try to explain the complicated directions, she takes him to the right road, but once there, the Kansas landscape looks unfamiliar to Dorothy also. She suddenly sees that roads are going in all directions from where they are standing, and she has no idea of how to return to the farmhouse. Finally she, Toto, and the Shaggy Man pick a road at random, and they soon find that they are in fairyland and much closer to Oz than to Kansas. Along the road they meet Button-Bright, a lost young American boy, and Polychrome, a daughter of the rainbow, also lost, and they have several interesting adventures before they reach Oz just in time to attend the birthday celebrations of Princess Ozma.

151

From the standpoint of plot, *The Road to Oz* is one of the weakest books in the series: only one of the adventures has any suspense to it; the mysterious object of the journey (the birthday celebration) is apparent early in the story; and Ozma's explanation that she confused the roads to bring Dorothy to Oz for the party is unsatisfactory. Why did she not use the Magic Belt? However, from the standpoint of the development of Oz, *The Road to Oz* is one of the most important books in the series.

There is a unity about the four Oz books published between 1907 and 1910 that indicates that Baum had in mind some sort of overall plan. After the further adventures of the Scarecrow and the Tin Woodman in *The Marvelous Land of Oz*, his readers had let him know that they also wanted to learn more about the other characters from *The Wonderful Wizard of Oz*, especially Dorothy. This request probably also made him realize that it was his original story and not the stage play that had the most claim on his readers' affections, since he subsequently dropped the references to the plot of the play. All four books concern journeys that Dorothy makes to Oz, and after reintroducing the little Kansas girl as well as the Cowardly Lion in *Ozma of Oz*, the Wizard in *Dorothy and the Wizard in Oz*, and Toto in *The Road to Oz*, he attempted to round off and end the series in *The Emerald City of Oz* by having Dorothy and her Aunt Em and Uncle Henry go to live in Oz.

The amount of the story set in Oz increases in each successive book, almost as though Baum needed time to come to terms with the country that he originally had no intention of developing (in *The Road to Oz*, twelve out of twenty-four chapters are set in Oz). Within the framework of these four books, *The Road to Oz* fits beautifully. Its pastoral, sunny nature makes it a perfect foil for the darkness and danger of *Dorothy and the Wizard* and sets off, by giving a much needed breathing space, the serious and ominous story of *The Emerald City*. Thus, *in context*, the serenity of and absence of violent and threatening incidents in *The Road to Oz* are assets. The very lack of a strong plot enabled Baum to concentrate more fully on the nature of Oz itself, and the book, in addition to clearing up more of the past confusion, contains a radical reinterpretation of Oz and of Baum's entire imaginary world.

The alterations and reinterpretations are best seen in their proper places in the story. The first unusual thing that one notices about this book is that it contains Dorothy's first non-life-threatening entrance into fairyland, as though she has stepped across some line of enchantment. At first, the landscape seems no different from the familiar Kansas country-side, and it is not until she and her friends visit a city of talking foxes that she finds out what has happened. She asks the Fox King, "[W]e are in Kansas now, are n't we?" and is surprised to learn that Foxville "is nearer to Oz than it is to Kansas."[40] This peaceful transition makes Oz seem closer to America than do the transitions in any of the other books in the series, and Ozma's later explanation that she enchanted the roads to bring Doro-thy to the birthday celebration does little to dispel that feeling.

One of the strengths of the book lies in the three new charac-ters whom Baum introduced: the Shaggy Man, Button-Bright, and Poly-chrome. They all became popular with his readers and reappear in later books. He had a genius for creating unusual and interesting characters, and one of his best is the Shaggy Man, who may have been inspired by James Whitcomb Riley's popular poems about "The Raggedy Man," the hired man who is so good with children. "Hobo" and "bum" are the wrong words to use to describe the Shaggy Man because there are no indications that he was forced by circumstances or any deficiencies within himself to be what he is. Terminology from the 1960s best describes him: he has "dropped out" and is "doing his own thing." He is a wanderer who wants only to love and be loved by everyone; he cares nothing for money, and his shaggy appearance is not a sign of his poverty, but a badge of his individu-ality. The society of Oz, as Baum reinterprets it in this book, suits the Shaggy Man perfectly, and he asks if he may be permitted to live there, a request that Ozma grants "for a time, at least. If he proved honest and true she promised to let him live there always, and the shaggy man was anxious to earn this reward."[41]

Baum knew well that such an individualist was not often wel-comed in American society: "In the big, cold, outside world people did not invite shaggy men to their homes, and this shaggy man of ours had slept more in hay-lofts, and stables than in comfortable rooms."[42] And it is a fine example of Baum's ideal of tolerance and understanding that in Oz the Shaggy Man is treated with as much respect and honor as the most powerful ruler. Baum is especially sensitive when he has Ozma, while providing the Shaggy Man with a new wardrobe of silks, satins, and velvets, respect his individuality and make those new clothes as quaintly shaggy as his old ones.

These are not sentiments that are peculiar to this one book; they run throughout Baum's writings—he had great sympathy for unusual and individual people. When Polychrome remarks, "You have some queer friends, Dorothy," the little Kansas girl answers, "The queerness does n't matter, so long as they 're friends."[43]

The Shaggy Man, like the humbug Wizard, belongs to that class of Baum's adult male characters who could be labeled "misfits of society." In fact, the majority of his good male characters fall either into that category or into the nonhuman one (the Scarecrow, the Tin Woodman). It seems that Baum did not have much faith or confidence in the aggres-sive American male who was bringing "civilization" to this new country. It is obvious that Baum had somewhat advanced or unorthodox ideas about power and authority. More often than not, his rulers are women and children, and even though he poked fun at the suffragette movement in *The Marvelous Land*, Jinjur and her female army are opposed by Glinda the Good and *her* female army, and the rule of Oz is not restored to the male Scarecrow but given to the rightful ruler, the child Ozma. Baum's male figures provide protection for the children on their journeys, but the real authority belongs to the female characters such as Glinda the Good and Ozma. The Wizard, who had built and ruled the Emerald City, now stands "modestly behind Ozma's throne" in *The Road to Oz*.[44]

Oz is more clearly the goal and purpose of the journey in *The Road to Oz* than it was in the previous two books, and Baum emphasized

154

that other fairylands exist outside the borders of Oz, a change that he had introduced in *Ozma*. He also stressed the isolation of Oz among those other fairy countries by stating in even stronger terms the dangers of the desert surrounding Oz. When the road leads Dorothy and her companions to the edge of that desert, they find a sign that reads:

ALL PERSONS ARE WARNED NOT TO VENTURE UPON THIS DESERT *For the Deadly Sands will Turn Any Living Flesh to Dust in an Instant. Beyond This Barrier is the* LAND OF OZ *But no one can Reach that Beautiful Country because of these Destroying Sands.*[45]

It is by the Shaggy Man's ingenuity that the travelers are able to cross the desert unharmed; it is another of his deeds that carries weight with Ozma when she comes to consider letting him live in Oz.

Once the characters are in Oz, Baum immediately tackled the problem of the color scheme of the country—which he had largely avoided since *The Marvelous Land of Oz*—and he arrived at a workable compromise among all the various statements he had made about color in Oz, including the illusory color of the Emerald City in *The Wizard*. Thus when they reach the Winkie Country, Dorothy explains "that 'most everything here is yellow that has any color at all,'" and it is clear from the descriptions that Baum meant the blossoms on the trees and the flowers rather than the trunks, stems, and leaves.[46] The grass may be either green or "yellowish green," but there is no doubt that anything that is naturally green in our world retains green as its base hue in Oz. This compromise, while avoiding the monotony of the color scheme in *The Marvelous Land*, also enabled Baum to include more color descriptions than appear in *Ozma* and *Dorothy and the Wizard*.

The exterior of the Emerald City is still basically green, but now gold is also present in its decoration, while the interiors and the clothes of its people can be any color.[47] Baum did give a subtle nod to his older ideas when he described the Little Guardian of the Gates as still wearing green spectacles, the only person so described.[48] The compromise, however, is not consistently used in the later books, although it is the version of the color scheme most often indicated.

Tik-Tok and Billina are sent to meet the travelers, and they escort them to the new tin palace of the Tin Woodman, the Emperor of the Winkies. At this point, Baum linked his modern fairy tales to the older tradition when he has Dorothy say at the sight of the new palace, "It's the fairy dwelling of a fairy prince," and one realizes how well the enchanted Woodman fits that tradition.[49]

Baum's reinterpretation of Oz in this book affects three major areas: the nature of the society of Oz, the nature of the people of Oz, and the nature of the fantasy world in which Oz exists. The Tin Woodman introduces the first of these subjects when the Shaggy Man remarks of the new palace that "it must have cost a lot of money."[50] The Tin Woodman answers:

> *"Money! Money in Oz! . . . What a queer idea! Did you suppose we are so vulgar as to use money here?"*
>
> *"Why not?" asked the shaggy man.*
>
> *"If we used money to buy things with, instead of love and kindness and the desire to please one another, then we should be no better than the rest of the world. . . . Fortunately money is not known in the Land of Oz at all. We have no rich, and no poor; for what one wishes the others all try to give him, in order to make him happy, and no one in all Oz cares to have more than he can use."[51]*

Thus despite the fact that money has played a part in previous Oz books, Baum dispensed with it on his way to making Oz an ideal world. A little later in the Emerald City, the Tin Woodman elaborates on the way society in Oz is organized: "To be sure they [the people of Oz] work . . . this fair city could not be built or cared for without labor, nor could the fruit and vegetables and other food be provided for the inhabitants to eat. But no one works more than half his time, and the people of Oz enjoy their labors as much as they do their play."[52]

156

The second, and even more important, facet of Baum's reinterpretation is introduced shortly before the travelers reach the Emerald
City. It is certain that Baum's readers had noticed the absence of Jack
Pumpkinhead in *Dorothy and the Wizard in Oz,* and Baum reintroduced
that popular character with the explanation that when his head spoiled,
Ozma carved him another one. By this time, he has discarded three
heads—all properly buried with markers—and he lives in the middle of a
large pumpkin field to be near his source of supply. When the travelers
reach "Jack Pumpkinhead's private graveyard," Dorothy is quite surprised
and says, "But I thought nobody ever died in Oz." The Tin Woodman
answers, "Nor do they; although if one is bad, he may be condemned and
killed by the good citizens."[53] In two sentences, Baum banished natural
death from Oz. He soon pointed out that the people of Oz are still prey to
accidents, and he would elaborate this reinterpretation and bring it more
into line with his past statements about people dying in Oz in the remaining books of the series, but the great change occurs here: Oz has become
more than a haven from danger; it has become a haven from death itself.

It is interesting that Baum made this modification to Oz in this
particular story, for the plot contains no threat to any of the principals that
would have made the change necessary; indeed, the portion of *The Road to
Oz* that takes place in Oz is exceptionally sunny, happy, and trouble-free.
The change actually creates major inconsistencies with the earlier books
without explaining any previous discrepancies, but it may have been that
Baum was looking ahead to his next book, in which the inhabitants'
immortality is important to defusing the darker aspects of the story line
and in guaranteeing the continued existence of his Other-world even
though he planned for the real world and Oz to go their separate ways. Or
perhaps, on his way to building an ideal world, Baum, with his intuitive
understanding of fantasy, just felt that the change was right and natural.

Before going on to the third area—the nature of the fantasy
world—several minor alterations in *The Road to Oz* should be mentioned:
Oz is once again more rural, and the Emerald City is the only city in the
country.[54] There are also the usual inconsistencies: the Tin Woodman is

now counted among the four subrulers, but Glinda the Good and the Good Witch of the North have not been restored to their positions as rulers; in fact, the Good Witch of the North, a nebulous figure at best, just about disappears from the series after this book. Glinda's position, however, is very different. As the most powerful magic worker, she is second only to Ozma in the hierarchy of Oz, and she is developing into the real, maternal spirit of that fairyland. To be placed again among the subrulers would actually lessen her importance.

There is also one example of carelessness about direction that presages a major confusion about directions that occurs later. When the travelers enter Oz on the west side (the Winkie Country), they start for the Emerald City on "a fine road leading toward the northwest."[55] That direction would, of course, take them in the opposite direction from the Emerald City. On the whole, however, the discrepancies are fewer than in some of the previous books.

The third facet of the reinterpretation occurs in the finale of the book. A birthday celebration that occupies the final fifth of a book and that is not supported by plot lines of mystery or suspense could make for dull reading. However, this is not the case in *The Road to Oz*. Baum wrote that "perhaps there has never been in any part of the world at any time another assemblage of such wonderful people as that which gathered . . . to honor the birthday of the Ruler of Oz," and for once, an author did not overstate the facts.[56] Baum not only included among the guests all the important characters from the previous books in the series, as well as the new characters from this book, but also introduced characters who have hitherto had no connection with Oz. Thus with ever mounting pomp and circumstance, the foreign visitors begin to arrive to honor the Princess of Oz: "His Gracious and Most Edible Majesty, King Dough the First, Ruler of the Two Kingdoms of Hiland and Loland. Also the Head Booleywag of his Majesty, known as Chick the Cherub, and their faithful friend Para Bruin, the rubber bear"; "a band of Ryls from the Happy Valley," "a dozen crooked Knooks . . . from the great Forest of Burzee," and "the most Mighty and Loyal Friend of Children, His Supreme Highness—Santa Claus"; "Her Gracious Majesty, the Queen of Merryland," accompanied by the Candy Man of Merryland and four wooden soldiers; and "Her Sublime and Resplendent Majesty, Queen Zixi of Ix! His Serene and Tremendous Majesty, King Bud of Noland. Her Royal Highness, the Princess Fluff."[57]

The presence of these characters, for the first time, places all of Baum's imaginary creations in the same fantasy world, while also affirming the premier position of Oz in that world. And the characters bring more than their birthday gifts to Oz; they bring their histories, their adventures, and their strange, exotic countries as well. The reader is fairly overwhelmed with all the memories and associations from the other books. Indeed, the effect is not so very different on first-time readers who are not familiar with Baum's other fantasies because these characters and the scraps of their histories that are given conjure up wonderful visions of unknown and fascinating countries stretching beyond the borders of Oz— a great fantasy world just waiting to be explored.

Once Oz has been elevated to the center of Baum's fairy world, the birthday celebration with its grand banquet, royal procession, and spectacular entertainments does not disappoint. At its climax, the Wizard sends the foreign visitors, including Button-Bright, home in gigantic, sparkling soap bubbles that are guided by Santa Claus, although Dorothy prudently chooses the Magic Belt as her means of returning to Kansas. The Wizard's feat is purely the result of his mechanical inventions, but to the people of Oz, it seems as much magic as that performed by Glinda and the Good Witch of the North. Finally, as the last soap bubble floats away into the distance, Polychrome's father lets down his radiant rainbow into the celebration to reclaim his daughter. Surely in the realms of fantasy there has never been a celebration to match it.

Baum's *Road to Oz* is a tour de force of place. With almost no plot and little danger or suspense, he created one of the most exhilarating and satisfying of his works of fantasy. John R. Neill enhanced the book with his most beautiful and detailed drawings, and although there were no color plates, the book was printed on various colors of paper that created a rainbow effect when leafing through the pages.

Baum began his introduction to *The Road to Oz* by writing, "Well, my dears, here is what you asked for: another 'Oz Book' about Dorothy's strange adventures," indicating that he realized the strength of his readers' attachment to Oz. But he wanted to write other stories, and he concluded his introduction with the startling announcement: "Since this book was written I have received some very remarkable news from The Land of Oz, which has greatly astonished me. . . . But it is such a long and exciting story that it must be saved for another book—and perhaps that book will be the last story that will ever be told about the Land of Oz."[58] That farewell to Oz was to be *The Emerald City of Oz,* and in it Baum unleashed his creative imagination.

THE EMERALD CITY OF OZ

In contrast to *The Road to Oz, The Emerald City of Oz* abounds in plots. For the first time in his fantasies, Baum utilized double, and sometimes triple, plot lines, alternately following separate sets of characters and bringing them all together at the end of the story. For the sake of clarity and ease of summary, the various concurrent and interconnected plots will be presented separately.

The first involves the Nome King, whose anger has festered and grown since his defeat in *Ozma of Oz.* He determines to conquer Oz, and to ensure the success of his goal, he sends his general to gather allies from the most evil creatures who live around Oz: the Whimsies, the Growleywogs, and the Phanfasms. To solve the problem of the desert— deadly alike to mortals and immortals—the Nome King sets his Nomes to

---

An example of John R. Neill's beautifully detailed style in The Road to Oz.

"O, JELLIA JAMB! I'M SO GLAD TO SEE YOU"

building a large tunnel to the Emerald City, a task eminently suited to his underground subjects.

The second plot line follows Dorothy. In Kansas, a series of reversals, including the cyclone and ill-health, have forced her Uncle Henry into bankruptcy, and he is to lose his farm. When Dorothy learns the extent of their troubles, she makes the secret signal to Ozma and is transported to Oz with Toto, followed shortly by her Uncle Henry and Aunt Em. In one of the realistic touches that Baum sprinkled throughout his books, the transition to Oz is not an easy one for Dorothy's elderly relatives. They are simple people used to hard work, and they have trouble adjusting to the splendor of Ozma's court and to having no useful work to do. While Ozma tries to find a solution to this problem, she sends the newcomers, accompanied by her Captain General, the Wizard, the Shaggy Man, and Billina, on a tour of some of the interesting and unusual places in Oz.

A third, subsidiary plot line follows Ozma in the Emerald City as she, via the Magic Picture, discovers and watches the progress of the Nome King's tunnel. All the strands converge at the end, when the Oz characters gather in the garden of Ozma's palace to meet the invading armies.

There is an air of tying up loose ends about *The Emerald City of Oz:* Dorothy, with her uncle, aunt, and Toto, at last comes to Oz to live; the Scarecrow, who has had no fixed home since he lost his throne, is given a corn-shaped mansion outside the Emerald City; and the humbug Wizard has begun a course of study with Glinda the Good to make himself a real wizard, thus transforming the last illusion remaining from *The Wonderful Wizard of Oz* into reality. That this book was to end the series also seems to have freed Baum's inventive imagination and made him more willing to deal with the Land of Oz itself. So completely has Oz dominated the previous books that it comes as a shock to realize that there has been almost no exploration of the country since *The Marvelous Land* and that Baum had not added any strange and unusual areas and races to Oz since the China Country and the Hammerheads in *The Wizard.* As it had originally been created, Oz was, more clearly than any of his other worlds, a fantasy version of America; it took time and distance for Baum to work out a new conception of Oz and to change the illusions into reality. Not until *The Road to Oz* did the new Oz emerge in a fairly well developed form and become integrated with Baum's other fantasy worlds.

The reinterpretation of Oz in *The Road to Oz* is repeated without change in *The Emerald City*, except that it is discussed at greater length; Baum presented the most complete, detailed, and realistic picture of the Emerald City and the society of Oz in the series (Appendix A).[59] In that description, he implied that there are sections of Oz that are not as "normal" as the Emerald City and the usual farming areas of the country, and he introduced seven of them in the tour that Dorothy, her relatives, and her friends make: the Cuttenclips, a village of paper dolls created and ruled by a young-appearing girl; the Fuddles, people who come apart and can be put back together like jigsaw puzzles; the kingdom of Utensia, peopled by kitchen utensils; Bunbury, a town inhabited by live baked goods; Bunnybury, a city of rabbits; Rigmarole Town, in which reside people who can never say what they mean; and Flutterbudget Center, where live all the people who worry excessively about improbable things that have not happened. The genesis of these strange places is clearly the odd countries encountered on the journey south in *The Wizard*. Some of the new places, such as Cuttenclip Village and Bunnyburg, have been set aside for the protection of the inhabitants by Glinda the Good, who, more than ever in this book, is the wise mother-figure of Oz; others, such as Utensia and Bunbury, are newly discovered; and still others like Rigmarole Town and Flutterbudget Center are "Defensive Settlements" established to protect the other inhabitants of Oz.[60]

Baum sometimes had trouble keeping his creative abilities under control, and the tour section of *The Emerald City* could easily have disintegrated into a mere travelogue except that it is interspersed with chapters that recount the progress the Nomes are making in gathering allies and building the tunnel to Oz. In that context, the tour emphasizes the variety and richness of the land that the Nomes hope to destroy, and the reader whose sense of impending doom is mounting cannot help but contrast the peace and innocence of the Oz characters with the evil machinations of the Nome King.

In *The Emerald City*, Baum did not restrict his facility for the creation of unusual races to Oz; he also conceived three nations of evil allies—each more terrible and frightening than the last—for the Nomes. Not until Tolkien's *Lord of the Rings* would there be another mustering of evil to oppose good to match it in a fantasy. And in the confrontation between good and evil that was, Baum thought, to end the Oz series, he provided the finest moment of Oz.

Many of Baum's ideas and ways of viewing the world were not mainstream for his time—some of them are, unfortunately, still not main-stream—and one of his most radical departures from common opinion is occasioned by the confrontation in *The Emerald City*. Dorothy and her companions' tour is cut short when they learn of the threat to Oz, and they rush to the Emerald City in a show of support for Ozma. When her friends and advisers are discussing the possibility of rallying the four nations of Oz to form an army, Ozma interrupts them: "But I do not wish to fight. . . . No one has the right to destroy any living creatures, however evil they may be, or to hurt them or make them unhappy. I will not fight—even to save my kingdom." She goes on to explain, "Because the Nome King intends to do evil is no excuse for my doing the same."[61] With the exception of the comic violence in Baum's earliest book, his works had increasingly expressed support for nonviolence and for the sacredness of all living things, and he made Ozma, the most important ruler in his imaginary world, the spokesperson for his strongest statement on the subject. Many times before, the sentiments had been expressed without any actual threat being imminent, but in this instance, the cost of uphold-ing those principles is the destruction of Oz. Ozma offers to send her friends to Kansas and safety, but one by one, they decide to stand by her. Even Uncle Henry and Aunt Em throw in their lot with Oz. Dorothy proves her worthiness of the rank she has in Oz by saying that "if the

Ruler of Oz must not desert her people, a Princess of Oz has no right to run away, either."[62] She has, in effect, finally reached her real home.

There is, of course, a happy ending, which reaches back to *The Wonderful Wizard of Oz* because it is the excellent brains given to the Scarecrow by the Wizard that come up with the means to neutralize the evil and save Oz by cleverness instead of violence. However, the ease by which Oz was almost conquered is a shock and casts an ominous significance on the various ways in which Dorothy and the Wizard have been able to enter Oz. These concerns are the impetus for the ending of the series. Ozma states the problem:

> *It seems to me there are entirely too many ways for people to get to the Land of Oz. We used to think the deadly desert that surrounds us was enough protection; but that is no longer the case. The Wizard and Dorothy have both come here through the air, and I am told the earth people have invented airships that can fly anywhere they wish them to go. . . .*
>
> *. . . [And] if the earth folk learn how to manage them we would be overrun with visitors who would ruin our lovely, secluded fairyland.*[63]

These are concerns that Baum had expressed as far back as *Dot and Tot of Merryland* (1901). He had been living in Chicago when that city's population doubled in the short space of ten years; he had seen farmland, meadows, and forests paved over, and he had not liked the crowded, dirty city streets and slums that often took their place. To him, such unbridled growth was destructive, not creative. He could, at least, keep his imaginary world free of it.

Ozma appeals to the supreme authority on magic in Oz, Glinda the Good, who has anticipated the ruler's request by the use of the Magic Record Book, a new device that records all the events that happen, and it is decided to remove Oz "forever from all the rest of the world" by making it invisible to all outside eyes.[64] Once the enchantment takes effect, anyone coming to the edge of the desert or flying over Oz will see nothing. In the short last chapter, "How the Story of Oz Came to an End," Baum "quotes" a note from Dorothy ending, "Toto and I will always love you and all the other children who love us."[65]

Even though Baum tied up many loose ends and provided what he believed was a satisfying conclusion to his series, there are still some problems with the text of *The Emerald City*. Having made the inhabitants of Oz immortals in *The Road*, Baum here referred to them as either "fairies" or "fairy people,"[66] unsatisfactory appellations because in Baum's other stories fairies are a separate immortal race and not the common inhabitants of a fairy country. He also provided Ozma, who hitherto has had no magic apart from the Magic Belt and the Magic Picture, with a magic fairy wand,[67] with no explanation of how she came to have it or any examples of its use. He also left the fate of the American characters up in the air and does not inform the reader whether or not they, by living in Oz, share the immortality of the regular inhabitants.

One blunder that was hinted at in *The Road* and is later to become more serious concerns directions. In *The Emerald City*, Baum wrote:

> *The mountains underneath which the Nome King's extensive caverns were located lay grouped just north of the Land of Ev, which lay directly across the deadly desert to the* east *of the Land of Oz. As the mountains were also on the edge of the desert the Nome King found that he had only to tunnel underneath the desert to reach Ozma's dominions. He did not wish his armies to appear above ground in the Country of the* Winkies, *which was the part of the Land of Oz* nearest *to King Roquat's own country.*[68]

The location of the Nome King's kingdom is exactly the same as that given in *Ozma*, except that the eastern country of Oz is the Munchkin Country. Somehow the positions of the Munchkin and Winkie Countries become switched in Baum's mind, probably as early as *The Road to Oz* because the northwesterly direction of the road to the Emerald City mentioned in that book would have been correct if the Winkie Country

166

lay in the east. The switch could be dismissed as carelessness on Baum's part except that it continued for several more books and was the source of some confusion.

There is a possible explanation for the switch that also would add strength to the argument that Oz was located in Baum's mind in the midst of the Great American Desert. If Baum, writing in Chicago, placed Oz to the west of the Great Plains (he would have been well aware of the west being the traditional direction for magical worlds), he probably pictured Dorothy's house landing in the nearest part of Oz across the desert. That would be the eastern section, the Munchkin Country, and Dorothy enters Oz from that direction again in *Ozma of Oz*. Therefore, it would seem natural that it would become fixed in Baum's mind that the Munchkin Country was the area of Oz nearest to our world. However, Baum himself changed direction, spending every winter from 1904 in California (except the winter he spent in Europe); the introductions of the three Oz books after *Ozma* are signed "Coronado," and in 1910, the year of *The Emerald City*, he and Maud moved to California permanently. If the Munchkin Country was still fixed in his mind as the side of Oz closest to him, it would now be, looking from California, on the west side of Oz, and the Winkie Country would lie on the east side.

This explanation is speculation, but it does reflect actual changes in his life that had a great effect on him. His fictional solution to Uncle Henry's money problems could very well have been wishful thinking, because the enormous debts incurred by *The Fairylogue and Radio-Plays* were becoming more pressing and probably influenced his and Maud's decision to move to California, where the cost of living was supposed to be lower than in Chicago. In some ways it was not a difficult decision because they both loved California, their children were grown, and the climate there was certainly better for someone in Baum's precarious state of health. Thus in 1910, they moved to Los Angeles, and soon after, with money Maud had inherited,[69] they built a house in a small suburb of Los Angeles, a lovely and peaceful place with more orange trees than houses. Its name was Hollywood.

167

Chapter Six

Beginning Again
1911–1916

When the children have had enough of them [the Oz books], I hope they will let me know, and then I'll try to write something different.

L. Frank Baum, "'Twixt You and Me" in
The Scarecrow of Oz (1915)

IT MUST HAVE BEEN WITH A MIXTURE OF RELIEF AND ANXIETY THAT L. FRANK BAUM ENDED HIS CONNECTION WITH OZ by concluding the series with *The Emerald City of Oz:* relief because he was at last free to write some of the other stories he had in mind and anxiety because he had stopped a very successful and profitable series and had no idea how well his new fantasies would be received.

The end of the Oz series had been planned quite a while before the last book appeared, but other forces were at work and *The Emerald City* coincided with one of the worst periods in Baum's life. He had not been able to pay off the debts from *The Fairylogue and Radio-Plays;* the move to California had not helped financially as much as he had hoped; and in 1911 the stage play of *The Wonderful Wizard of Oz* finally ended its phenomenal run around the country and money stopped flowing from that source. On June 3, 1911, Baum filed for bankruptcy in Los Angeles,[1] and in the process of settling his debts, he lost the rights to many of his earlier books.

THE SEA FAIRIES AND *SKY ISLAND*

For his new fantasy series, he stuck to what had proved to be his most successful formula: an American child, accompanied by an older companion, having adventures in fairyland. However, he tried to avoid the problem of being restricted to just one imaginary country by having his characters visit a different fairyland in each book. The main American characters in these fantasies are young Mayre Griffiths, called Trot, and her faithful companion, old Cap'n Bill Weedles. The setting is a coastal town in southern California. Cap'n Bill lives with Trot and her mother, and Trot's father is the captain of a ship at sea. It is easy to see that Baum lost no time in transforming his experiences in his new home into fantasy; having already populated the land with fairies, he now peopled the sea and the sky.[2]

The Sea Fairies (1911), the first of the Trot stories, most resembles Baum's nature fairy tale *Policeman Bluejay* in that many of the natural wonders of the sea are noted in the book, and Trot and Cap'n Bill, like Twinkle and Chubbins, must change their shapes to experience the fairyland of the sea. Their adventures are the result of an invitation from the Mermaids, who are Water Fairies and who fit the criterion of being created with the world that Baum set for land fairies in *The Life and Adventures of Santa Claus*.[3] In *The Sea Fairies*, however, the seemingly limitless extent of the ocean worked against the construction of a well-defined, bounded imaginary world.

Unfortunately, this interesting and beautifully illustrated book did not sell as well as the Oz books,[4] and in the next story, *Sky Island* (1912), Baum attempted to link the new series with the old by introducing two characters who appear in an Oz book. The second book is not a nature fairy tale but is pure fancy. "Place," an island in the sky divided by a fog bank into the countries of the Blues and the Pinks, is more clearly realized in *Sky Island* than the sea realm is in *The Sea Fairies*. Baum linked his sky adventure with Oz by using Button-Bright from *The Road to Oz* as one of the main characters. Button-Bright, having found a magic um-

170

brella, travels to California, where he meets Trot and Cap'n Bill. While taking his new friends for a trip, his directions for the umbrella are confused, and they end up on the island in the sky. A further link to Oz is made when Polychrome, the Rainbow's daughter and also from *The Road*, makes a short stop on the island to save Button-Bright and his friends from harm.[5]

Sky Island also did not sell well. Perhaps the series would have gained momentum if it had continued beyond two books. Nevertheless, both stories prove that Baum was still capable of telling interesting non-Oz tales, although both had little direct influence on his fantasy world.

BACK TO OZ

Even before *Sky Island* was published, Baum knew that he would have to return to Oz. He and his publisher briefly toyed with the idea of alternating Oz and "Trot" stories,[6] but Baum was not in a position to gamble; he really could not afford the time for more experimentation. His readers wanted more books about Oz, and he needed money, so he was literally forced by circumstances and public demand to explore further that ideal world of his imagination.

It was much easier for Baum to resume the Oz series at this point than it had been when he wrote *Ozma of Oz*, because he now had an established base to work from: he had extensively developed Oz and the fantasy world in which it exists; he had defined the nature of the society and the physical characteristics of the country; he had a repertory of plot devices at hand; and he had a large cast of characters to work with. However, these very things that eased his return to the series may be some of the reasons why the second half of the series is generally considered weaker than the first.

After Oz had become more or less "fixed" in *The Emerald City*, the succeeding stories had to be devised to be placed against, and to fit into, an existing background that was fairly stable. Because the stories and background were no longer developing concurrently, there is more of a sameness of tone about the later books. The second half of the series does contain some very good stories and Oz does continue to develop, albeit in less radical ways, but Oz now exists more or less independently of the stories that take place within its borders.

From time to time, Baum still expressed the hope that his readers would want stories other than those about Oz, but he most likely realized that there was little chance of that. He lived until 1919 and was productive almost until the end, but he never again published another non-Oz fantasy. One of the fascinating aspects of place in the later books is how he modified Oz to accommodate his various new story ideas.

THE PATCHWORK GIRL OF OZ

It was important to Baum and to his publisher that his return to Oz be successful. Reilly & Britton decided on a "large promotion of L. Frank Baum and all of his books for the year 1913,"[7] and Baum did his part by supplying not only a full-length fantasy, *The Patchwork Girl of Oz*, but also six short booklets under the general title *The Little Wizard Series*. These booklets, republished the next year in one volume as *Little Wizard Stories of Oz*, were intended for younger readers and do little beyond introducing the principal Oz characters, as the individual titles show: "The Cowardly Lion and the Hungry Tiger," "Little Dorothy and Toto." However, *The Patchwork Girl of Oz* is one of Baum's best stories.

A young boy, Ojo the Unlucky, and his "Unc" Nunkie live in the lonely Blue Forest in the Munchkin Country of Oz. They are very poor and almost out of food, so they decide to go where things are better. Ojo's uncle first takes him to visit their nearest neighbor, Dr. Pipt, the Crooked Magician and inventor of the Powder of Life, which brought Jack Pumpkinhead to life in *The Marvelous Land of Oz*. At the magician's house, they meet his wife, Margolotte, and the conceited, ill-tempered Glass Cat. Dr.

172

Pipt is busy stirring a new batch of the Powder of Life, which he will use to bring to life a life-size dummy made out of a patchwork quilt to be a servant for his wife. He has been cooking the mixture for six years, and it is just about done. Margolotte intends that the girl have only the mental qualities that will make her a good and docile servant, but when Dr. Pipt's wife is not looking, Ojo adds portions of all the bottles on the magician's "Brain Furniture" shelf.

When the Patchwork Girl comes to life, unfortunately, Unc Nunkie and Margolotte are so startled that they jump back against a shelf on which sits the magician's Liquid of Petrifaction. It spills, and both of them are turned into marble statues. There is no Powder of Life left, so Dr. Pipt must begin the six-year task again unless Ojo can find all the things needed to make the antidote to the Liquid of Petrifaction: "a six-leaved clover," "the left wing of a yellow butterfly," "a gill of water from a dark well," "three hairs from the tip of a Woozy's tail and a drop of oil from a live man's body."[8]

Thus begins Ojo's quest for the ingredients of the magic potion to restore the statues to life and to lose the "Un" from his name and become Ojo the Lucky. He is accompanied by Scraps, the Patchwork Girl, and the Glass Cat, both of whom want to see more of the world.

The adventurers first meet the Foolish Owl and the Wise Donkey, who are of no help at all, but soon they find the strange, square creature called a Woozy, who turns out to be pleasant and nice and not frightening at all. He is quite willing to give them the three hairs on his tail, but they are too firmly attached to be pulled out. The only answer is for the Woozy to join them on their journey.

They soon find a yellow brick road (not the one Dorothy traveled on), and they decide to go to the Emerald City to ask for Ozma's help. Almost immediately, they encounter some large and beautiful rainbow-colored plants, but the plants are not benign; they scoop up and envelop the travelers in their leaves. The group is rescued, though, by the Shaggy Man, who happens along on one of his rambles around Oz.

When he hears their story, he agrees to accompany them to the Emerald City, although he warns them that there is a law against picking six-leaved clovers.

The next day they encounter a giant porcupine, but are saved from harm by the Patchwork Girl, who acts like a large pin cushion. They are next stopped by a locked, iron gate, but it turns out to be an illusion that can be walked through if only they close their eyes. The gate has reality only when seen.

Once through the gate, they are in the more populated country surrounding the Emerald City, and soon they meet the Scarecrow and the Sawhorse, who are out on a short afternoon trip to visit Jinjur. The Scarecrow and the Patchwork Girl are immediately attracted to each other. Ojo, however, is very unhappy, because after hearing their plight, the Scarecrow tells him, "That Crooked Magician is breaking the Law by practicing magic without a license, and I'm not sure Ozma will allow him to restore your uncle to life."[9] Ojo has no firsthand knowledge of Ozma, whether she will understand his problem or not; therefore, when he spies a six-leaved clover and can pick it unseen, he does so, even though he knows that it is against the law.

They are met at the gate of the Emerald City by the Soldier with the Green Whiskers, who arrests Ojo for breaking the law. The others feel that there must be some mistake, but Ojo is led away to "prison," which is a comfortable home and where he is treated as an honored guest (which is the way the rare prisoner is treated in Oz). The rest of the party continues on to the palace, where they meet Dorothy and tell her their story.

The next day, Ojo is tried for his crime; although Scraps tries to defend him, he admits that he is guilty. Ozma explains why there has to be a law against the practice of magic by unauthorized people; then she forgives him. Neither she nor the Wizard can break the spell and change his uncle back to a living person, so she allows Ojo to keep the six-leaved clover and resume his quest. After he has found the other items (not all of which he remembers at that moment), she will allow Dr. Pipt to make the antidote before she takes away his unlawful magic powers. The Shaggy Man, the Glass Cat, and the Woozy stay in the Emerald City, and on the second leg of the journey, the Scarecrow and Dorothy elect to go with Ojo and Scraps to help them find the remaining items.

After a visit to Jack Pumpkinhead, from whom they learn much about some of the lesser known areas of Oz, the travelers head south to the Quadling Country, where there are wild, unexplored areas. After two days of walking, they meet the Tottenhots, a primitive tribe of mischievous people. Next they come upon a caged giant named Yoop, and they are able to pass through the narrow way in front of his cage only with the help of the Scarecrow.

None of these encounters helps them locate any of the items they need. But finally they encounter two strange nations of people living inside a mountain, where Ojo hopes he can find a dark well. The people are the Hoppers, who have only one leg and hop instead of walk, and the Horners, each of whom has a horn in the middle of his or her forehead. Ojo does learn that there is a dark well in the Horner country, but the two nations are at war, and the group from the Emerald City must end that war before the well can be found. Only after they settle the dispute does Ojo acquire his gill of water from a dark well. With renewed hope, they start off toward the Winkie Country, the only place a yellow butterfly can be found.

After an adventure with a trick river, they reach the palace of the Tin Woodman. While talking to him, Ojo suddenly realizes what is meant by "a drop of oil from a live man's body." He is able to catch a drop of oil that falls from the Tin Woodman's freshly oiled joints. Now all he needs is the left wing of a yellow butterfly. But here, in sight of success, Ojo is stopped. The Tin Woodman's kind heart will not let him permit a butterfly to be killed, and the others agree. They had not known that the butterfly would have to be killed.

The next day, the discouraged party starts back to the Emerald City accompanied by the Tin Woodman. When Ozma hears what happened, she agrees with the Tin Woodman's decision, but she also has some happy news. Glinda the Good has learned of Ojo's problem and has instructed the Wizard on how to break the spell. The marble statues and Dr. Pipt (now without his magic) have been brought to the Emerald City, and with real, lawful magic, the Wizard brings the two statues back to life.

There is a happy ending for everyone. The Patchwork Girl, the Glass Cat, and the Woozy are allowed to live in the Emerald City, and Ojo and Unc Nunkie are given a home just outside.

Baum did have a lot to work with when he resumed the series, but he also had some problems to surmount. He had created the fiction that he was merely the recording agent of events that happened in Oz, and he had cut that fairyland off from all contact with the outside world at the end of *The Emerald City;* and he had made Oz a paradise where "every inhabitant of that favored country was happy and prosperous," and "only peace and happiness reigned in Oz."[10] He was, in effect, faced with writing stories that occur *after* the traditional "and they lived happily ever after" fairy-tale ending.

But Baum was equal to both problems. He solved the first one neatly in the introduction to the new book, characteristically giving the credit to one of his readers. He wrote that one of the letters he had received suggested that he try to contact Oz by wireless; he did and had heard the present story. Baum had always placed great importance on his correspondence with his readers, taking their suggestions seriously and answering every letter. That collaboration grew even stronger when he had to continue the Oz books. He respected his readers' opinions and tried to please them. Oz seemed like a real place to them, and often they were sharp-eyed critics, pointing out to Baum some of the inconsistencies and lapses in logic that had crept into his stories. This resulted in some of the later stories being constructed to explain those lapses.

One important way in which Baum modified Oz to accommodate more stories is evident in *The Patchwork Girl:* he restored to Oz the sense of vast size that exists in *The Wizard,* but is somewhat ambiguous in

176

the subsequent books. Dorothy's journeys in that book take days to accomplish, except when she has the assistance of the Winged Monkeys, but in *The Marvelous Land*, Glinda reaches the desert from the Emerald City in an hour, and in *Ozma* the journey from the desert to the capital takes less than a day of leisurely walking. But here, once again, Oz is a land of great distances, and it is "a day's journey from the Emerald City" to Jack Pumpkinhead's house and "a two days' journey from Jack Pumpkinhead's house to the edge of the Quadling Country."[11]

This sense of space was necessary for the modification that Baum made to enable a seeming paradise to include the necessary obstacles and struggles that would generate plots. Actually, the "loophole" exists in the description given in *The Emerald City* to rationalize the presence of the Hammerheads and the Fighting Trees in Oz: "In spite of all I have said in a general way, there were some parts of the Land of Oz not quite so pleasant as the farming country and the Emerald City which was its center."[12] In *The Patchwork Girl*, Baum amplified this statement, having Dorothy explain that Oz is a fairyland "and lots of queer people live in places so tucked away that those in the Emerald City never even hear of 'em. In the middle of the country it's diff'rent, but when you get around the edges you're sure to run into strange little corners that surprise you."[13] Not only do the people in the Emerald City not know about all the strange places in their own country, but when his characters enter a wild part of the Quadling Country, Baum explained that "this part of the Land of Oz, while it belonged to Ozma and owed her allegiance, was so wild and secluded that many queer peoples hid in its jungles and lived in their own way, without even a knowledge that they had a Ruler in the Emerald City."[14] These areas "around the edges" of Oz generate most of the stories for the remainder of the series.

Baum made two other modifications to help generate future stories. First, he had Ozma outlaw the practice of magic in Oz, except, as she states, by "Glinda the Good and her assistant, the Wizard of Oz, both of whom I can trust to use their arts only to benefit my people and to make

177

them happier."[15] This is a logical development in a fairyland that has been plagued by Wicked Witches, and actually there was a precedent: in *The Marvelous Land of Oz*, "the Good Witch [of the North] . . . had forbidden any other Witch to exist in her dominions."[16] It also provided a logical means to involve the main Oz characters in those stories that begin in out-of-the-way places, because it is necessary to acquaint everyone in Oz with the laws and with Ozma's rule.

Second, Baum more often than before shifted the focus away from the main, and by now somewhat static, cast of characters, using smaller segments of the cast mixed with new characters. *The Patchwork Girl*, for example, begins in one of the forgotten areas of the Munchkin Country with the boy Ojo and his Uncle Nunkie. Only a good way into the story do Ojo and his companions—the Patchwork Girl, the Glass Cat, and the Woozy—meet the first of Baum's standard characters, the Shaggy Man, who escorts them to the Emerald City. In the city, many, but not all, of the main characters are introduced, but the journey is continued only by Ojo, Dorothy, the Patchwork Girl, and the Scarecrow. On that second part of the quest, they visit Jack Pumpkinhead and the Tin Woodman, but only Ojo and the Patchwork Girl are constants throughout the story.

One of the reasons for the success of this story is its resemblance to *The Wonderful Wizard of Oz*, which was, surprisingly, the only other book thus far in which Baum had utilized the quest motif inside Oz. Another resemblance to the earlier book is that within sight of the supposed end of the quest, the characters are balked; just as the Wizard fails to send Dorothy home, Ojo cannot obtain the last ingredient for the magic potion because it is the left wing of a yellow butterfly, and in Oz all living creatures are protected. In both books, it is Glinda who overcomes the difficulties, showing Dorothy how to return home and giving the Wizard the spell to restore the statues to life.

The quest is a good device to introduce logically various strange adventures and peoples. Baum created a second yellow brick road to explain why Ojo's experiences in the Munchkin Country are different from Dorothy's,[17] but Baum's sparing use of such places and peoples in his earlier Oz books is more satisfying. His prolific imagination made it too easy for him to go beyond the bounds of the story and introduce exotic locales and quaint characters for their own sakes, some of which fit uneasily into Oz. As Warren Hollister noted: "The Dainty China Country has a habit of turning up repeatedly, in various guises, throughout the Oz series."[18] Perhaps the lack of other outlets for Baum's creativity—non-Oz fantasies—is the reason that this trait is more prominent in the second half of the series.

An addition to Oz that jars somewhat in *The Patchwork Girl* is Baum's introduction of a bread tree in Ojo's garden and bun-trees, cake-trees, creampuff bushes, and chocolate-caramel plants in that of the Crooked Magician. This idea is not extensively developed, however, and there is only one reference to these kinds of plants within the settled parts of Oz.[19] One of the great attractions of Oz is its resemblance to our own world, but these food plants hearken back to Baum's too-sweet fairyland of Mo. In fact, he may have been thinking of Mo when he added these plants to Oz because there is also a direct link with that earlier creation in *The Patchwork Girl*. Ojo stops for advice at the house of a Foolish Owl and a Wise Donkey, and the donkey turns out to be the very same Wise Donkey from Mo who happened "to visit the Land of Oz on the day it was shut off from the rest of the world."[20]

Otherwise, Oz remains the same, familiar place. Baum began the story by describing everything in the Munchkin Country as blue, but he realized his mistake, and later when his characters are in the Quadling Country, he explained the arrangement of colors that he had arrived at in *The Road to Oz:* "But they knew they were still in the Country of the Quadlings, because everything had a bright red color. Not that the trees and grasses were red, but the fences and houses were painted that color and all the wild-flowers that bloomed by the wayside had red blossoms."[21]

Surprisingly, *The Patchwork Girl of Oz* was the first book of the

179

series to be set totally within the borders of Oz. Baum had, of course, written himself into a corner by cutting Oz off from the rest of the world with the Barrier of Invisibility, but such a problem was hardly insurmountable to someone with Baum's inventive ability. That Baum did not reconnect Oz to the real world, even though his next two books involve new American characters in Oz, is an indication that he felt very strongly about preserving his fairyland from outside intrusion and that his own thinking about the nature of Oz had changed. To him Oz was increasingly becoming an ideal world to contrast with the real world, very much like the Land of Paradise in *Policeman Bluejay*.

TIK-TOK OF OZ

Baum's bankruptcy made his real world a not very pleasant place, but *The Patchwork Girl* was a successful return to Oz and that gave him hope. He had faced financial reverses before and had not been defeated; his active mind was still developing new projects. During the next few years, he saw the achievement of a long-planned goal, and he was involved in one of the most interesting and unusual enterprises of his career. Those projects were very important for the next three Oz books—*Tik-Tok of Oz* (1914), *The Scarecrow of Oz* (1915), and *Rinkitink in Oz* (1916)—because these stories are unusual in the series in that they all originated in different forms before their appearances as Oz books. (In fact, with its beginning in the Munchkin Country, the journey on a yellow brick road to the Emerald City to ask its ruler for help, the subsequent trips south and west, the frustration of the quest in sight of success, and the final intervention by Glinda to put things right, *The Patchwork Girl of Oz* can be viewed as an adaptation of the first Oz book, and it, too, could be said to have originated in a different form.)

Knowing the strength and consistency of Baum's interests, one is not surprised that those projects involved the theater. Even the dismal failure of *The Woggle-Bug* in 1905 had not killed his theatrical ambitions. Subsequently, he had worked on several different ideas for the stage, the most persistent one being to change *Ozma of Oz* into a musical extravaganza. The script went through several versions and titles, including *The Rainbow's Daughter, or the Magnet of Love*,[22] before it was finally produced in Los Angeles in the spring of 1913 as *The Tik-Tok Man of Oz* with music by Louis F. Gottschalk.[23] The play did not have the phenomenal success of *The Wizard*, but its short run was profitable and successful enough to wipe out the stigma of Baum's past failure.[24]

To capitalize on the hoped-for success of the play, Baum turned it into his Oz book for 1914, *Tik-Tok of Oz*. The book, like *The Patchwork Girl*, opens in a remote area of Oz, this time a tiny valley named Oogaboo bordering the desert in the far-northern corner of the Winkie Country. Its queen is Ann Soforth, an ambitious woman who wants to rule more than "eighteen men, twenty-seven women and forty-four children."[25] She decides to conquer the world, starting with the rest of Oz, and to accomplish her goal, she raises an army of sixteen officers and one private. Glinda, however, learns about the plan from her Magic Record Book and confuses the army's way so that they are transported across the desert from Oz to the desolate land above the domain of the Nome King near Ev. There, in an encounter with a monster called a Rak, Private Files demonstrates that only the privates in an army have the courage to fight.

The scene then shifts to a shipwreck at sea. The only survivors are a little girl from Oklahoma, Betsy Bobbin, and a small mule named Hank, who, on some of the wreckage, float to the beach of a lovely, but seemingly deserted country. It is the Rose Kingdom, where beautiful rosebushes, each with a girl's face in the center, are tended in a greenhouse by the Royal Gardener. Despite the beauty of the country, it is not a pleasant place, for the law forbids strangers from entering it. Just as Betsy and Hank find this out and feel threatened, another stranger falls through the glass roof of the greenhouse. It is the Shaggy Man, who had been in an apple tree outside. The penalty for breaking the law is to "be condemned by the Ruler and put to death."[26] However, the interlopers cannot be "condemned by the Ruler" because there is no ruler at that moment. They are told that there is not one ripe on the bush where the royals grow, but Betsy thinks that one of them, a lovely princess, is ripe, and she and the Shaggy Man pick her. Her name is Ozga, and she is a cousin to Ozma. Unfortunately, the roses will not accept a female ruler, and with their thorns, they drive the Shaggy Man, Betsy, Hank, and Ozga out of the Rose Kingdom into the land above the Nome Kingdom.

This is actually where the Shaggy Man was going because he is searching for his lost brother, who he fears is a prisoner in the Nome King's domain. The others offer to help him, and quickly their group is increased by Polychrome, the Rainbow's daughter who has once again lost her father's bow, and by the Shaggy Man's friend Tik-Tok, the clockwork man, whom they find down a well. Once wound up, he seems no worse for wear, and he tells them that Shaggy's brother is indeed a prisoner of the Nome King and that Glinda sent him to help rescue the brother. Before he could join the Shaggy Man, however, Tik-Tok encountered the Nome King, who was so angry about the attempted rescue that he threw Tik-Tok down the well in which they had found him. Just as all this is explained, Queen Ann and her army come along and try to capture Betsy and her friends. The end result is that Private Files resigns from the army because he refuses to conquer people who are not enemies, Tik-Tok becomes the new private, and both groups join forces to try to conquer the Nome King, Ruggedo. (The Nome King's name is Roquat in *Ozma of Oz*, but in *Tik-Tok of Oz*, Baum changed it to Ruggedo and explained in a footnote: "This King was formerly named 'Roquat,' but after he drank of the 'Waters of Oblivion' [in *The Emerald City of Oz*] he forgot his own name and had to take another."[27])

Ruggedo has protected the entrance to his kingdom with a series of obstacles, but when these barriers are easily surmounted by the rescue party, he becomes desperate and causes them to fall into the Hollow Tube. By doing this, he defies the great and mysterious Tititi-Hoochoo, who lives at the other end of the tube on the other side of the earth. The group is not harmed when they emerge from the other end of the tube, but they have arrived in a very strange land, inhabited by beautiful people who all look similar and who are all kings and queens. Betsy and the others soon find out that this is a fairyland almost as beautiful as Oz and even more powerful, for it is "one of the chief residences of fairies who minister to the needs of mankind."[28] The inhabitants are prominent fairies such as the King of the Animals and the Queen of Light, with her attendants Sunlight, Moonlight, Starlight, Daylight, Firelight, and Electra. Because there are so many kings and queens there, their supreme ruler is the only Private Citizen, the Great Jinjin, Tititi-Hoochoo, who unlike the other inhabitants does not have a heart, only "a high degree of Reason and Justice."[29] This fairyland is also the home of the Original Dragon, who is as old as the world, and his family.

The next day, the Great Jinjin judges that the intruders are innocent of any intentional wrongdoing and that the guilty person is the Nome King, who must be punished. As his "Instrument of Vengeance," he chooses a young dragon named Quox to return with the Shaggy Man, Betsy, Polychrome, and the rest to help them conquer Ruggedo and remove him from his kingdom.

When they reach the other side of the world, Queen Ann is so confident that her "army" can conquer the Nomes that Quox agrees to let them try first. But they are all captured and some transformed into objects—except Polychrome, who manages to escape and summon Quox. The dragon easily conquers Ruggedo by producing eggs, which are the things most feared by Nomes. Ruggedo is so terrified that he flees into the upper world, and when he tries to return, the eggs are there to stop him. The others are rescued and transformed back to their proper shapes, and Kaliko, Ruggedo's High Chamberlain, who is kinder than his master, is made the new king. Quox's task accomplished, he leaves.

The Shaggy Man still must find his brother, and Kaliko tells the rescuers that the man they seek lives in the Metal Forest in a secret cavern of the Nome Kingdom and is called the "Ugly One" because Ruggedo transformed him. Only a kiss will break the enchantment, but no one remembers whether it is "the kiss of a Mortal Maid, . . . a Mortal Maid who had once been a Fairy, . . . or the kiss of one who is still a Fairy."[30] However, since among themselves, Betsy, Ozga, and Polychrome satisfy all those requirements, they all agree to kiss the Shaggy Man's brother and the enchantment is broken.

They celebrate with a feast given by Kaliko, and even the former Nome King is allowed to attend. Because he is in a repentant mood, he is forgiven and allowed to live in the Nome Kingdom. Then the travelers begin leaving. Polychrome's father comes for her, and suddenly Queen Ann and her army disappear. Far away in the Emerald City of Oz, Ozma, Dorothy, and the Wizard have been watching them in the Magic Picture. When Queen Ann and her army talked about how happy they were in Oogaboo and how they wished that they were back there, the Wizard sent them home. He also sent Ozga with them because she and Files would not want to be separated. Finally, the remaining companions—Betsy, Hank, the Shaggy Man, and his brother—begin their journey through the desolate land. In the Emerald City, there is much discussion about whether to invite the strangers into the Land of Oz. It is finally decided in their favor, and they are transported to Oz. The story ends as Dorothy and Ozma get acquainted with their new friend Betsy, and Hank gets to know the other animal characters that live in Ozma's palace. Hank finds that he can talk in Oz, and Dorothy finds out, to her amazement, that Toto has been able to talk all the time they have been there; he just had not needed to.

By the time the book appeared, the play *The Tik-Tok Man of Oz* was no longer running, and Baum was careful to note in his introduction that the book differed in many ways from the play, although it is easy to pick out elements that probably originated in the stage version: the romantic interest between Ozga and Private Files, the comic animal character, the beautiful chorus of Rose Maidens. What Baum did not mention was that the plot of the book is very similar to that of *Ozma of Oz*, the original source for the stage play.

Instead of Dorothy and Billina, Betsy Bobbin and her pet mule Hank are washed ashore after a shipwreck.[31] In *Ozma*, Dorothy and Billina are met by an unpleasant race of creatures called Wheelers; in *Tik-Tok*, the Wheelers are replaced by the equally unwelcoming plant inhabitants of the Rose Kingdom. In this section, Baum combined the successful poppy scene (girls dressed as flowers) from *The Wizard* musical with attributes from the vegetable kingdom of the Mangaboos in *Dorothy and the Wizard in Oz*. Betsy and the Shaggy Man "pick" the ripe, but unwanted, princess from the royal bush, just as Dorothy and the Wizard do in the earlier book. The Rose Princess, Ozga, a cousin to Ozma, differs from the Mangaboo princess in that she is a fairy with a heart who becomes a mortal when rejected as the ruler of the Rose Kingdom and driven from her kingdom to wander with Betsy and the Shaggy Man. It is tempting to speculate about the unconscious symbolism of this section. As the characters are being forced out of the Rose Kingdom, Baum wrote: "'For my part,' said Princess Ozga of Roseland, with a gentle sigh, 'I must remain forever exiled from my Kingdom.'"[32] This was the only instance where Baum referred to the Rose Kingdom as Roseland. "Roseland" is very like "Rose Lawn."

Tik-Tok was introduced in *Ozma of Oz*, being discovered by Dorothy in Ev, and he plays an important part in that story. Here he is the title character, again encountered outside Oz, and again playing an important part in the story. Ozma and her army are replaced by Queen Ann Soforth and her even more comic-operetta army from the small kingdom of Oogaboo. Baum added the Rainbow's daughter, Polychrome, from *The Road to Oz*, *Sky Island*, and the play.

Besides the fact that Baum never left his child characters for long without some kind of adult protection, the character of the Shaggy Man is very necessary to this story. In *Ozma of Oz*, the purpose of the journey to the Nome Kingdom is to rescue the royal family of Ev; here the purpose is to rescue the Shaggy Man's brother. In fact, the section of the plot that concerns rescuing prisoners from the underground land of the Nomes

dates even further back than *Ozma of Oz;* it dates back to Baum's unpublished fantasy *King Rinkitink,* in which Prince Inga and his party must
rescue his parents.[33] An echo of that earlier story can be heard in the
similarity of the hero's name, Inga, to that of the Rose Princess, Ozga.

Although the basic structure of *Tik-Tok of Oz* is the same as that
of *Ozma of Oz,* many of the surface incidents are quite different. The
addition of the fairyland on the other side of the world is especially
interesting, as it joins the Forest of Burzee and the Forest of Lurla as one
of the main residences of the fairies. And although Baum did not develop
that fairyland in later books, he once again suggested that Oz is only a part
of a larger and quite marvelous fantasy world.

Despite its stage origins, *Tik-Tok of Oz* is not a bad story, and it
plays a significant part in the continuing development of Oz. It contains
two alterations of major importance.

The first is evident as soon as one opens the cover of a first edition
of this book. For endpapers, Baum provided the first official maps of Oz,[34]
and they give Oz a substance and a stability that it had lacked. The front
endpapers present Oz alone and show the country in its final, rectangular
form. Many of the places appearing in this and the previous books are
located on it, plus several locales that had not yet appeared in books: the
Skeezers in the Gillikin Country; the Yips in the Winkie Country; and
Mount Munch in the Munchkin Country—all these places on the outer
borders of Oz. The desert is also given a different name in each direction:
the Impassable Desert, the Deadly Desert, the Great Sandy Waste, and
the Shifting Sands. One glaring error stands out because Baum placed the
Winkie Country on the east side of Oz, as he had in the text of *The
Emerald City,* although he had the countries in their proper positions in
The Patchwork Girl.[35] (Someone noticed this error before the book was
issued and reversed the normal compass points of east and west in an
attempt to correct it.) This map adds a great degree of reality and con-
creteness to Oz, but of even more interest is the map that forms the rear
endpapers. It shows Oz and its surrounding desert as the centerpiece of a
whole continent of fairylands! In *The Road to Oz,* Baum had drawn all his

imaginary countries together into the same Other-world, but he had given no information about their geographical relationships. Now he actually shows the reader how they are connected. The fact that their positions on the map do not always agree with the textual descriptions is overridden by the centrality of Oz and the interconnectedness of Baum's entire Other-world.

Besides the reality given to Oz by being set in a detailed map, the country also gains in richness by being set among so many other exotic countries, most of them with their own histories and special ambiences. These other countries also gain from being placed around Oz. In fact, it becomes extremely difficult for a reader who has followed Baum to this point in his career to go back to the first part of the Oz series or to those earlier individual fantasies and divorce any of them from Baum's entire Other-world; all his various creations have become too firmly a part of one great fantasy world. The appearance of these maps is, in fact, the culmination of Baum's proclivity, evident as far back as 1901, to draw his various worlds together.

The other major alteration that appears in *Tik-Tok of Oz* profoundly affects the very nature of Oz. Until this time, the most general impression of the location of Oz had been that it is in our world, hidden away and difficult to get to, but a magical, marvelous, undiscovered part of America. In fact, the reason given in *The Emerald City* for making Oz invisible is so that it will *remain* uncivilized and undiscovered as airships begin to reach areas once considered inaccessible. Now, in *Tik-Tok*, Oz becomes something more than a hidden fairyland in our own world. Oz is part of a continent, a fairy continent, and the impression left by this book is that Oz has been removed from our own world and now exists apart from it.

This, of course, raises again the question of just what Oz represents. Is Oz an American paradise, an ideal world, or heaven? It may be

Map of Oz from Tik-Tok of Oz *(1914), with the east and west compass points reversed, as they originally appeared.*

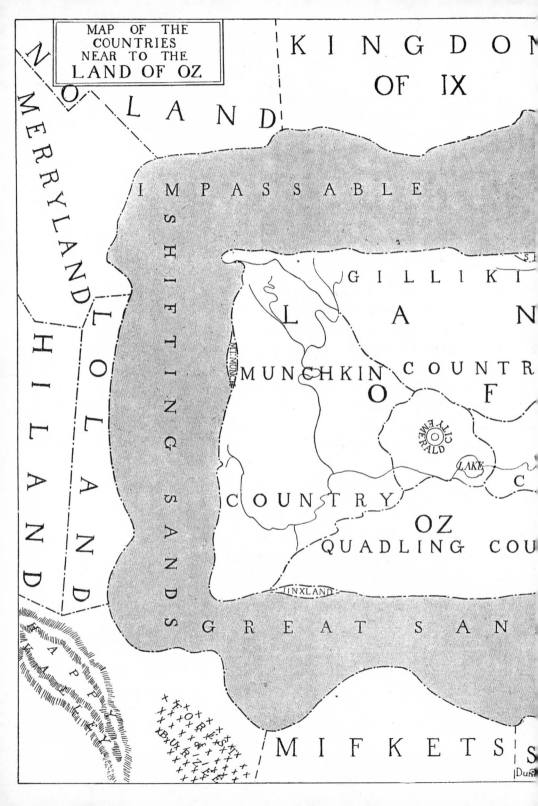

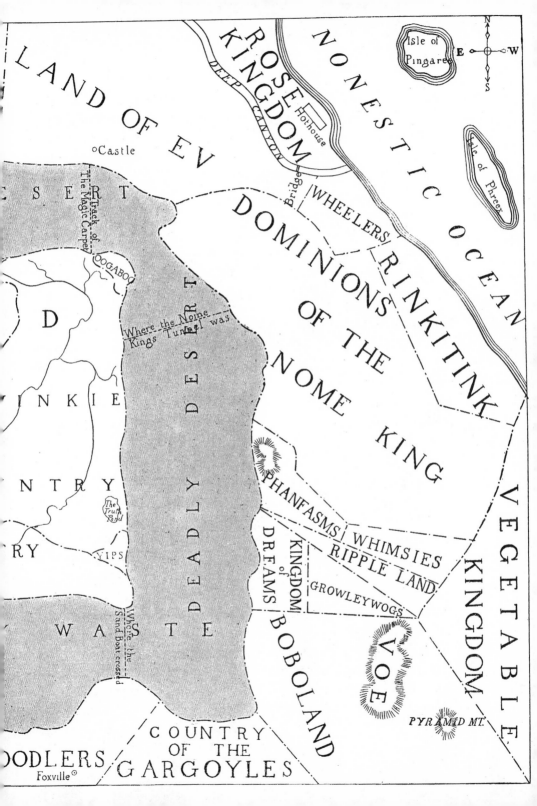

that at one time or another Oz is all of these; certainly, the emphasis differs in different books. In *Tik-Tok,* the argument leans toward the idea of heaven. Baum does not seem to have been a particularly religious person, at least in an orthodox way, and it is impossible to prove that he ever thought of Oz as a version of heaven. Certainly, he made it clear that although Oz is the most beautiful and desirable of all fairylands, there are other places more powerful, such as Burzee and the fairyland on the other side of the world in *Tik-Tok of Oz.* But it is difficult to disregard the religious overtones, whether Baum himself was consciously aware of them or not. The one point that is made clear in this book is that one must be worthy of Oz to gain entrance.

Too much should not be read into Betsy's life-threatening entrance into fairyland because it is merely a duplication of Dorothy's entrance in *Ozma of Oz,* except that in this instance Baum has the ship actually wreck and sink, with the inescapable implication that all the other people on board perished. It is at the completion of the adventures in the Nome King's domain that a new element enters the history of Oz. The rescue has been accomplished, and the Wizard has transported all the characters back to Oz, with the exception of Betsy, Hank, the Shaggy Man, and his brother, who are left at the entrance to the Nome Kingdom. Always before at this point in the story, the choice has been between living in Oz or returning home. Now, however, in Baum's Other-world, home is no longer part of the choice. The possibilities before Betsy and the others are either to go to Oz to live or to wander forever in those fairylands outside Oz, and the choice is not theirs to make. By removing the option of returning home from his American characters and by transferring to Ozma the judgment of the worthiness of those characters to live in Oz, Baum strengthened the idea of Oz as a version of heaven. Ozma's is not an arbitrary or simple decision: "The Land of Oz is not a refuge for all mortals in distress,"[36] she says (that is, suffering does not always equate with worthiness). God-like, she has watched their adventures in the Magic Picture and must weigh their performances and characters. The Shaggy Man's brother, appearing only at the end of the story, is the unknown quantity, and Ozma states the problem: "This brother seems a kindly, honest fellow, but he has done nothing to entitle him to a home in the Land of Oz."[37] The Shaggy Man is already a part of Oz, and ultimately, it is his love that wins a place in Oz for his brother, who with Betsy and Hank are allowed into Oz. Thus another of Baum's stories follows the pattern of death (the shipwreck), purgatory (the difficult adventures outside Oz), and heaven (Oz).

That this pattern was intentional and not merely a result of this story's similarity to *Ozma of Oz* is made clear by Baum's next book, *The Scarecrow of Oz*. In it, Baum reintroduced Trot and Cap'n Bill as well as Button-Bright, whom they meet on their adventures. In contrast to their safe and gentle entrances into fairyland in *The Sea Fairies* and *Sky Island,* the beginning of their adventures in this book is violent and life-threatening: their small rowboat is caught in and destroyed by a whirlpool. And again, after many dangerous and difficult adventures in which the characters prove themselves, they are allowed into Oz at the end. This time, it is Glinda who pronounces judgment: "I think we shall like them very much, for they are just the kind of people to enjoy and appreciate our fairyland and I do not see any way, at present, for them to return again to the outside world."[38]

Baum gave little information about Betsy, but the reader knows that both Trot and Button-Bright have loving parents in America. Time and again, Dorothy's love for her Aunt Em and Uncle Henry take her back home, but Oz has changed, and Trot and Button-Bright have no such choice; for them Oz is the end and the fulfillment of the journey.

These journeys of Betsy, Cap'n Bill, Trot, and Button-Bright to Oz also raise another important point. Although Baum would write six more Oz books and although the plot device of having Americans adventure in fairyland and end up in Oz was the most popular pattern for his stories among his readers, and probably the easiest for Baum to write, he

Map of countries surrounding Oz from Tik-Tok of Oz, *with the east and west compass points reversed, as they originally appeared.*

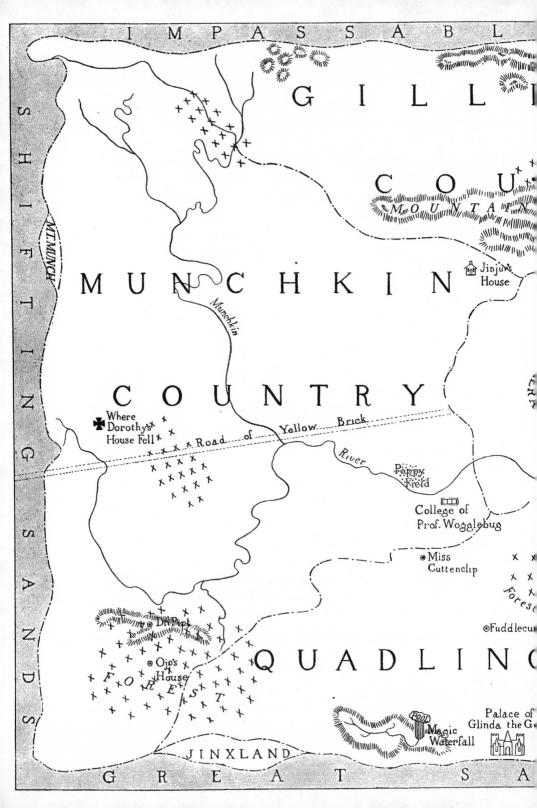

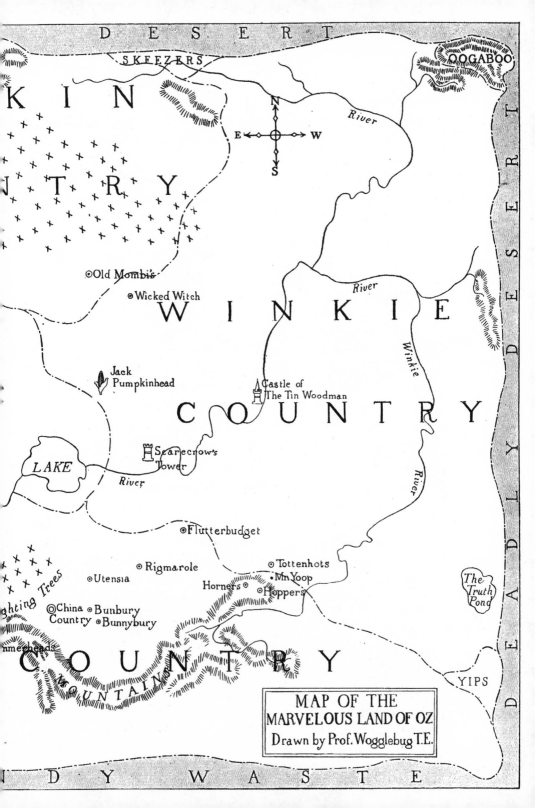

did not use it again. That fact emphasizes both the isolation of Oz and Baum's removal of that fairyland from the outside world of America, and it raises some interesting questions: Why did he as the creator not dispense with the Barrier of Invisibility? Even though he did bridge it several times, there is no indication that he ever contemplated removing it. Why did he close Oz to new American characters? And why does Oz become, especially in the latter half of the series, less like the fantasy version of the United States that Oz had been in *The Wonderful Wizard of Oz*?

Baum wrote intuitively, and his stories and especially his characters have an intuitive logic about them. When stuck at a point in a story he was writing, he once complained that his characters would not do what he wanted them to.[39] The answer was to let them do what *they* wanted to do, and they obviously did not want to be discovered and "civilized." From early in his career, Baum had been concerned about some of the directions America was taking—directions that decreased the wonder, beauty, and quality of life in the country. He knew what some American character types would do to Oz if he opened it up indiscriminately to them; he had seen what had happened when the West was opened up for "civilization." He could at least protect his imaginary worlds. First, he had closed and protected Merryland, and then he had removed himself to more traditional types of fairy tales. When circumstances forced him to return to Oz, he was able to develop that country to suit his own vision of an American paradise, but the real America continued to evolve in a totally different way. It and Oz grew farther apart until Baum felt that he had to protect his vision by removing it from America, and Oz became, like heaven, journey's end and the reward for those truly worthy.

THE SCARECROW OF OZ

The first half of *The Scarecrow of Oz*, published in 1915, takes Trot and Cap'n Bill from California through a series of adventures to a small secluded borderland of Oz in the Quadling Country. After being sucked down by the whirlpool, they are assisted by the Sea Fairies to an underwater cave, and they have a journey underground as dark and terrifying as anything in *Dorothy and the Wizard in Oz*. Early on, they are joined by a large, bird-like creature called an Ork who enables them, when they reach the surface again, to fly across the ocean to the great fantasy continent of which Oz is a part.

For the first time, Baum himself referred to Oz and the countries surrounding it as a continent, and it is apparent that he was following the map that appeared in *Tik-Tok* because first Trot and Cap'n Bill pass over a small island that appears on that map,[40] and later an inhabitant of Jinxland assures them that that country "is on the Map of Oz,"[41] which it is. Baum had neglected to add one of his major fairy countries to his map, however, and he rectified that oversight in this story by having his characters alight on one of the mountains surrounding the Valley of Mo. Baum now positioned his very first imaginary country near the desert that bounds Oz and even added new information that fits right into that edible country of Mo, where the rain is lemonade and the snow is popcorn: he tells us that the winds of Mo are perfumed and that it is possible to tell which direction the breeze is blowing merely by its aroma.[42]

In Mo, Trot and Cap'n Bill are joined by Button-Bright, the Philadelphia boy who shares their adventures in *Sky Island,* and with the help of the Ork and some other birds, they continue their journey across the desert toward Oz. But Baum did not forget the Barrier of Invisibility, which he described as "a great cloud of pink-tinted mist."[43] They fly through it for a distance, unable to see anything, until the landscape of Oz suddenly appears spread out below them. In a variation on his treatment of color in Oz, Baum alerts the reader that the travelers have reached the Quadling Country of the South: "Over all this delightful landscape—which from Trot's high perch seemed like a magnificent painted picture—was a rosy glow such as we sometimes see in the west at sunset. In this case, however, it was not in the west only, but everywhere."[44] This is Baum's only specific reference to the color scheme of Oz in this book.

Douglas Greene believes that the introduction of Trot and Cap'n

Bill in this story may have been Baum's use of material originally "planned as the third Trot book."[45] This is quite probable, since the first part of the book follows the pattern of the other two Trot stories, a series of adventures and meetings with odd characters in unusual fairylands. Also, the variety of scenes and the chain of incidents in the first half of the story are at odds with the static setting and more connected plot of the second half. As will be seen, Baum combined two different stories to make this book and the seams are sometimes noticeable.

Most of the second half of the book is taken up by an adventure in Jinxland that illustrates how adaptable the border countries far from the rule, and sometimes the knowledge, of Ozma could be. In a kingdom so cut off from the rest of Oz as Jinxland is (by mountains and a deep gulf), Baum could disregard or suspend many of the "givens" of Oz and tell his story without regard to them. The adventure in Jinxland is, in fact, an unusual one to be set in Oz, being a traditional romantic tale that ends in a marriage. Grown-up romance was something Baum was usually careful to keep out of Oz.

This section of the story involves a beautiful princess in love with a gardener's boy (in reality of noble birth) and her cruel uncle, the king, who has the heart of the princess frozen by a wicked witch to kill her love for the boy. Baum saved this section from mere conventionality by making Pon, the gardener's boy, a parody of a romantic, noble youth who, as Trot observes, "isn't any great shakes."[46] Trot and Cap'n Bill become involved in Pon's plight and try to help him, but they have little success alone, and Cap'n Bill is transformed into a grasshopper by the wicked witch. The Scarecrow is brought into the story by Glinda, who, after reading of the situation in her Magic Record Book, sends him to Jinxland to help. With this additional aid, the cruel king and the wicked witch are defeated and the happy ending is achieved.

There are strong echoes of *The Wonderful Wizard of Oz* in this story that were not unintentional. Trot, like Dorothy, first meets the Scarecrow in a cornfield, and this wicked witch is brought under control by a magic potion that causes her to shrink in imitation of the melting of the Wicked Witch of the West in the earlier book.

After the happy ending in Jinxland, the travelers enter Oz proper, the good and great place, where "for the first time . . . Trot and Cap'n Bill were free from anxiety and care."[47] The book ends with a celebration in the Emerald City, where the rest of the familiar Oz characters are reintroduced.

Baum was clever in adapting Jinxland to accommodate incidents that are, in many respects, un-Oz-like. That section of the story had, in fact, originated as the plot of a motion picture made in 1914 entitled *His Majesty, The Scarecrow of Oz,* which combined elements of *The Wizard* and *The Marvelous Land* with these new, original incidents. Thriftily, Baum incorporated these new plot elements into his current Oz book.

Most of the things in *The Scarecrow of Oz* that affect Oz are in the nature of additions and clarifications, but the story does contain one point of major significance: a reinterpretation of one of the most familiar of the characters: Ozma. This is Baum's description of her in this book: "Born of a long line of Fairy Queens, Ozma is as nearly perfect as any fairy may be, and she is noted for her wisdom as well as for her other qualities."[48] Always before, Baum had pointed out that the ruler of Oz was a real girl not so very different from Dorothy,[49] but he seems to have changed his mind and made the ruler of his premier fairyland a fairy also. The change was not the result of carelessness because he did go into more detail about it in future books, and the change became a vital one in the final development of Oz.

THE OZ FILM MANUFACTURING COMPANY

It seems almost as though fate had directed Baum's trek across America. He had arrived in Chicago at one of the brightest points in that city's history; the eyes of the world were focused on the World's Columbian

Exposition, and the city was becoming a magnet for writers and artists. Later, he moved to Hollywood thinking that he would be living in a quiet suburb, but almost before he had had time to settle down, he found himself in the middle of one of the most active, interesting, and fastest-growing sections of the country, all caused by the infant movie industry having discovered southern California. Given Baum's passion for the theater and his earlier experiment with film in *The Fairylogue and Radio-Plays*, it was inevitable that he would be drawn to the new industry.

Baum had lost no time in taking an active part in his adopted area, helping to found a social club in Los Angeles called the Uplifters.[50] Like the Press Club in Chicago, this new company of like-minded men did much to inspire Baum to new goals, the most ambitious being to start a movie studio. The money for this venture was raised among the Uplifters in ten days, and in the late spring of 1914, the Oz Film Manufacturing Company opened. It occupied an entire city block on Santa Monica Boulevard and was one of the best equipped studios of the day.[51]

Luckily, Baum had learned his lesson with the *Radio-Plays*, and he put none of his own money into the project. He was given stock in return for relinquishing the movie rights to his books and for writing scripts for the films. The plan was to film all his stories as well as his stage plays, and production got under way with *The Patchwork Girl of Oz*, quickly followed by *The Magic Cloak (Queen Zixi)* and *His Majesty, the Scarecrow of Oz*. Two of the actors who appeared in some of these films were Hal Roach, who later had his own studio, and Mildred Harris, who was later the first of Charlie Chaplin's wives.[52]

The young company faced enormous obstacles: the lawsuits filed by the Motion Picture Patents Company, owners of the Edison patents, that crippled or destroyed many of the independent companies of this era;[53] the lack of theaters under the new company's control;[54] and the same problem that had plagued Baum in his later theatrical ventures, the taste of the adult public. He believed that theatrical adaptations, stage or screen, that were faithful to his original stories could be successful, but the adult public disagreed and refused to patronize films for children. His company then turned to more adult subjects, filming *The Last Egyptian* from a novel that Baum had published anonymously in 1908 and *The Gray Nun of Belgium* from an original script, but it was already too late. After only a year and a half, the Oz Film Manufacturing Company was closed. It is sad that Baum could not know that his belief in his stories would be vindicated by the 1939 MGM production of *The Wizard of Oz*, a film that is, in most respects, faithful to the original book and is today considered one of the truly great motion-picture classics.

Although Baum planned other projects, the end of the film company also marked the end of his professional theatrical career. He was, however, able to indulge his love of the theater in another way, because between 1914 and 1917, he wrote the books and lyrics for the annual outings of the Uplifters. He enjoyed writing these plays, with titles such as *Stagecraft, the Adventures of a Strictly Moral Man* and *The Uplift of Lucifer; or, Raising Hell (An Allegorical Squazosh)*,[55] and he must have gained a great measure of satisfaction from seeing them produced for an apprecia-tive audience. It seems only just that his up-and-down career in the theater he loved so much should end on this pleasant note.

RINKITINK IN OZ

While the Oz Film Manufacturing Company was operational, it required a great deal of Baum's time and energy. That and a marked decline in his health[56] are most likely the main reasons that he resurrected the un-published, full-length fantasy manuscript he had written in 1905 and reworked it into his Oz book for 1916, *Rinkitink in Oz*. It is lucky for us that he did, for the story comes from his most creative period and provides one of the high spots of the second half of the Oz series.

In revising the manuscript, Baum seems to have left the original story of the island kingdom of Pingaree and the king of Rinkitink fairly much intact. (For a summary of the original plot, see Chapter 4.) Atypically for the Oz series, the book does not end with the banquet and celebration in the Emerald City because after all the obstacles are overcome, tasks accomplished, and enchantments broken, Baum reverted to his original ending, which recounts the festivities on Pingaree when the royal family returns without any accompanying characters from Oz. At the beginning of his revision, he placed Pingaree and Rinkitink in their geographical relationships to Oz and the fairy continent according to his recent map, but Oz and Oz characters have nothing else to do with the plot until very near the end when Dorothy and the Wizard arrive in the Nome King's domain just in time to rescue the king and queen of Pingaree.

It is good that this fine story was finally published, but the addition of the Oz element is not entirely successful. Dorothy and the Wizard appear almost out of nowhere and accomplish the victory that clearly should have been Prince Inga's (and probably was in the original version). The Nomes, having appeared in three other books in the series, ease somewhat the introduction of Oz, but as has already been suggested, one of the reasons Baum had not published this story was that he had adapted the section in the Nome Kingdom for use in *Ozma of Oz.* Even though the Nome Kingdom episode originated in the original version of this story, by the time *Rinkitink* appeared, Baum had already used it twice more! In reworking this part of the original story, he now faced another problem: the Nome Kingdom had also undergone development. The character and description of the Nome King in *Rinkitink* is very similar to that given in *Ozma,* but by this point in the series, he is not the same king. At the end of *Tik-Tok,* the first Nome King, Ruggedo, is deposed, and his kindly High Chamberlain, Kaliko, is made king. It is the name Kaliko that Baum used in *Rinkitink,* but it is the earlier king he described.

Baum's use of his map to give the reader the positions of the countries in *Rinkitink in Oz* and relate them to Oz does much to add to the sense of the totality of his Other-world, but Oz plays such a small part in the story that there is no occasion for any new development. Baum realized that his readers might be puzzled by this "Oz" book and explained in his introduction: "Indeed, I think you will find this story quite different from the other histories of Oz, but I hope you will not like it the less on that account."[57] He promised to write an Oz book for the next year that would tell about the adventures of some of the most popular of the Oz characters. By 1917 when that book, *The Lost Princess of Oz,* appeared, there had been some serious changes in Baum's life.

Chapter
Seven

Resolution of Conflict
1917–1919

For, after all, dear reader, these stories of Oz are just yours and mine, and we are partners. As long as you care to read them I shall try to write them.

L. Frank Baum,
"To My Readers" in
The Lost Princess of Oz (1917)

L. Frank Baum's life was an unusually eventful one that took him across the entire breadth of America, but the wandering had not been the result of free choice on his part. Without the reversals he and his family suffered in the early 1880s, he would most probably have been content to remain in Syracuse, New York. There are, however, absolutely no indications that he ever regretted the last move to California. With the comfortable and spacious home that he named Ozcot and his large garden in which he grew prize flowers and kept a flock of chickens, just as he had when he was a boy,[1] Baum was at last able to re-create some of the grace and serenity of his lost Rose Lawn.

It was good that he had the peaceful haven of Ozcot because the work and worry involved with the Oz Film Manufacturing Company had done great harm to his always fragile health. The problems with his heart became more severe; he developed the painful tic douloureux in his face; and he began having severe gall bladder attacks.[2] In fact, he wrote the promised new Oz book, *The Lost Princess of Oz*, while he was in continual pain.[3] It was in the introduction to that book that for the first time he implied that he was content to give up his hopes of writing other kinds of fantasies and continue to add to the Oz series: "As long as you care to read them I shall try to write them."[4]

The last four Oz books are unusual in that, with the exception of only two chapters in one of the stories, they are set entirely within the borders of Oz, almost as though Baum, having reconciled himself to writing only Oz fantasies during the time left to him, wanted to explore that fascinating fairyland more extensively himself. There are good things in each of these four books, with few obvious traces of Baum's physical suffering and the sometimes difficult conditions under which he wrote them. They are also more consistently plotted than some of the books immediately preceding them, and there is a sense that, at last, the Oz series had Baum's undivided attention, that these fantasies were conceived as Oz books and not as springboards for or adaptations of stage or movie plays. It may be symbolic of this central position that the Oz series had now attained in Baum's creative life that *The Lost Princess of Oz* is the first (and the only) of his Oz books to open in the Emerald City, the very center of his fantasy world.

THE LOST PRINCESS OF OZ

Baum had always acknowledged his debt to his readers for their encouragement and suggestions. He had written in the Introduction to *The Emerald City of Oz:* "Perhaps I should admit on the title page that this book is 'By L. Frank Baum and his correspondents,' for I have used many suggestions conveyed to me in letters from children."[5] That "collaboration" probably became even more important to him when his health problems made it more difficult for him to work, and he admitted that the basic idea for his Oz book for 1917, *The Lost Princess of Oz*, was suggested by an eleven-year-old girl who said, "I s'pose if Ozma ever got lost, or stolen, ev'rybody in Oz would be dreadful sorry." And Baum noted, "That was all, but quite enough foundation to build this present story on."[6]

One morning in the Emerald City, Dorothy cannot find Ozma.

No one has seen her, and when her friends try to look in the Magic Picture to find their ruler, they find the picture also gone. The mystery deepens when in the Quadling Country, Glinda discovers that her Magic Record Book, one of the treasures of Oz, and all her other magic implements have been stolen. Later the Wizard is dismayed to find his magic bag of tools also missing.

These are, however, not the only important thefts that day. Far away at the southern tip of the Winkie Country in the hitherto unknown Country of the Yips (which does appear on the 1914 map), Cayke the Cookie Cook discovers that her golden, diamond-studded dishpan has been stolen, and without it, she cannot bake the delicious cookies she is known for. (The dishpan has other magic properties that she knows nothing about, but Baum does not explain what a dishpan has to do with baking.) In the Country of the Yips also lives a frog the size of a man who dresses in splendid clothes and has convinced the people that he is the wisest being in the world. Cayke begs his help, and seeking a wider audience for his imagined magnificence, he agrees to go with her out into Oz to try to find the dishpan.

In the Emerald City, Ozma's friends decide to search Oz in all directions for some trace of her. The group that goes to the Winkie Country consists of the Wizard, Dorothy, Betsy, Trot, Button-Bright, the Patchwork Girl, the Cowardly Lion, Betsy's mule Hank, the Sawhorse, and Toto. They soon learn from a shepherd about a part of the Winkie Country that is wild and unknown and that might harbor wicked people. It seems possible that Ozma might be hidden in such a place, so they set off in that direction. In quick succession they encounter the Merry-Go-Round Mountains, spinning rubber hills; a disconcerting revolving land-scape; and the City of Thi, where the Thists live. These last are strange creatures with diamond-shaped heads and heart-shaped bodies who eat thistles, use mechanical dragons for transportation, and are ruled by the High Coco-Lorum. The searchers learn nothing of Ozma there, but do hear about the unnaturally strong people living in the next city.

The next day, between the cities, they find an orchard with all

205

kinds of fruit trees to supply food for their breakfast. Button-Bright loses himself, as is his wont, and he finds the only peach in the orchard. It has a golden pit, and he is told by a Bluefinch that it is an enchanted peach placed there by someone called Ugu the Shoemaker.

Button-Bright is found again, and the group next comes to the city of the Hercus, who are ruled by Vig, the Czarover. These people are immensely strong because their leader feeds them zosozo, which is a form of energy. They are excessively thin, frail-looking people, but they are served by giants who fear their masters' great strength. It is here that the rest of the group from the Emerald City hear about Ugu the Shoemaker and learn his history: how he was descended from a long line of magicians, how he discovered and studied their magic books, and how he left the city of the Hercus and built himself a wicker castle. It seems to everyone that Ugu is the most likely person to have stolen Ozma.

The scene shifts to the journey of the Frogman and Cayke and details the events of their journey, which include a dip in the Truth Pond for the Frogman that cures him of his arrogance and conceit, a ride with a sullen ferryman, and the discovery of a small kingdom of bears in the forest. The encounter with the ferryman sheds interesting light on Baum's respect for wild creatures. The ferryman cannot understand what the Frogman or any other animal in Oz says, and his speech to them is only meaningless sounds. The man's condition is punishment for deliberate cruelty to animals. He is sorry for what he did, but he must live forever cut off from the animal kingdom. His cruelty has destroyed the bond of communication.

The adventure in the forest is longer and more developed. This area of the forest called Bear Center is populated by stuffed teddy bears. Their king is the Big Lavender Bear, who is able to produce illusions of real people and objects just as the Magic Picture does and who possesses the wind-up Little Pink Bear, who will give the true answer to any question put to him about the present or past. By the magic of the Big Lavender Bear, the Frogman and Cayke learn that it was Ugu the Shoemaker who stole the dishpan. Having become interested in their situation, the king and his Pink Bear decide to accompany them on their search for Ugu.

Both parties are now approaching each other, and the next morning they meet and join forces, not far from Ugu's wicker castle. Like many of Baum's villains when they are threatened, Ugu tries to block the rescuers' way with magic obstacles that, with the Wizard's knowledge, they are able to overcome until they enter the castle and the very room where Ugu is. He has, however, one last trick, and he turns the room upside down, making them prisoners.

This time they are saved by Dorothy, who in secret had been practicing with the Nome's King's Magic Belt. She turns the room right side up and transforms Ugu into a dove. Unfortunately, before they can find out what happened to Ozma, Ugu escapes in the golden dishpan; its magic property is that it will transport anyone to anyplace in Oz in an instant. With the help of the Pink Bear, Ozma is discovered imprisoned in the golden peach pit in Button-Bright's pocket, and they are all able to return to the Emerald City, happy at the success of their mission—all, that is, except Cayke, who pines for her dishpan.

The story has a happy ending when the Tin Woodman and the Scarecrow find the dishpan in the Quadling Country and bring it to the Emerald City. Ugu also appears in the city and asks forgiveness for his evil ways. He refuses to be turned back into his old shape, since he knows that he makes a better dove than he ever did a man.

Having Ozma kidnapped and her friends search for her was a good idea that enabled Baum to use a large number of his main characters. With each book he had added new characters to Ozma's court until, by this time, he had an almost unwieldy permanent cast, and his readers expected the most prominent ones, at least, to make an appearance in each new story. He also had developed the settled part of Oz into a peaceful and, above all, safe place to live where the inhabitants are protected from outside harm by Ozma, the benevolent Glinda, and the Wizard, as well as by various magical implements such as the Magic Picture, the Magic

Record Book, and the Nome King's Magic Belt. Thus it was a problem to build a story that would include many of the main characters and could somehow sidestep all the magical aids he had created to protect them. The idea of having Ozma stolen allowed him to do just that.

He made Ozma's kidnapper, Ugu, an unlawful magician who is ambitious to be the most powerful magic worker, as well as the ruler, of Oz. To that end, Ugu steals not only Ozma, but also all the magic tools in the country, with the exception of the Nome King's Magic Belt, which was not originally from Oz. Thus having reduced the magic in Oz to the level of that in the first two books, Baum was able to separate his cast of permanent characters into four different groups, one to search each of the four countries of Oz. His story follows only one group, but it is a large one comprising fourteen beings at the end!

Probably because Baum had to manipulate such a large number of characters, the journey is a bit lumbering at the beginning, and some of the adventures, though interesting, seem to have no purpose other than to introduce strange and unknown inhabitants of Oz. However, this may result from there being no indication that the search party is even going in the right direction until Chapter 11. Also, the first hint of who might be the villain is not given until the same chapter. And it is not until Chapter 19 that the connection between the kidnapping and the theft of the magic instruments is revealed. The reader knows that the group of searchers including Dorothy and the Wizard will be the successful one, but the first half of the book has the feel of wandering in the dark with no clear goal in sight. Perhaps, though, the story's major problem within the context of the series is the climactic rescue. In previous books, Baum had developed the Magic Belt into the most powerful magic tool in Oz, and it is unsatisfactory to have it so conveniently introduced at the end and to have Dorothy seem unfamiliar with its powers. She had both captured it *and* used it in *Ozma of Oz*.

Baum's treatment of Oz in this story is quite satisfactory, however. The map of Oz he had drawn, while eliminating the flexibility he had utilized in the earlier books to fit the country to his stories, had the effect of causing him to treat Oz in a more consistent manner. There are no major changes or reinterpretations of that fairyland in *The Lost Princess,* but there are several refinements.

In view of what happened to Oz after Baum's death, it should be mentioned again that he did not indiscriminately sprinkle the landscape of Oz with odd characters and settlements. He had already stated that there were many unknown parts of Oz around the edges of the country, and in *The Lost Princess,* he is quite specific about the location of the strange peoples and places the travelers come across:

> *The settled parts of the Winkie Country are full of happy and contented people who are ruled by a tin Emperor named Nick Chopper, who in turn is a subject of the beautiful girl Ruler, Ozma of Oz. But not all the Winkie Country is fully settled. At the east, which part lies nearest the Emerald City, there are beautiful farmhouses and roads, but as you travel west you first come to a branch of the Winkie River, beyond which there is a rough country where few people live, and some of these are quite unknown to the rest of the world. After passing through this rude section of territory, which no one ever visits, you would come to still another branch of the Winkie River, after crossing which you would find another well-settled part of the Winkie Country, extending westward quite to the Deadly Desert that surrounds all the Land of Oz and separates that favored fairyland from the more common outside world.*[7]

It is in the "rude section" between the rivers that the adventures of the story take place. Note also that in the text, Baum placed the Winkie Country in its correct location in Oz.

A refinement Baum made that adds greatly to the sense of place in this story is the inclusion of a map showing the section of Oz containing the Winkie Country with the routes of the travelers and the strange places they visit marked on it. Baum had learned from his readers' letters how successful the maps in *Tik-Tok of Oz* had been, and he sent his publisher a "Map of the Search for the Lost Princess" to use in this book.[8] That map, combined with the precise textual descriptions, gives the reader a definite sense of sharing a journey in a recognizable country.

A further refinement in this story was to make it certain that the ruler of Oz, Ozma, is no ordinary girl. She is now definitely "a powerful fairy."[9] He had made that change in *The Scarecrow of Oz,* but the repetition of it several times in *The Lost Princess* makes it clear that the change was intentional, although the fairy powers she possesses are not mentioned.

THE TIN WOODMAN OF OZ

The constant pain that Baum endured while writing *The Lost Princess* finally forced him to consent to an operation in December 1917 to remove his gall bladder and appendix. He survived the operation, but it further damaged his heart, and it soon became apparent that he would never again be well enough to leave his bed.[10] Despite all this, he worked on his Oz book for 1918, *The Tin Woodman of Oz.* Perhaps he found solace by escaping from his limited environment into that safe and happy world his imagination had created.

His readers' comments also provided the inspiration for this book. In *The Wonderful Wizard of Oz,* the Tin Woodman explains how his love for a Munchkin girl led to his ax being enchanted and to his becoming a man of tin with no heart.[11] Many of Baum's readers had asked him what had become of the Munchkin girl, and Baum constructed his new story to answer their questions.

The search for the Munchkin girl, now given the name Nimmie Amee, is initiated by a young wanderer called Woot who stops at the castle of the Tin Woodman to ask for a meal. After hearing the histories

Map showing the route of the search party in The Lost Princess of Oz *(1917).*

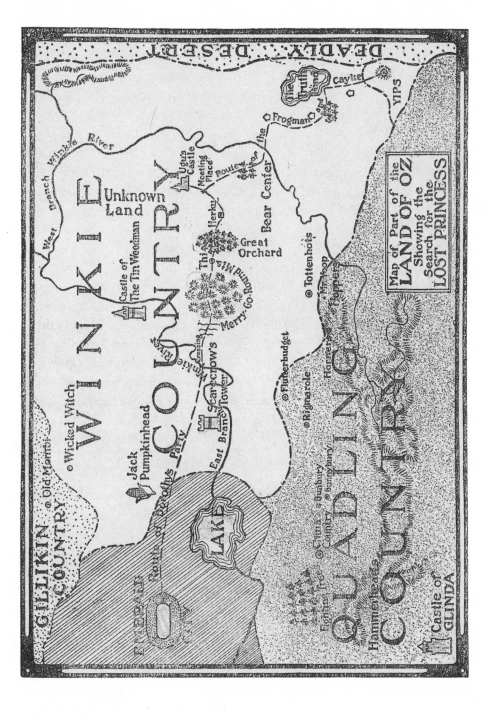

of the Scarecrow and the Tin Woodman, Woot asks what became of the girl, and the Tin Emperor decides that it is his duty to find her and make her Empress of the Winkies.

Woot and the Scarecrow accompany the Tin Woodman, who, because of the personal nature of the mission, decides that the travelers will avoid the Emerald City on their way to the Munchkin Country. By doing so, they are forced to pass through a wild and unknown part of the Gillikin Country where they have some interesting and some unpleasant adventures. They first encounter the City of Loonville, where the inhabitants are rubber balloons. These strange creatures are not friendly, but they pose little danger because they are so easily punctured. The group's next adventure has more serious consequences. They meet Mrs. Yoop, the wife of the captured Yoop from *The Patchwork Girl* and herself a giantess. At first she seems pleasant, but she is a Yookoohoo, which Baum explains is "an Artist in Transformations," and that makes the travelers uneasy. She shows her true nature when she transforms the Tin Woodman into a tin owl, the Scarecrow into a bear stuffed with straw, and Woot into a green monkey. They then learn that their old friend Polychrome has also been captured and changed into a yellow canary.

The prisoners are able to escape by stealing the magic apron that allows Mrs. Yoop to open and close the doors of the castle, but their troubles are not over for they are threatened by a jaguar in the forest and Woot is chased by a dragon family hoping to make him their dinner. Because of their transformations, they decide to delay their quest and go south to ask Glinda for help in regaining their true forms. They first stop at Jinjur's ranch, which is nearby, and there they meet Ozma and Dorothy. Ozma is able to come to their rescue and in an exhibition of magic unlike anything she has before displayed, she restores them to their normal shapes so that they are able to continue their original mission.

Ozma practices magic in The Tin Woodman of Oz. *Her character underwent quite a transformation after her first appearance in* The Marvelous Land of Oz.

Back in the Tin Woodman's native forest in the Munchkin Country, they find a rusted Tin Soldier very like the Tin Woodman, and, after oiling his joints, they are surprised to hear that his history is similar to the Woodman's. He, too, fell in love with Nimmie Amee and had his sword enchanted by the Wicked Witch of the East so that it cut off parts of his body until he was made entirely of tin. He also feels that it is his duty to find the girl, but she no longer lives in the forest. Further surprises greet the travelers when they visit the tinsmith and hear that, having discovered some magic glue at the witch's lair after she had been destroyed by Dorothy's house, he made a man out of the cast-off human parts of the two tin men. The tinsmith is able to tell them that Nimmie Amee now lives near the desert border of the Munchkin Country near Mount Munch. After more adventures that include a journey through an Invisible Country, encounters with a gigantic beast called a Hip-po-gy-raf and a family of educated pigs, and a trip through a rabbit hole, the searchers finally locate her. Both the Tin Woodman and the Tin Soldier are dismayed and shocked to find Nimmie Amee happily married to the composite man made by the tinsmith from their body parts!

The Tin Woodman of Oz shares the structural problems that are more or less common to all the books (except *Rinkitink*) in the latter part of the series. These stories often depend too strongly on series of brief, undeveloped adventures among communities of strange creatures to fill out the plot, and the result frequently is that the narrative thread is lost for a time. Baum had a genius for inventing exotic and wonderful fantasy places; the problem was that sometimes his imagination ran away with him. The way he exercised that ability in the last part of the Oz series played a part in changing the way we view Oz itself. This tendency to let his invention run free is noticeable in Baum as early as the journey to the south section in *The Wonderful Wizard of Oz*, but inside his premier fairyland, he kept it under better control until his return to Oz in 1913. It is true that *Dorothy and the Wizard in Oz* and *The Road to Oz* are little more than tours through odd and magical countries, but those countries are outside Oz. They add to the geography of the fantasy world that Oz is a part of, but they also point out the uniqueness of Oz within that world. Oz remains in those books very much like the real world, not a magical country but a country in which magical things may exist or happen. Magic is still the exception, not the rule.

In the latter part of the series, Baum poured his inventive ability into Oz, bringing Oz closer to the spirit of his early, totally fantastic country of Mo, and thus lessening its reality. It should be remembered, though, that Baum now had no other outlet than the Oz series for his imaginative countries, and the fact that he funneled all his creative energies into Oz may be another indication that he had become reconciled to his readers' preference for Oz stories above his other types of fantasies.

Baum was also, in the latter half of the series, more inclined to use magic to extricate his characters from awkward situations and to help them overcome obstacles. In the first six books, Glinda is the principal source of good magic in Oz, and her magic is limited. In the last eight books, magic workers, magic implements, and the use of magic increase enormously.

All these problems appear in *The Tin Woodman of Oz*, but the basic plot is stronger and more inventive than those of the books surrounding it. Part of the story's appeal lies in the look back at, and continuation of, events in *The Wonderful Wizard of Oz*, but its main significance here comes from the fact that it presents Baum's last major reinterpretation of Oz.

When the Tin Woodman recounts his history, Baum added more details, but in the main, he was faithful to the original version given in *The Wizard*, except that now the evil woman for whom the girl was a servant was actually the Wicked Witch of the East. This change allowed the girl to gain her freedom when the witch was destroyed. The Tin Woodman's return to his old home in the forest sparked Baum's imagination to some of his most original and disturbing flights of fancy, which have a modern sense of the absurd about them. In a cupboard at the tinsmith's shop, the Woodman finds a head that, being the head of an Oz man, is very much alive and carries on a conversation with him. The most bizarre part of the incident is that it is the Tin Woodman's own head, which his enchanted ax had cut off long before. The episode creates some interesting confusion about identity, that is only increased when the Tin Woodman and the Tin Soldier meet the composite man, who was created out of parts of them both.

Such incidents would have been impossible in Oz as it was originally created in *The Wizard*, but changes such as making its inhabitants immortal in *The Road to Oz* had opened the way for all kinds of paradoxical situations. Baum's readers had not been slow in spotting those paradoxes and inconsistencies, but far from being hurt by their criticisms and questions, he welcomed and encouraged them. (It would be interesting to know how many future literary scholars got their first experiences with textual criticism from the Oz books.) It is probable that the description and reinterpretation of Oz that Baum inserted into *The Tin Woodman* was his way of answering some of those questions (Appendix B).[12] His readers were asking for the internal logic that George MacDonald believed must be a part of successful fantasy.[13] Oz in *The Wizard* has that consistency, as it does in many of the other books if taken individually. But the series had now progressed through eleven books, and the cumulative picture the reader built up over the course of them began to look much less consistent. Baum was not able to rewrite the series and bring everything into line, but he could present a new version of Oz history to answer some of the most pressing questions.

The principal problem he addressed was the immortality of the inhabitants, and while repeating what he had said in *The Emerald City*, that no one died or was sick in Oz but that in rare instances a person could be destroyed, he went on to deal with the American characters: "Another strange thing about this fairy Land of Oz was that whoever managed to enter it from the outside world came under the magic spell of the place and did not change in appearance as long as they lived there."[14] And he went even further and explained how it all came about and why people of all ages existed in Oz:

> *Oz was not always a fairyland, I am told. Once it was much*
> *like other lands, except it was shut in by a dreadful desert of*

sandy wastes that lay all around it, thus preventing its people from all contact with the rest of the world. Seeing this isolation, the fairy band of Queen Lurline, passing over Oz while on a journey, enchanted the country and so made it a Fairyland. And Queen Lurline left one of her fairies to rule this enchanted Land of Oz, and then passed on and forgot all about it.

From that moment no one in Oz ever died. Those who were old remained old; those who were young and strong did not change as years passed them by.[15]

This new version of the origin of Oz solves many problems. Baum was able right away to explain that the Wicked Witch of the East is destroyed by Dorothy's house because "she was very old and was all dried up and withered before Oz became a fairyland."[16] But it also created new problems.

It probably seemed fitting to Baum that since Oz had developed into such a splendid fairyland, it should be ruled by an exceptional being such as a fairy, but by making Ozma one of Queen Lurline's band, he had to discard her whole history as it is presented in *The Marvelous Land* and repeated with variations in several of the subsequent books. He had, though, prepared the way by mentioning in two of the later books that she is a fairy. Firmly established as "a real fairy,"[17] Ozma also becomes a magic worker as powerful as Glinda and the Wizard in *The Tin Woodman of Oz*, and she demonstrates her ability when she transforms the travelers back to their original forms.

However inconsistent this new version of Oz may be with those presented from *The Road* on, it is more logical than the others and is satisfying in that it draws Oz closer to the source of power and home of the fairies, the Forest of Burzee. Baum obviously confused Zurline, the Queen of the Burzee Wood Nymphs, and Lulea, the Queen of the Fairies, when he wrote Queen Lurline.[18] Unfortunately, even before he became an invalid, Baum seems to have trusted too much to his own memory for names and incidents in his previous stories.

217

Besides being a more logical version of Oz history, it is an ingenious one. Baum's physical condition forced him to work more slowly on this story than was his custom, and the extra time he had to think about it is apparent. He also seems to have had time to consider his too-large cast of characters, because at the end of *The Tin Woodman*, he sends Woot out to wander happily again and the Tin Soldier to a post in a faraway part of the Gillikin Country; neither settles in the Emerald City.

THE MAGIC OF OZ

In the introduction to his next book, *The Magic of Oz* (1919), Baum mentioned his "long and confining illness" when apologizing to his readers for not answering all their letters. It is amazing that Baum, despite his physical condition, could continue to create magical, happy books about Oz; but for him, his whole life long, living had meant creating—to stop would be to die. What is even more amazing is that his stories actually begin to improve again until they reach a level, though not as high as his best works, of which he could rightfully be proud. *The Tin Woodman of Oz* meanders a bit, but the level of invention is high. *The Magic of Oz* depends heavily on some of the earlier stories for its plot, but it dispenses with the travelogue and is much more tightly constructed, using double and sometimes triple plots.

The first of those has the Nome King, Ruggedo, appearing as the deposed king of the Nomes he becomes at the end of *Tik-Tok*, but again, just as in *The Emerald City*, he plans to try to conquer Oz. To do this, he enlists the help of a discontented boy, Kiki Aru, from Mount Munch in the Munchkin Country who has learned a secret word that will effect any kind of transformation. The Nome King's plan is to go to the wild forest area of the Gillikin Country, transform the animals into men, and use them as an army.

The other main plot refers back to *The Road to Oz*, which brings Dorothy to Oz for Ozma's birthday. In *The Magic of Oz*, it is again almost

218

time to celebrate the ruler's birthday,[19] and Dorothy and Trot are trying to discover unusual presents to give to Ozma. Trot and Cap'n Bill hear about a Magic Flower that grows on an island in a river near the northern border of Oz and to the east of the forest where the Nome King intends to raise his army. Led by the Glass Cat, they go to the island but find that the island is also magic because they take root there and become prisoners.

Dorothy and the Wizard, for their gift, decide to go to the forest in the Gillikin Country to ask some of the monkeys to come to the Emerald City and perform for Ozma and her guests. Accompanied by the Cowardly Lion and the Hungry Tiger, Dorothy and the Wizard arrive in the forest just as the Nome King and Kiki Aru are rallying the animals, but after a struggle involving much magic, the Wizard manages to defeat them in time to rescue Trot and Cap'n Bill from the magic island.

In the same manner as in *The Emerald City*, the Nome King and Kiki Aru are rendered harmless by drinking from the Fountain of Oblivion, which makes them forget all their evil ways. Baum, perhaps feeling that this might be his last book, gave the now harmless little Nome a home in Oz "where he was quite content and passed his days in innocent enjoyment."[20]

The book's climax is Ozma's birthday banquet, at which the whole cast of familiar Oz characters is assembled. This banquet, however, pales in comparison with the glittering celebration that Baum created for *The Road to Oz*. It consists only of the members of Ozma's court, but that court has grown so numerous that it is a large party even without the splendor afforded by foreign visitors.

The Magic of Oz is aptly named, for magic abounds in it. What all the new mechanical inventions were doing for people in America, magic was doing for the people of Oz. Indeed, for the good of the story, magic is almost too abundant; it touches almost every aspect of the adventure, except transportation. If food or lodgings are needed while traveling, the Wizard supplies them, or if no path is found in a dense forest, the Wizard's magic ax cuts one. The ultimate effect is that the sense of wonder is actually lessened because magic becomes the norm. Baum was, in a sense, competing with the actual world, and by increasing the magic in his fantasy world, he may have been trying to keep the interest of his readers, who were exposed every day to the new technological wonders of the real world.

Despite the addition of even more magic, the land of Oz remains unchanged from the version presented in *The Tin Woodman*. The adventures again take place among the inhabitants of wild and unknown parts of the country, but Baum explained: "Still, these unknown subjects are not nearly so numerous as the known inhabitants of Oz, who occupy all the countries near to the Emerald City. Indeed, I'm sure it will not be long until all parts of the fairyland of Oz are explored and their peoples made acquainted with their Ruler."[21] The frontier in Oz was disappearing as quickly as that in the United States.

It is outside Oz that Baum added some refinements to his world. Only a little more than two chapters of this story do not take place in Oz, but that section is important because it demonstrates that even this late in Baum's career, when he knew that he would never again write other kinds of fantasy, he still viewed his many past creations as part of only one large and varied imaginary world.

When Kiki Aru, high up on Mount Munch on the eastern edge of Oz, discovers the magic word that will cause transformations, he changes himself into a hawk so that he can fly out of Oz over the Shifting Sands (the name of the desert on that side of Oz) to escape detection by Glinda and Ozma for illegally practicing magic. Once he is across, Kiki Aru visits in quick succession Hiland, Loland, Merryland, Noland, Ix, and Ev, where he meets the Nome King. Except for the stop in Ev, these visits are in no way necessary to the story; their sole function seems to be to highlight the interlocking nature of the fantasy countries of Baum's imagination.

In Ev, the boy has trouble getting food because he has no money, "for in the Land of Oz they do not use money at all."[22] By this device, Baum made it clear that in his mind his alterations to Oz do not extend to his other imaginary countries, despite the fact that they surround Oz. He

220

thus emphasized still more that in his continent of the imagination, Oz is quite different and very special.

GLINDA OF OZ

The Magic of Oz did not turn out to be Baum's last fantasy; he was able to finish *Glinda of Oz* (published in 1920), the best of the last four Oz books. The level of invention is very high; no unnecessary incidents impede the narrative; and the plot grows naturally out of the background as it had evolved in Baum's last major revision in *The Tin Woodman*.

The story concerns Ozma's attempt to prevent a war between the Flatheads and the Skeezers, two hitherto unknown tribes of people who live near the northern border of Oz. The Flatheads live on the top of a mountain and are a strange race whose heads are flat just above their ears where their brains should be; however, all carry a can of brains given to them by the fairies who made Oz a fairyland. They are ruled by the Supreme Dictator, who has stolen the canned brains from several of his subjects and has become a sorcerer. The Skeezers are normal-looking people who live in a beautiful island city in a lake near the mountain of the Flatheads. The city is enclosed by a large glass dome, and their Queen Coo-ee-oh, a powerful and cruel Krumbic witch, has constructed marvelous, magical machinery by which she can submerge the glass-domed island in the lake in times of danger.

Ozma and Dorothy's mission of peace fails when they are unable to persuade the two rulers to acknowledge the authority of Ozma and to obey the laws of Oz forbidding fighting and unlawful magic, and they are taken captive by Queen Coo-ee-oh. The Skeezer queen submerges the city before the first engagement with the Flatheads, and Dorothy and Ozma's plight becomes more serious when Coo-ee-oh, having left the city by a submarine boat, is defeated and transformed into a jeweled swan by the Supreme Dictator of the Flatheads. They and the rest of the Skeezers are prisoners in the submerged city because as a swan, Coo-ee-oh has lost all memory of the magic words needed to raise the city and work the machinery of the boats and the bridge.

The focus of the story now shifts from conflict to rescue as all of Ozma's counselors (most of the familiar Oz characters), led by Glinda, rush to the lake of the Skeezers to attempt to rescue the ruler of Oz and Princess Dorothy. Glinda and the Wizard are aided by three girls, Adepts at Magic, who had been the original rulers of the Flatheads before being transformed into fish by Coo-ee-oh and who had been restored to their proper shapes by Red Reera the Yookoohoo (a mistress of transformation like Mrs. Yoop). At first, even the combined knowledge of these magic workers is unsuccessful, but after the water level of the lake is lowered enough to allow them entrance into the city through the top of the dome and after the machinery is examined, they find the proper way to operate it, and the city is raised.

A new queen is chosen for the Skeezers, and after the Supreme Dictator is deposed, the three Adepts at Magic are restored as rulers of the Flatheads. Glinda causes the heads of these strange people to assume the normal shape, with the brains inside instead of in cans. Both the Skeezers and the Flatheads, now renamed Mountaineers, pledge loyalty to Ozma and the laws of Oz.

Just as in *The Magic of Oz*, Baum made no major changes to his fairyland in *Glinda of Oz*, which may indicate that in his mind, his premier fairyland had reached its final stage of development; certainly the plot of *Glinda* grows naturally out of all that has gone before. The area occupied by the Skeezers appears on Baum's 1914 map, and the Flatheads are cleverly linked to Baum's final version of the history of Oz by the gift of canned brains from Queen Lurline and her fairy band. That unlicensed magic is unlawful in Oz and that it is Ozma's duty as ruler to enforce the law had been established as far back as *The Patchwork Girl* (1913), but until this book, Ozma has not been directly involved with the far-flung parts of her realm. There are indications that if Baum had been able to write more stories, there would have been more plots involving Ozma settling disputes and extending her benevolent rule to all the undiscovered corners of Oz. Baum has Ozma say, "It is my duty to be acquainted with every tribe of people and every strange and hidden country in all Oz." And Dorothy replies, "Time doesn't make much diff'rence in the Land of Oz . . . so, if we explore one place at a time, we'll by-an'-by know all about every nook and corner in Oz."[23] What Ozma intends is to become acquainted with the far-flung areas of her realm; she says nothing about civilizing or changing those regions.

In the series, Oz was being explored in a way that resembled Baum's own experience with America. At the time of *The Wizard* in 1900, much of this country, especially the Far West and the Deep South, were unknown to him. But as the series progressed so did Baum's acquaintance with the United States, until he had traveled to almost every major section.[24] The parts that were still unknown to him were, like Oz, the areas around the edges and certain other wild and inaccessible parts within the country. There was also a correlation between Oz and Baum's America in Ozma's goal of extending the benefits of her rule to all parts of Oz. During his lifetime, he had seen the western United States become more fully explored and the western territories brought into full equality with the rest of the union as states. However, one cannot escape the conclusion that the benefits of Ozma's rule would be more unobtrusive and natural than what was done in the name of civilization in Baum's America.

Glinda of Oz, named for the supreme sorceress of Oz, contains a greater number and variety of magic workers than any of Baum's other stories: besides Glinda, the Wizard, and Ozma, there are the Supreme Dictator, a sorcerer; his wife, a witch; Coo-ee-oh, a Krumbic witch; the three Adepts at Magic; and Red Reera, the Yookoohoo. Yet this proliferation of magic is not the flaw that it is in several other of the books because Baum seems to have recognized the problem, and he set limits on the magic and brought order out of the confusion.

The magic of the fairies depends on "the secret laws of nature" and is "granted them to bring comfort and happiness to all who appeal to them."[25] Ozma is "the most powerful fairy in Oz," but other fairies have powers different from hers, and Glinda and the Wizard are more powerful still.[26] When Dorothy confidently asserts that Ozma will understand the magic machinery of the Skeezer island, Ozma disagrees, "I'm afraid not, my dear. It isn't fairy magic at all; it is witchcraft."[27]

Red Reera is a Yookoohoo and thus is restricted to magical transformations, but the magic of the other magic workers (sorceress, sorcerer, witches, wizard, and adepts) utilizes "chemicals and herbs and . . . tools,"[28] and therefore the extent of their powers depends on the intelligence, diligence, research, and experience of the various individuals. Coo-ee-oh "had a rare genius for mechanics,"[29] and her machines that control the island are unfamiliar to Glinda and the Wizard and difficult for them to comprehend.

Baum thus divided the magic workers in his Other-world into two groups representing nature (fairies) and science (wizards, witches). Because it comes from nature, Ozma's fairy magic is inherently good and cannot be perverted (there are no evil fairies in Baum's stories), yet the magic of the other magic workers is, like science, neither good nor bad, but depends on the moral nature of the person wielding the power. Both Glinda and the Wizard are good people, and their magic is good; the Supreme Dictator is evil, as is his magic; the three Adepts at Magic are good, but their magic instruments are perverted to evil use when stolen by Coo-ee-oh.

This dichotomy illustrates Baum's attitude toward nature and science throughout his career. To him, nature was inherently good, but the technological advances of science were no better or worse than the people controlling them. At times, he appears to have adopted a negative attitude toward the scientific and technological innovations that were changing his America, but it was not the innovations themselves he distrusted—they were fairy-tale wonders to him. He distrusted the ability of himself and the rest of his generation to use them wisely and unselfishly "for the good of the world."[30] Baum put his faith in the children. He devoted his adult career to them and tried to open their eyes to the natural wonders of the world and to develop their imaginations by giving them a real "American" fairyland, in the hope that they would learn to use the magic of the modern world wisely to enhance nature and not destroy it.

THE LAST JOURNEY

L. Frank Baum did not live to see the publications of his last two Oz books. About *Glinda of Oz*, Martin Gardner wrote, "I have often fancied that the sunken island on which Dorothy was trapped beneath a lake was an unconscious expression of Baum's own sinking emotions."[31] In that context, the great array of magic workers whom Baum assembled in his story to try to raise the island would also take on new meaning. However, doctors in the actual world are human and not magic workers. Baum died in May 1919 at Ozcot in Hollywood. For much of May 5, he was unconscious, but he rallied in the evening and talked to Maud for a little while before lapsing back into unconsciousness. Early on the morning of May 6, he spoke one more sentence before dying. It is reported that what he said was, "Now we can cross the Shifting Sands."[32]

At the end of *Glinda of Oz*, Baum left his characters in the sunshine of a summer's day on their way back to the Emerald City. We, his readers, can easily follow them there in our minds because we know what to expect; the brilliant and sparkling City of Emeralds is as familiar to us as our own native city or town. The little Guardian of the Gates will be there to welcome them, just as he did when Dorothy, the Scarecrow, the Tin Woodman, and the Cowardly Lion made their first journey to see the Great Oz, and the people of the city will turn out to celebrate the safe return of their adored ruler, Ozma, and the beloved little girl from far-off Kansas who is now their Princess Dorothy. And all the members of the rescue party will also receive hearty welcomes and cheers.

While the celebration and rejoicing are taking place, perhaps we, with the bird's-eye view possible to us, will rise above the activity, seeing the jeweled city set amid green meadows dotted with wild flowers and, farther out, the neat well-kept farms of the rural countryside. Then, as we continue to rise, we will catch a glimpse of the glittering tin castle in the west and the glowing ruby palace in the south; dark forests and mist-shrouded mountains will come into view, many containing areas and peoples still unknown. Soon the whole, vast, rectangular-shaped country, with its four distinct kingdoms and the jeweled city in the center, will be laid out before us. We will then see the rosy-tinted Barrier of Invisibility, which protects this favored land, and, beyond that, the added protection of the desert, with its shifting sands and noxious gases.

But we must rise even higher because there is more to be seen. Ringed around the desert border of Oz are other countries: the magical Valley of Mo, with its happy and contented people; the twin kingdoms of Hiland and Loland, where a gingerbread man is king; the seven Valleys of Merryland, with their clowns, newborn babies, candy people, and fairy wax-doll queen; the Happy Valley, where Santa Claus works to make children happy; the mystical Forest of Burzee, where the fairies have lived since the world began; the kingdoms of Noland and Ix, where King Bud is learning to become a good ruler and where Queen Zixi remains radiant and young in the eyes of her subjects; the Land of Ev, with its handsome royal family; and the merry kingdom of Rinkitink, which is washed by the purple waters of the Nonestic Ocean. And still there is more to be seen because the whole fantasy continent is now spread out before us. We may notice an island in the sky hovering about this world or the strange and unusual islands that dot the ocean; we may see some of the Sea Fairies sporting on the white-capped waves; and we may remember stories of the long-ago enchanted Island of Yew, which disappeared from this magical world. We will also observe other countries surrounding Oz, and in particular, we may notice one, the Kingdom of Dreams,[33] that the author did not live to write about. However, we know that this whole marvelous and varied continent lapped by the waves of an unknown sea is a Kingdom of Dreams and that it all came out of the imagination of one man: Lyman Frank Baum.

The growth and evolution of Baum's imaginary Other-world has now been traced from its beginning with the Valley of Phunnyland (Mo) and the little Dorothy who hears a marvelous story from a rabbit through its final manifestation in *Glinda of Oz*. It was neither an orderly nor a completely planned development, and so many unanticipated and extraliterary factors played parts that it is a wonder that the development was not more chaotic than it was. That Baum's tying together of his various imaginary countries was not totally unplanned is evident from the links and references among such diverse books as *A New Wonderland, American Fairy Tales, The Life and Adventures of Santa Claus,* and *Queen Zixi of Ix;* even *John Dough and the Cherub* contains subtle references to other Baum stories. Oz, however, was the unexpected element in Baum's plan.

Oz was actually discovered first by children. When Baum's creative energies were set in motion with the phenomenal success of *Father Goose, The Wonderful Wizard of Oz* was to him only one of the great variety of stories that poured out of his imagination. It was his young readers who first recognized the uniqueness and fascination of that marvelous land. It was not a place his readers wanted to visit only once; they wanted to go there again and again. At first, Baum mistakenly attributed the continued success of the book to the success of the stage version, and he wrote a second book about Oz more in hopes of another stage triumph than from a desire to develop Oz further. In the meantime, he continued to develop his fictional world in his own way without reference to Oz. One can imagine that he was somewhat bewildered when the success of the second Oz book, the utter failure of its stage adaptation, and the less than overwhelming success of his other fantasies finally forced him to realize that, of all his creations, Oz held supreme place in the affections of his readers.

It was a dilemma. The original story had not been constructed to have a sequel, and the "sequel" he did write was intended as the basis of a stage musical and only confused the matter of Oz. What he finally did was to develop Oz slowly and to focus most of the attention on Dorothy's journeys to that land, because he had realized that, to his readers, Oz was the beautiful, wished-for place and not the slightly sinister land of illusion he had originally conceived.

In his fifth book about Oz, Baum drew that country into his existing imaginary world, which included Merryland, Burzee, Ix, and the rest of his other countries, and he affirmed the supreme position of Oz in that world by having his characters from those other fantasies honor the ruler of Oz. Also in that book, he began the transformation of Oz into an ideal world by removing both money and death from that favored country, and he continued the process in his sixth book, where, probably because he thought he was ending the series, he felt free to give his most detailed description of the organization and nature of that fairy society. It is likely that Baum still did not completely grasp the power and reality that his imaginary world held for his readers. He thought that by bringing Dorothy to Oz to live and by cutting that fairyland off from the rest of the world, demand for more Oz books would cease, but it was not Dorothy's journeys to Oz that his readers wanted. They wanted more about Oz itself.

Baum's attempt to leave Oz and write about new imaginary places was short-lived, and once Oz became his only outlet for his imaginary creations, he poured them into this existing Other-world, exploring more and more odd corners of it. He also organized his entire Other-world by drawing maps that showed how Oz related to all his other fairy countries, and he revised the history of Oz to link it with his earlier fairy mythology and give his marvelous land an appropriate ruler. By the end of his life, he had created the most spectacular and detailed fantasy world to come from the pen of an American writer.

The question is: Why Oz? Why did Oz capture the imaginations of his readers? *The Wonderful Wizard of Oz* is not the only good story he wrote. Many people maintain that *Queen Zixi of Ix* is a better book, and the myth-tinged imaginary world in *The Life and Adventures of Santa Claus* is certainly richer than Oz as that country was first conceived. The most generally accepted answer is that the uniqueness and appeal of Oz lie in its American quality. Whether consciously or unconsciously, Baum put more of his own experiences in *The Wizard* than in any of his other fantasies. Dorothy's travels in Oz are his own travels in America: from the East to the frontier of the West, to Chicago, and to the southern extent of his sales territory. He was himself an exile far from home, and the country that Dorothy discovers is America seen by Baum and transformed by his imagination. His readers recognized before he did that Oz is an authentic

American fairyland, that it is a place—unlike the German forests of the Brothers Grimm or the English Wonderland of Lewis Carroll—that can be just over the hill or beyond the prairie in this land of limitless possibilities.

Even when Baum began to develop Oz, it did not lose its American qualities, and that development reflects Baum's own increasing experiences with the United States, sometimes in a negative way as when he made Oz not what America is, but what it could be. At times, the development of Oz was erratic and confused, but so was the development of America. Edward Wagenknecht wrote, "It would be comparatively simple to make the history of Oz a somewhat more highly finished record, but the chances are nine out of ten that you would at the same time make it somewhat less American."[34]

Baum's imaginary world passes the primary test of successful fantasy: his imaginary continent, with Oz set in its center, *is* an authentic and recognizable Other-world. In a very real sense, however, Baum's total Other-world exists outside his books and stories because it is a composite of all the facts and scraps of information—the "introductory interiors"—contained in his whole body of work. It is in this way that Baum's creation most resembles Doyle's Sherlock Holmes. The character of Holmes, as it is built up over the course of the stories about him, ultimately forms a whole that exists in no one of them and, in fact, exists quite apart from the stories. It is the same for Oz. There is no one book the reader can go to that contains the totality of Baum's Other-world; *that* exists quite apart from the books. The "existence" that these creations have outside the narratives in which they figure is what makes them such real, living entities that actually seem to have a life apart from their creators. Sherlock Holmes is still solving cases long after Doyle's death; every year sees the publication of new Holmes stories by various writers. The same is true with Oz; that marvelous fairyland continues to be explored and mapped in new books and stories. Baum's Other-world did not die with him.

229

Epilogue

Oz After Baum

And when I say imagination, I am talking of one of the greatest factors and forces in human progress. Stunt, dwarf, or destroy the imagination of a child and you have taken away its chances of success in life. Imagination transforms the commonplace into the great and creates the new out of the old. No man ever made a new invention or discovery without imagination, and invention and discovery have made human progress.

"Interview with Mr. Frank G. [*sic*] Baum" (1909) in *The Advance*.

FOR A LONG TIME, L. FRANK BAUM WAS IGNORED BY THE CRITICS. Except for Edward Wagenknecht's pioneering study *Utopia Americana* (1929),[1] there was little written about Baum until the mid-1950s when several things occurred to draw attention to him. The centennial of his birth was 1956; that year, too, *The Wonderful Wizard of Oz* entered the public domain, and new editions began to multiply; the first exhibition devoted to Baum and his entire body of work was organized by the Columbia University Libraries; and the classic MGM film *The Wizard of Oz* was first shown on television.

Today many, but not all, of the critical battles about Baum have been fought. He has taken his place as America's greatest writer of children's fantasy; he has been acknowledged by critics in the United States and England to have created the first distinctly American fairy tale and the first distinctly American Other-world; and he has been credited with having originated an American fantasy tradition. One wonders why this evaluation took so long.

There are two obvious reasons. First, while the Oz series proved to have a life of its own, continuing after Baum's death more or less continually until 1951, his other books went out of print and were forgot-

231

ten. Critics and librarians too often classed his Oz books with the myriad other children's series that they also ignored, not bothering to separate Baum's stories from the Oz books by other authors or the Oz series from those series less worthy of consideration. And second, Baum wrote expressly to please children. With only few exceptions, he excluded from his writings those elements that he had been forced to add to his stage adaptations in an attempt to please adult tastes as well.

Baum's death had little effect on the demand for Oz, and his publisher, Reilly & Lee, with the consent of Maud Baum, engaged a young Philadelphia writer, Ruth Plumly Thompson, to continue the Oz series.[2] This was, of course, a commercial decision because Baum's books had been a mainstay of the publisher, but without public demand and interest, the series would have quickly died. Ruth Plumly Thompson's high-spirited and imaginative books sustained that public demand and interest for nineteen more years. A new Oz book for Christmas had become a tradition in a great number of American households, where for many children, Oz and Santa Claus were twin images of Christmas. Thompson's first book, *The Royal Book of Oz* (1921), carries Baum's name on the title page with the phrase "Enlarged and Edited by Ruth Plumly Thompson," and the introduction, signed by Maud Baum, states that Baum left "some unfinished notes," which Thompson "enlarged."[3] That, however, was a fiction of the publisher; the entire book was written by Thompson.[4] Her next story, *Kabumpo in Oz* (1922), carries the legend "Founded on and continuing the Famous Oz Stories by L. Frank Baum 'Royal Historian of Oz'" on the title page, as do all subsequent books of the series.

The transition from Baum to another writer was eased by the fact that John R. Neill continued as the illustrator. Thompson published a book a year through 1939, when she retired to write other things. Then Neill began to contribute an Oz book a year as well as illustrate them, but his association with Oz as an author was brief because he died in 1943. Such was the strength of Oz that there had not been a year without a new book from 1913 through 1942, but after Neill's death, the series was continued more sporadically. New books appeared in 1946, 1949, and 1951—the first two by Jack Snow and the last by Rachel R. Cosgrove. Then, in 1963, the last Oz book to be published by the official publisher, Reilly & Lee, appeared. It was *Merry Go Round in Oz* by Eloise Jarvis McGraw and Lauren McGraw Wagner, and was illustrated by Dick Martin. The series had reached a total of forty volumes, only fourteen of those by L. Frank Baum. Thus it is somewhat misleading to speak of the Oz series as consisting of those books by Baum and those by "other authors." That division tends to minimize the achievement of Baum's successor Ruth Plumly Thompson, who with nineteen of the official books of the series wrote more about Oz than anyone else. The five authors besides Baum and Thompson account for only seven of the forty books.

Reilly & Lee was, on the whole, fortunate in its selection of writers for the subsequent Oz books. Ruth Plumly Thompson (1891–1976) was an inspired choice to continue the Oz series. Even though her writing style was quite different from Baum's, her ability to invent odd and entertaining characters and incidents was almost equal to his. And it is in her characters that the real spirit of Oz is found in her books. Many of them—such as the two American boys Peter and Speedy, Kabumpo the elegant elephant, the Red Jinn, Pigasus, Captain Salt, and Sir Hokus—have been very popular. But her amusing characters and the breathtaking variety of incidents with which she packed her books disguise, to a large extent, the fact that her stories are more traditional fairy tales than are Baum's. That she changed the spelling of "nome" back to its original spelling of "gnome" indicates her traditional approach; "gnome" with a "g" links the word back to northern European folklore. The majority of her books have at least one old-fashioned European- or Arabian Nights–style kingdom as a source of much of the action, and her favorite plot has a prince or a princess (or both) who is enchanted (or disguised) saving his or her kingdom, regaining the throne, or saving Oz from being conquered. Five of her books end with a royal wedding; in two others, a separated king and queen are reunited; and in another, it is predicted that one of her American characters will return, marry a princess, and rule a kingdom.

Her style has been called brisk, "robust," and "enthusiastic,"[5] and where Baum usually had girls as his central characters, Thompson preferred boys. All her American characters who travel to Oz are male, and it is easy to identify one of the influences on her in the boys' adventure books of the late nineteenth century, with their pirates, nobles in disguise, highwaymen, and damsels in distress. But there was also another side to her style because among Oz authors "she was unexcelled in her ability to suggest the beauty and magic of evening, whether it was the dark blues and purples of an autumn night in the forest seen from the cozy warmth and red and orange glow of a camp fire, or the blue and silver of a summer evening in a garden lit only by Chinese lanterns or fireflies."[6]

When John R. Neill (1877–1943) began writing Oz books, he had already given visual life to that imaginary world and its inhabitants for almost forty years. He filled his books with both verbal and visual whimsy. His richly detailed drawings always provide a running commentary on the story being told by Baum or Thompson, often adding amusing, fanciful, and sometimes even factual information not in the actual text. For example, it has been noted that he continued W. W. Denslow's practice in *The Wonderful Wizard of Oz* of drawing the buildings in Oz to look as if they had faces. In Neill's books, the houses are given life, personalities, and tempers. In his version of Oz, anything can be alive.

While John R. Neill continued to use characters created by Ruth Plumly Thompson, in addition to contributing many more himself, the next author, Jack Snow (1907–1956), took a different approach. An avid fan of Baum's fantasies, Snow consciously tried to imitate Baum's style, and in his two well-plotted and interesting stories, he reduced the population of Oz to only those characters Baum had created, although in the course of his books, he did add new characters of his own.

Rachel R. Cosgrove (b. 1922), in her wonderfully titled *The Hidden Valley of Oz*, also took this restrictive approach to the large population of Oz celebrities, and the adventures shared by Dorothy, the Scarecrow, the Tin Woodman, the Cowardly Lion, the Hungry Tiger, and her two

American characters often evoke an earlier Oz even more clearly than Snow's stories.

The last Oz book in the Reilly & Lee series is one of the best written, but Eloise Jarvis McGraw and Lauren McGraw Wagner presented a different vision of Oz. In addition to restoring many of the trappings of the traditional, European fairy tale favored by Thompson, they visualized Oz as a European landscape. When the American boy who is the main character arrives in Oz, he is struck by the foreign appearance of the country. He thinks that Oz looks just like "the pictures of England he had seen in books," and to emphasize the similarity, he is soon met by a group of fox hunters.[7]

All these later authors brought different kinds of imaginations and abilities to their books. Each was a talented individual with specific ideas about the direction the series should take, and ideally each should be considered individually. Edward Wagenknecht has cautioned about considering the entire Oz series as a whole: "Oz is L. Frank Baum's creation, the product of his mind. Others can at best do no better than glean in the fields he reaped, which are also the fields he planted. . . . And if we do not distinguish carefully between his work and the work of his successors, we may well be asking him to carry a heavier burden than he ought to carry."[8] Wagenknecht was reminding the reader that Baum was the true creator of Oz, but considering the series as a whole is also unfair to the later authors because their individual achievements are often lost or overlooked.

This is not the place to discuss all the changes made to Baum's Other-world by the later authors, but something must be said about three of the most important because these *have* often saddled him with "a heavier burden than he ought to carry."

1. Oz became overpopulated with both odd characters and exotic places. As early as *The Tin Woodman of Oz*, Baum recognized the problem inherent in his large cast of permanent characters, and he added no new characters to Ozma's court in his last three books. He was also very precise about placing the strange, new places he introduced in unexplored, wild

areas that are well defined in their relationships with the known and settled areas of the country. After Baum, the already large cast was retained, and new characters were added to the Emerald City in almost every book until Ozma's court had reached unmanageable proportions and some drastic pruning was necessary. Similarly, Oz and the countries surrounding it became littered with small kingdoms, towns, villages, and magical places. Of course, to generate new stories it was necessary to create new characters and places, but Baum's careful distinction between the safe, known areas of Oz and the wild, unknown areas was obscured; the newly created places invaded all parts of Oz, also obscuring one of the correspondences between the development of his fairyland and that of America.

2. Many more characters from the real world were introduced into the stories. Baum himself overused the plot of an American child's journeys to and from Oz, but except for the special circumstances in *Tik-Tok of Oz* and *The Scarecrow of Oz*,[9] he dispensed with it after *The Emerald City*. He had cut Oz off from the real world, and the American characters who enter Oz after that do not have the option of returning home. Whatever Baum's reasons for removing Oz from to-and-fro contact with the outside world, he remained consistent about it, which made Oz more of a paradise or heaven-like place, safe from all the troubles of the real world. This structure, which Baum had built up during the second half of his series, was discarded in the stories published after his death. All the later authors made Oz more easily reached by outsiders. Oz stopped being the wished-for place over the horizon, always a little farther off, and became a fairly attainable destination that American children visited on rainy days and summer vacations. It also became easier to reach Oz from the countries surrounding it, and a common plot of the later books is the attempt to conquer Oz; the Nome King was revived as a villain and attempts the feat several times.

3. Oz lost much of its American ambience. This is perhaps the most problematic change that the later authors made to Baum's Otherworld. Baum used traditional fairy-tale themes in his stories, but he fil-

236

tered them through his unique imagination to fit the American character of his stories. He used the *themes,* not the original outward manifestations of those themes. The Tin Woodman is an odd image of "a fairy prince."[10] He is an American product built of scraps of tin, with a kind heart and a great sense of justice that make him a prince among men. He is not a knight in shining armor, but he is made of armor, and his protection of the weak and helpless makes him the equal of any traditional knight. However, the later Oz books employed almost every cliché of the European-style adventure and fantasy story. Oz and the area surrounding it became filled with new places such as small Germanic duchies, Gypsy camps, Arabian Nights realms, and oriental kingdoms, with the attendant royal families, medieval knights, princesses in distress, bandits, and pirates.

These changes were probably inevitable given the circumstances: continuing another author's work *is* an impossible situation for a writer, and Baum's transforming vision, which could look at America and see it in terms of wonder and fantasy, was unique to him. To expect the first and primary author who continued the series, Ruth Plumly Thompson, to have intuitively grasped the direction in which Baum's world would have been developed and to have slavishly imitated his style is to ask *her* "to carry a heavier burden than [s]he ought to carry." Thompson was a talented and creative author in her own right, with her own unique brand of fantasy. Had she been less original and more of an imitator, the series probably would not have remained vital for as long as it did. She was particularly gifted in creating funny and lovable characters, and it is in the characters—Baum's original ones and her new creations—that the Oz ambience came to reside.

The sense of place, however, became less pronounced as the series progressed, possibly because that was the area where Baum's genius was the strongest. He created Oz and the imaginative world in which it is located, and the fantasy world of Thompson and the other authors could be successful only because of the base that Baum provided. The farther away from Baum the later books got, the weaker they became in the sense of place. The point is that unless, as Wagenknecht advises, we "distin-

237

guish carefully between his work and the work of his successors," Baum's
Other-world loses its whole structure and coherence; the countries outside Oz lose their unique histories and significance, and they and Oz
become indistinguishable from scores of other conventional fantasy/ad-
venture settings.

Reilly & Lee's attempt to revive the series in 1963 was not successful, but
even after the firm discontinued the series for good, Oz continued to live
on. In 1957 a schoolboy, Justin Schiller, began an Oz fan club. There had
been many such clubs in the past, but Schiller's club attracted several Oz
enthusiasts who were also artists, writers, and scholars. Today, the International Wizard of Oz Club has more than two thousand members from
all parts of the world, and the club journal, the *Baum Bugle,* has grown
into a beautifully produced magazine that is a unique blend of articles that
appeal to children, collectors, and scholars. The club also has a special
publications program, which has published many books important for the
study of Baum, including the first book publication of his *Animal Fairy
Tales* and the *Bibliographia Oziana,* a bibliography of the Oz books and
related items. The club has also continued the Oz series, luring Ruth
Plumly Thompson back to Oz with *Yankee in Oz* in 1972 and *The Enchanted Island of Oz* in 1976. Thompson died in 1976, and in 1980 the
club published a second book by Eloise Jarvis McGraw and Lauren Lynn
McGraw, *The Forbidden Fountain of Oz.* In 1986 appeared *The Ozmapolitan of Oz* by Dick Martin, the artist who illustrated the last Oz book
published by Reilly & Lee. And the latest book in the club's series—but
certainly not the last—is *The Wicked Witch of Oz* (1993), a long completed
but previously unpublished story by "official" Oz author Rachel R. Cosgrove (Rachel Cosgrove Payes). In addition, Books of Wonder, a children's book store in New York City, is publishing a series of reprints and
facsimiles of books by Baum and other Oz authors. In 1995 it published
John R. Neill's fourth Oz book, *The Runaway in Oz,* which had been
completed before Neill's death but not illustrated. (Both this book and

The Wicked Witch of Oz are beautifully illustrated by Eric Shanower.) There seems to be no end in sight to the demand for "more about Oz."

Reilly & Lee, the International Wizard of Oz Club, and Books of Wonder are not the only organizations to continue the Oz series. One aspect of the phenomenon of the continued "life" of Oz has not yet been mentioned. After Baum died, his readers also began writing their own Oz stories. After all, the children were Baum's publicly acknowledged collaborators; he commented on this in his prefaces, mentioning when a child's idea had given him the basis for a plot and encouraging his readers to send him their ideas, however fantastic. Baum credited the great inventions of his day to imagination; he hoped that imagination would create adults who would be able to use those new inventions more wisely than his own generation; and he firmly believed that fairy tales helped imagination to develop in children. He probably would have had mixed feelings about his publisher's original decision to continue the Oz series with other authors,[11] but he would have wholeheartedly approved of the stories by his former "collaborators" because those stories were concrete examples of the exercise of their imaginations.

The first public manifestation of this trend among his readers appeared in 1926 when the magazine *Child's Garden for Cheerful and Happy Homes* published a twelve-part story, "Invisible Inzi of Oz" by Robert (nine years old) and Virginia (thirteen) Wauchope.[12] Maud Baum allowed the publication of this story, but Oz was copyrighted so there is little further public evidence until after several of the Oz books had entered the public domain and Reilly & Lee had discontinued the series. Then more Oz books began to be published privately in formats ranging from photocopies of typewritten pages with crude illustrations to beautifully produced books with color plates.[13] It is probably not an exaggerated estimate to say that the number of unofficial Oz books greatly exceeds the number of official ones. In recognition of this phenomenon, the International Wizard of Oz Club in 1971 established a separate yearly magazine, *Oziana,* that is devoted to publishing short stories by Baum's readers. Books of Wonder has a separate imprint, Emerald City Press, to publish new Oz books by various authors. The books and stories that have achieved some sort of public presentation are, however, only a small portion of those that have been written, and it is probably fair to say that a large number of American children have gotten their first experience of creative writing by trying to construct a new Oz adventure.

The Oz phenomenon can be bewildering to critics and other adults who were not exposed to Baum's stories as children. They recognize his virtues, and they see quite clearly his faults as a writer, but they sometimes miss the magic of his Other-world. That is understandable because in one sense all children's literature is beyond adult criticism, since it is written for a group of readers with perceptions and interests that are totally different from those of adults. Baum, much more than the British writer Lewis Carroll, with whom he is sometimes compared, wrote unashamedly for children, and ideally, he should first be encountered by children.

No matter what adult criteria and literary theories are applied to books for children, the simple fact remains that the "best" children's books are those that the children love the best, because most often they are the better judges of which stories open their eyes, minds, and imaginations and impel them on to new and more complex experiences. In a very popular nineteenth-century novel that Baum most likely read, Edward Bulwer-Lytton's *The Caxtons,* a wife mentions to her scholar-husband her concerns about their child being fonder of fairy tales than of more "improving" stories; he answers, "All that wakes curiosity is wisdom, if innocent—all that pleases the fancy now, turns hereafter to love or to knowledge. And so, my dear, go back to the nursery."[14] Baum believed that childhood was the most important time in any person's life[15]—that truly "the child is the father of the man."

There is ample evidence that L. Frank Baum and his immortal fantasy world have succeeded in waking curiosity, love, and knowledge in countless American children—succeeded as no other American writer of fairy tales has. Edward Wagenknecht has described the impact Baum had on his life:

> *"The Wizard of Oz" opened up to me the whole wonderful, inexhaustible world of literature. . . . [Baum] was preparing me to explore the worlds of other, greater, more difficult writers later on—Dickens and Scott and Shakespeare and Chaucer and Spenser. . . . Perhaps I should never have loved any of them so well if I had not had Baum to show me the way.*
>
> *Yet he showed me more than that. He showed me what I wanted to do. For it was when I read "The Wizard of Oz," . . . when I was six years old, that I made up my mind that I too would be a writer of books.*[16]

And the magic has been in no way restricted to Baum's masterpiece, *The Wonderful Wizard of Oz*. Gore Vidal began with one of the others in the series:

> *Like most Americans my age (with access to books), I spent a good deal of my youth in Baum's Land of Oz. I have a precise, tactile memory of the first Oz book that came into my hands. It was the original 1910 edition of* The Emerald City. *I still remember the look and the feel of those dark blue covers, the evocative smell of dust and old ink. I also remember that I could not stop reading and rereading the book. But "reading" is not the right word. In some mysterious way, I was translating myself to Oz, a place which I was to inhabit for many years while, simultaneously, visiting other fictional worlds as well as maintaining my cover in that dangerous one known as "real." With* The Emerald City, *I became addicted to reading.*[17]

Other writers and scholars, too, have recorded their debts to Baum, and even a partial listing of them is impressive: Anthony Boucher, Martin

Gardner, Shirley Jackson, Philip Wylie, Russel B. Nye, Ray Bradbury, James Thurber, C. Warren Hollister, and C. Beecher Hogan. These writers and scholars, like the "published" unofficial Oz stories, are only the most visible segment of the masses who have loved and been influenced by Baum's stories. There is, of course, no way to estimate the effect of Baum's Other-world on those readers who first had their imaginations exercised by his stories, but who went into less public professions.

It is recorded in the biography of Baum that when he was a boy, "much of his time was spent alone in some favored spot in the house or a corner of the yard, where he kept happy for hours with the fey playmates his imagination created."[18] His enchanted childhood at Rose Lawn opened his eyes and imagination to the natural wonders of the world. When he grew up, that sense of wonder remained, and he created out of the raw materials of his native country a marvelous Other-world into which he invited the children of America. They have accepted the invitation in large numbers, and they have found that world to be an enchanted place. When they return home, they are changed. Suddenly, all around them they see beauty and magic and wonder where they never saw it before: the prairie becomes an enchanted landscape; the forests are peopled with fairies; the clouds are great cities in the sky; and the hard, brilliant sunshine of America makes raindrops on leaves sparkle like emeralds. The children are greatly surprised because when they look to the east at the distant, blue slopes of the Appalachians; to the north at the purple shadows of the dense forests; to the west at the flat sea of yellow grain; and to the south at the rich, red soil, they suddenly realize that they never really left home at all. Oz has always been there all around them. L. Frank Baum only raised the veil that had covered their eyes and their imaginations.

Appendix A

Baum's Description of Oz, 1910

THE EMERALD CITY IS BUILT ALL OF BEAUTIFUL MARBLES in which are set a profusion of emeralds, every one exquisitely cut and of very great size. There are other jewels used in the decorations inside the houses and palaces, such as rubies, diamonds, sapphires, amethysts and turquoises. But in the streets and upon the outside of the buildings only emeralds appear, from which circumstance the place is named the Emerald City of Oz. It has nine thousand, six hundred and fifty-four buildings, in which lived fifty-seven thousand three hundred and eighteen people, up to the time my story opens.

All the surrounding country, extending to the borders of the desert which enclosed it upon every side, was full of pretty and comfortable farmhouses, in which resided those inhabitants of Oz who preferred country to city life.

Altogether there were more than half a million people in the Land of Oz—although some of them . . . were not made of flesh and blood as we are—and every inhabitant of the favored country was happy and prosperous.

No disease of any sort was ever known among the Ozites, and so no one ever died unless he met with an accident that prevented him from living. This happened very seldom, indeed. There were no poor people in the Land of Oz, because there was no such thing as money, and all property of every sort belonged to the Ruler. The people were her children, and she cared for them. Each person was given freely by his neighbors whatever he required for his use, which is as much as any one may reasonably desire. Some tilled the lands and raised great crops of grain, which was divided equally among the entire population, so that all had enough. There were many tailors and dressmakers and shoemakers and the like, who made things that any who desired them might wear. Likewise there were jewelers who made ornaments for the person, which pleased and beautified the people, and these ornaments also were free to those who asked for them. Each man and woman, no matter what he or she produced for the good of the community, was supplied by the neighbors with food and clothing and a house and furniture and ornaments and games. If by chance the supply ever ran short, more was taken from the great storehouses of the Ruler, which were afterward filled up again when there were more of any article than the people needed.

Every one worked half the time and played half the time, and the people enjoyed the work as much as they did the play, because it is good to be occupied and to have something to do. There were no cruel overseers set to watch them, and no one to rebuke them or to find fault with them. So each one was proud to do all he could for his friends and neighbors, and was glad when they would accept the things he produced.

You will know, by what I have here told you, that the Land of Oz was a remarkable country. I do not suppose such an arrangement would be practical with us, but Dorothy assures me that it works finely with the Oz people.

Oz being a fairy country, the people were, of course, fairy people; but that does not mean that all of them were very unlike the people of our own world. There were all sorts of queer characters among them, but not a single one who was evil, or who possessed a selfish or violent nature. They were peaceful, kind-hearted, loving and merry, and every inhabitant adored the beautiful girl who ruled them, and delighted to obey her every command.

In spite of all I have said in a general way, there were some parts of the Land of Oz not quite so pleasant as the farming country and the Emerald City which was its center. Far away in the South Country there lived in the mountains a band of strange people called Hammer-

Heads. . . . [They] never harmed any but those who disturbed them in the mountains where they lived.

In some of the dense forests there lived great beasts of every sort; yet these were for the most part harmless and even sociable, and conversed agreeably with those who visited their haunts. . . .

Not so tame were the Fighting Trees, which had a forest of their own. If any one approached them these curious trees would bend down their branches, twine them around the intruders, and hurl them away.

But these unpleasant things existed only in a few remote parts of the Land of Oz. I suppose every country has some drawbacks, so even this almost perfect fairyland could not be quite perfect. Once there had been wicked witches in the land, too; but now these had all been destroyed; so, as I said, only peace and happiness reigned in Oz.

For some time Ozma has ruled over this fair country, and never was Ruler more popular or beloved. She is said to be the most beautiful girl the world has ever known, and her heart and mind as lovely as her person.

L. Frank Baum, *The Emerald City of Oz,* illustrated by John R. Neill (Chicago: Reilly & Britton, 1910), 29–33.

Appendix B

Baum's Description of Oz, 1918

OZ WAS NOT ALWAYS A FAIRYLAND, I AM TOLD. Once it was much like other lands, except it was shut in by a dreadful desert of sandy wastes that lay all around it, thus preventing its people from all contact with the rest of the world. Seeing this isolation, the fairy band of Queen Lurline, passing over Oz while on a journey, enchanted the country and so made it a Fairyland. And Queen Lurline left one of her fairies to rule this enchanted Land of Oz, and then passed on and forgot all about it.

From that moment no one in Oz ever died. Those who were old remained old; those who were young and strong did not change as years passed them by; the children remained children always, and played and romped to their hearts' content, while all the babies lived in their cradles and were tenderly cared for and never grew up. So people in Oz stopped counting how old they were in years, for years made no difference in their appearance and could not alter their station. They did not get sick, so there were no doctors among them. Accidents might happen to some, on rare occasions, it is true, and while no one could die naturally, as other people do, it was possible that one might be totally destroyed. Such incidents, however, were very unusual, and so seldom was there anything to worry over that the Oz people were as happy and contented as can be.

Another strange thing about this fairy Land of Oz was that whoever managed to enter it from the outside world came under the magic spell of the place and did not change in appearance as long as they lived there. So Dorothy, who now lived with Ozma, seemed just the same sweet little girl she had been when first she came to this delightful fairyland.

246

Perhaps all parts of Oz might not be called truly delightful, but it was surely delightful in the neighborhood of the Emerald City, where Ozma reigned. Her loving influence was felt for many miles around, but there were places in the mountains of the Gillikin Country, and the forests of the Quadling Country, and perhaps in far-away parts of the Munchkin and Winkie Countries, where the inhabitants were somewhat rude and uncivilized and had not yet come under the spell of Ozma's wise and kindly rule. Also, when Oz first became a fairyland, it harbored several witches and magicians and sorcerers and necromancers, who were scattered in various parts, but most of these had been deprived of their magic powers, and Ozma had issued a royal edict forbidding anyone in her dominions to work magic except Glinda the Good and the Wizard of Oz. Ozma herself, being a real fairy, knew a lot of magic, but she only used it to benefit her subjects.

L. Frank Baum, *The Tin Woodman of Oz*, illustrated by John R. Neill (Chicago: Reilly & Britton, 1918), 156–58.

Notes

Prologue:
AMERICAN ARCADIA

1. Humphrey Carpenter, *Secret Gardens: A Study of the Golden Age of Children's Literature* (London: George Allen & Unwin, 1985).

2. Brian Attebery, *The Fantasy Tradition in American Literature: From Irving to Le Guin* (Bloomington: Indiana University Press, 1980), 82.

3. J. R. R. Tolkien, "On Fairy-Stories," in *Tree and Leaf* (Boston: Houghton Mifflin, 1965), 10, 40.

4. Ibid., 41.

5. C. Warren Hollister, "Oz and the Fifth Criterion," *Baum Bugle* 15 (Christmas 1971): 7–8.

6. Carpenter, *Secret Gardens,* 13.

7. George MacDonald, "The Fantastic Imagination," in *The Gifts of the Child Christ: Fairytales and Stories for the Childlike,* edited by Glenn Edward Sadler (Grand Rapids, Mich.: Eerdmans, 1973), 1: 23–24.

8. Tolkien, "Fairy Stories," 26.

9. Carpenter, *Secret Gardens,* 16.

10. Tolkien, "Fairy Stories," 69–70.

11. Christopher Morley, preface to *The Complete Sherlock Holmes,* by Sir Arthur Conan Doyle (Garden City, N.Y.: Doubleday, 1930), 5–6.

12. Attebery, *Fantasy Tradition,* 153.

13. Carpenter, *Secret Gardens,* 16.

14. L. Frank Baum, *The Lost Princess of Oz,* illustrated by John R. Neill (Chicago: Reilly & Britton, 1917), [13].

15. Raylyn Moore, *Wonderful Wizard, Marvelous Land* (Bowling Green, Ohio: Bowling Green University Popular Press, 1974). Moore does a very good job of showing how Baum's ideals and philosophy were relevant to the generation of the 1960s, but I cannot agree totally with her interpretation of Baum's character and motives.

16. Martin Gardner, introduction to *The Surprising Adventures of The Magical Monarch of Mo and His People,* by L. Frank Baum, with pictures by Frank Ver Beck [*sic*] (New York: Dover, 1968), vii.

Chapter 1:
CHARMED YOUTH AND YEARS OF STRUGGLE

1. Frank Joslyn Baum and Russell P. MacFall, *To Please a Child: A Biography of L. Frank Baum, Royal Historian of Oz* (Chicago: Reilly & Lee, 1961), 20. During the forty years of its existence (1957–present), the *Baum Bugle,* a journal devoted to Baum and Oz, has published a multitude of articles dealing with almost every aspect of Baum's life, and there have been numerous articles in other magazines (see Bibliography); but one of the best single works about him remains this biography by his son and Russell MacFall. In the main, my survey follows the facts as given in *To Please a Child,* with additions and corrections from other sources. The interpretation of and weight given to these facts, as well as any conclusions and speculations, are my own and come from my lifelong study of Baum. Only a broad outline of Baum's life is necessary for this study, and while Michael Patrick Hearn is presently working on a new biography that should be definitive, the outline of Baum's life should remain basically the same.

2. Baum and MacFall, *To Please a Child,* 18.

3. Ibid., 20.

4. Ibid., 21.

5. Ibid., 20.

6. L. Frank Baum, *Dot and Tot of Merryland*, pictures by W. W. Denslow (Chicago: Hill, 1901), 16.

7. Baum and MacFall, *To Please a Child*, 20.

8. Michael Patrick Hearn, "L. Frank Baum: Chicken Fancier," *Baum Bugle* 30 (Autumn 1986): 23.

9. Ibid.

10. Clara M. Houck, "Journey to Oz," *Baum Bugle* 26 (Autumn 1982): 15.

11. A copy of *The Rose Lawn Home Journal* is reproduced in *Baum Bugle* 30 (Spring 1986): 13–16.

12. Michael Patrick Hearn, "L. Frank Baum: Amateur Printer," *Baum Bugle* 30 (Spring 1986): 17.

13. Baum and MacFall, *To Please a Child*, 29.

14. Ibid., 30–32.

15. Ibid., 32.

16. Ibid.

17. Ibid., 33.

18. Ibid.

19. Ibid., 34.

20. Ibid., 35.

21. Ibid., 45.

22. Quoted in Matilda J. Gage, "The Dakota Days of L. Frank Baum: Part I," *Baum Bugle* 10 (Spring 1966): 5.

23. Baum and MacFall, *To Please a Child*, 46, 52.

24. Ibid., 53–54.

25. Ibid., 54. Another parallel to the fictional Ambersons is that George Amberson Minafer is forced to take a job in a chemical company to support what was left of his once magnificent family (Booth Tarkington, *The Magnificent Ambersons*, illustrated by Arthur William Brown [Garden City, N.Y.: Doubleday, Page, 1918], 485).

26. Baum and MacFall, *To Please a Child*, 55.

27. Ibid., 55–56.

28. Ibid., 57.

29. Edith Van Dyne [L. Frank Baum], *Aunt Jane's Nieces and Uncle John* (Chicago: Reilly & Britton, 1911), 169–70.

30. Baum and MacFall, *To Please a Child*, 57–58.

31. Gage, "Dakota Days: Part I," 5.

32. Matilda J. Gage, "The Dakota Days of L. Frank Baum: Part II," *Baum Bugle* 10 (Autumn 1966): 8.

33. Ibid.

34. Ibid., 9. It is interesting that Baum saw a connection between Edward Bulwer-Lytton and H. Rider Haggard, since it was later demonstrated that Bulwer-Lytton was an influence on and a source for Haggard (Herman Styles Ficke, "The Source of Rider Haggard's *She*," *Texas Studies in English* [1926]: 178–80). For a more recent discussion of the connection between the two authors, see Norman Etherington, introduction to *The Annotated She: A Critical Edition of H. Rider Haggard's Victorian Romance* (Bloomington: Indiana University Press, 1991), xxiv–xxv.

35. Gage, "Dakota Days, Part II," 9.

36. Quoted in Baum and MacFall, *To Please a Child*, 69–73.

37. Matilda J. Gage, "The Dakota Days of L. Frank Baum: Part III," *Baum Bugle* 10 (Christmas 1966): 11.

38. Baum and MacFall, *To Please a Child*, 78–79.

39. Ibid., 80.

40. Ibid., 86.

Chapter 2:
THE DISCOVERY OF THE OTHER-WORLD

1. L. Frank Baum, "Yesterday at the Exposition," *Chicago Sunday Times-Herald*, 2 February 1896, 34, reprinted in *Baum Bugle* 20 (Autumn 1976): 16–17.

2. Peter E. Hanff, introduction to *By the Candelabra's Glare (1898)*, by L. Frank Baum (Delmar, N.Y.: Scholars' Facsimiles & Reprints, 1981), v.

3. Ibid., vii. Hanff stated that *Adventures in Phunniland* was the copyrighted title. Martin Gardner wrote that Baum "originally called it *The King of Phunnyland*" (introduction to *The Surprising Adventures of The Magical Monarch of Mo and His People*, by L. Frank Baum [New York: Dover, 1968], vi). *The King of Phunnyland* probably was the title chosen after the book had been accepted for publication.

4. Frank Joslyn Baum and Russell P. MacFall, *To Please a Child: A Biography of L. Frank Baum, Royal Historian of Oz* (Chicago: Reilly & Lee, 1961), 87.

5. Ibid., 88. For a good, brief description of that era, with emphasis on Way & Williams, see Hanff, introduction to *By the Candelabra's Glare*, v–vi.

6. Baum and MacFall, *To Please a Child*, 93.

7. Quoted in ibid., 92.

8. According to Baum and MacFall, "Baum continued to publish *The Show Window* until 1902, when it was sold to Nickerson and Clark, publishers of another trade journal. In their hands it became *The Merchant's Record and Show Window*. It was finally absorbed into the *Display World*, which is still [1961] published in Cincinnati" (ibid., 96).

9. Gardner, in his introduction to *The Magical Monarch of Mo*, quoted an inscription in the copy of *A New Wonderland* that Baum gave to the wife of his son Robert. It explained part of the publishing history of the book:

This book was received by me on October 8th, 1900, although the date of publication was announced for September 20th. Mr. Russell [the New York publisher] tells me he has printed ten thousand as a first edition. . . . It was the first children's book I ever wrote—written in 1896—but it was not offered for publication until after *Mother Goose in Prose* appeared. Then Way & Williams accepted it; but failed (1898) the year it was to be published, and the MS was transferred to H. S. Stone & Co., who agreed to bring it out the fall of 1898, but let it drag until too late to secure a proper illustrator. I then took the MS away from them and in the summer of '99 sent it to Russell. He accepted it too late for publication that year, so it was not issued until now. . . . The boys heard most of these stories before I wrote them down. (vi)

10. L. Frank Baum, *The Surprising Adventures of the Magical Monarch of Mo and His People*, with Pictures by Frank Verbeck (Indianapolis: Bobbs-Merrill, 1903). The book's spine title, front-cover title, and page headings were shortened to *The Magical Monarch of Mo*. The pagination of the text of the 1968 Dover reprint is the same as that of the first edition.

11. Baum, *Magical Monarch of Mo*. Because the information in the discussion of this book—and the following books by Baum—is often drawn from various points in the book, note numbers will sometimes be given only at the end of a paragraph and all sources for facts in that paragraph included in one note. In *Magical Monarch*, Baum referred to the stories as "Surprises" (indicated by "S" in the notes) rather than "chapters": king escapes (S. 4); donkey (S. 4); cast-iron man (S. 6); wicked wizard (S. 9); a prince (S. 11); naughty dragon (S. 14).

12. Gardner, introduction to *Magical Monarch of Mo*, ix.

13. Ibid., x.

14. Daniel G. Hoffman, *Paul Bunyan: Last of the Frontier Demigods* (Philadelphia: University of Pennsylvania Press for Temple University Publications, 1952), 17.

15. Ibid.

16. Ibid., 16.

17. Baum, *Magical Monarch of Mo:* telephone (S. 4, 49); electric lights (S. 7, 94); bicycle (S. 11, 164); chewing gum (S. 9, 128).

18. Ibid.: king's head (S. 2); dog (S. 3); lion (S. 7); prince (S. 8).

19. Ibid.: "are . . . beautiful" (S. 1, 7); "no . . . live" (S. 8, 113); "wild . . . world" (S. 8, 118).

20. Ibid.: taffy (S. 3, 30); "jackson-balls and gum-drops" (S. 3, 30); jelly (S. 3, 32); chocolate (S. 11, 161); "a rough . . . candy" (S. 8, 109); "composed . . . maple sugar" (S. 11, 165); milk (S. 1, 6); root beer (S. 4, 47); maple syrup (S. 11, 165); fruit cake (S. 4, 47); cheese (S. 1, 6); "candied . . . lake" (S. 5, 58); "pond . . . cream" (S. 12, 199).

21. Ibid.: "All . . . bushes" (S. 1, 7); caramels (S. 2, 11); cream puffs (S. 5, 54); plum puddings (S. 13, 205); everything . . . grows on trees (S. 1, 6); medicine tree (S. 4, 50).

22. Ibid.: night and rays (S. 1, 6); snow (S. 7, 86–87); rain . . . Tannhäuser (S. 1, 7).

23. Ibid.: wilder region (S. 7); giant couple (S. 11); desert (S. 3, 31); "whose . . . bars" (S. 6, 69); sea (S. 6, 77).

24. L. Frank Baum, *A New Wonderland*, pictures by Frank Verbeck (New York: Russell, 1900), 3.

25. Baum, *Magical Monarch of Mo:* Alaska or South America (S. 11, 173); yellow hen (S. 13, 223).

26. Ibid.: "there is . . . Mo" (S. 8, 109); Purple Dragon (Ss. 2, 4, 13, 14); Gigaboo (S. 8); King Scowleyow (S. 6, 69); more dangerous threat (S. 1, 7–8) ["the King can not die; therefore a prince is a prince to the end of his days and his days never end"]; two stories: "The Peculiar Pains of Fruit Cake Island" (S. 4); "Prince Fiddlecumdoo and the Giant" (S. 11).

27. In his introduction to *By the Candelabra's Glare,* Hanff describes the first edition of *Mother Goose in Prose:*

The book contained fourteen inserted black-and-white drawings in Parrish's most elaborate style. The cover design included an illustration printed in full color and was printed on both front and back covers of the book. The spine was stamped in gold. In keeping with the significance of the project, Way and Williams issued twenty-seven sets of proofs of Parrish's drawings, each signed in pencil by the artist and with a limitation leaf signed by L. Frank Baum. The proof prints were printed on Japan vellum and were contained in portfolios consisting of cloth hinges and wood-veneer panels. (viii)

28. L. Frank Baum, *Mother Goose in Prose,* illustrated by Maxfield Parrish (New York: Bounty Books, 1986), 10, 15.

29. Baum and MacFall, *To Please a Child,* 90.

30. Ibid., 98.

31. L. Frank Baum, *By the Candelabra's Glare (1898),* with an Introduction by Peter E. Hanff (Delmar, N.Y.: Scholars' Facsimiles & Reprints, 1981), [xxvii].

32. Baum and MacFall, *To Please a Child,* 87.

33. Ibid., 100–101.

34. Ibid., 101.

35. Douglas G. Greene and Michael Patrick Hearn, *W. W. Denslow,* with an introduction by Patricia Denslow Eykyn (Mt. Pleasant: Clarke Historical Library, Central Michigan University, 1976), 83–85.

36. L. Frank Baum, introduction to *Father Goose: His Book,* pictures by William W. Denslow (Chicago: Hill, 1899).

37. In *Meet Me in St. Louis* (1942; reprint, New

York: Bantam Books, 1958), Sally Benson's nostalgic look back at life in St. Louis in 1903 and 1904, one of the most popular of the rhymes, "Did You Ever See a Rabbit Climb a Tree?" was one of the references used to evoke the period. The reference was retained in the 1944 MGM film adaptation, also titled *Meet Me in St. Louis*.

38. Baum and MacFall, *To Please a Child*, 113–14.

39. David L. Greene and Peter E. Hanff discuss all seven titles considered for the book in "Baum and Denslow: Their Books, Part One," *Baum Bugle* 19 (Spring 1975): 7–11. Those titles were *The City of Oz*, *The City of the Great Oz*, *The Emerald City*, *From Kansas to Fairyland*, *The Fairyland of Oz*, *The Land of Oz*, and *The Wonderful Wizard of Oz*. See also "The Original Title Page for The Wonderful Wizard of Oz," *Baum Bugle* 16 (Autumn 1972): 3 and front cover.

40. Greene and Hearn, *Denslow*, 90–91.

41. There exists an advertisement from Baum's time in Aberdeen that reads: "Baum, The Printer of Aberdeen, Solicits your Job Printing" (reprinted in Matilda J. Gage, "The Dakota Days of L. Frank Baum: Part III," *Baum Bugle* 10 [Christmas 1966]: 11).

42. Until recently, only in the rare first edition of *The Wonderful Wizard of Oz* could the design be seen exactly as Denslow and Baum conceived it, but in 1987 an excellent facsimile was published by Books of Wonder and Morrow.

43. Greene and Hearn, *Denslow*, 92–93. I am indebted to Greene and Hearn's discussion of the design of *The Wizard* and would refer the reader to their more detailed description.

44. Baum and MacFall, *To Please a Child*, 121.

45. Ibid., 123.

46. It is possible that while writing *The Wizard*, Baum actually intended the name Oz to refer only to the Wizard himself and not to the country, but the title finally chosen for the book and the final version of the text gave the name a larger reference (Jay Delkin, "The Meaning of 'Oz,'" *Baum Bugle* 15 [Autumn 1971]: 18–20).

47. Two of the titles considered contained the word "fairyland," but both were considered after the text was completed and were quickly discarded (Greene and Hanff, "Baum and Denslow," 11). At this point, Baum obviously did not want to link his new country to the traditional European idea of fairyland.

48. L. Frank Baum, *The Wonderful Wizard of Oz*, with Pictures by W. W. Denslow (Chicago: Hill, 1900), chap. 2, 24. My references are to the first edition, but there have been so many editions of this book that the chapter number will also be given for ease of reference.

49. Ibid.: "cut . . . world" (chap. 2, 24); deserts (chap. 2, 26); farther from Kansas (chap. 15, 186); overnight (chap. 1, 16–19); two days (chap. 15, 187).

50. Ibid., chap. 2, 23–26.

51. Ibid.: people (chap. 2, 20); houses (chap. 3, 33–34); wealth (chap. 3, 34); money (chap. 11, 122) ["At one place a man was selling green lemonade, and when the children bought it Dorothy could see that they paid for it with green pennies"]; man-made objects (chap. 3, 34) ["All [houses] were painted blue, for in this country of the East blue was the favorite color. . . . she came to a house rather larger than the rest. On the green lawn before it . . . "], (chap. 22, 248) ["The Quadlings . . . were dressed all in red, which showed bright against the green grass and the yellowing grain"].

52. Ibid., chap. 15, 187.

53. Ibid.: Gayelette and Quelala (chap. 14, 172–74); Wizard's history (chap. 15, 187); war (chap. 12, 146); Golden Cap returned to monkeys (chap. 23, 256).

54. Martin Gardner and Russel B. Nye, *The Wizard of Oz and Who He Was* (East Lansing: Michigan State University Press, 1957), 197.

55. Baum, *Wonderful Wizard of Oz*, chap. 2, 20.

56. Hezekiah Butterworth, *Zigzag Journeys in the White City with Visits to the Neighboring Metropolis* (Boston: Estes Lauriat, 1894), 90–92.

57. Ibid., 95.

58. Ibid., 125 [with a photograph of the Midway and the captive balloon].

59. Baum, *Wonderful Wizard of Oz,* chap. 16, 199.

60. For a good discussion of some of the films and books inspired by *The Wonderful Wizard of Oz,* see Allen Eyles, *The World of Oz* (Tucson: HPBooks, 1985), 73–91.

61. Baum wrote to his brother on April 8, 1900: "I only need one hit this year to make my position secure, and three of these books seem fitted for public approval. But there—who knows anything!" (quoted in Baum and MacFall, *To Please a Child,* 118–19). The books for 1900 were *The Songs of Father Goose, The Army Alphabet, The Navy Alphabet, The Wonderful Wizard of Oz, The Art of Decorating Dry Goods Windows and Interiors,* and *A New Wonderland.*

Chapter 3:
EXPLORATION OF THE OTHER-WORLD

1. Douglas G. Greene and Michael Patrick Hearn, *W. W. Denslow,* with an introduction by Patricia Denslow Eykyn (Mt. Pleasant: Clarke Historical Library, Central Michigan University, 1976), 102.

2. Ibid., 103.

3. Frank Joslyn Baum and Russell P. MacFall, *To Please a Child: A Biography of L. Frank Baum, Royal Historian of Oz* (Chicago: Reilly & Lee, 1961), 98.

4. Greene and Hearn, *Denslow,* 96.

5. Baum and MacFall, *To Please a Child,* 106–7.

6. L. Frank Baum, *Dot and Tot of Merryland,* pictures by W. W. Denslow (Chicago: Hill, 1901), 48, 224.

7. Ibid., 43.

8. Ibid., chaps. 6, 7.

9. Ibid., chap. 8.

10. Ibid., chap. 9.

11. Ibid., chaps. 10–14.

12. Ibid., 112.

13. Ibid., 113. The queen's "thinking machine" is an early example of Baum's use of magical mechanical devices (that is, machines run by magic rather than electrical power).

14. Ibid., 218.

15. Baum and MacFall, *To Please a Child,* 171.

16. Scott Olsen, "The Coronado Fairyland," *Baum Bugle* 20 (Winter 1976): 2.

17. Baum, *Dot and Tot of Merryland,* 125–26.

18. L. Frank Baum, "Modern Fairy Tales," *Advance,* 19 August 1909, reprinted in *Baum Bugle* 9 (Christmas 1965): 4.

19. J. R. R. Tolkien, "On Fairy-Stories," in *Tree and Leaf* (Boston: Houghton Mifflin, 1965), 5–6, 8.

20. Baum, *Dot and Tot of Merryland,* chap. 15.

21. Ibid., chaps. 16, 17.

22. Ibid., chap. 18.

23. Douglas G. Greene, "The Periodical Baum: An Annotated Checklist," *Baum Bugle* 19 (Autumn 1975): 5–6.

24. Peter E. Hanff, introduction to *By the Candelabra's Glare (1898),* by L. Frank Baum (Delmar, N.Y.: Scholars' Facsimiles & Reprints, 1981), xii–xiii.

25. Baum and MacFall, *To Please a Child,* 159.

26. L. Frank Baum, *American Fairy Tales* (Chicago: Hill, 1901). Because the pages of the first edition were not numbered, I have used a facsimile edition with added page numbers: L. Frank Baum, *American Fairy Tales,* illustrated

by N. P. Hall, Harry Kennedy, Ike Morgan, and Ralph Fletcher Seymour, with a new introduction by Martin Gardner (New York: Dover, 1978), 17.

27. L. Frank Baum, introduction to *Father Goose's Year Book: Quaint Quacks and Feathered Shafts for Mature Children*, illustrated by Walter J. Enright (Chicago: Reilly & Britton, 1907).

28. Baum, *American Fairy Tales*, 51.

29. Ibid., 79, 81.

30. Ibid., 165.

31. Greene, "Periodical Baum," 6.

32. L. Frank Baum, *The Runaway Shadows; or A Trick of Jack Frost's* (Douglasville, Ga.: Pamami Press, 1979), 8, reprinted in *Baum Bugle* 6 (April 1962): 11.

33. L. Frank Baum to Henry Clay Baum, 8 April 1900, in Baum and MacFall, *To Please a Child*, 118-19.

34. Richard Crowder, *Those Innocent Years: The Legacy and Inheritance of a Hero of the Victorian Era, James Whitcomb Riley* (Indianapolis: Bobbs-Merrill, 1957), 113-14.

35. Baum and MacFall, *To Please a Child*, 157.

36. L. Frank Baum, *The Master Key: An Electrical Fairy Tale*, illustrated by F. Y. Cory (Indianapolis: Bowen-Merrill, 1901), 11.

37. Ibid., 242, 243.

38. Ibid., 23.

39. Ibid., 237.

40. Ibid., 243.

41. Michael Patrick Hearn, *The Annotated Wizard of Oz* (New York: Potter, 1973), 371.

42. Baum and MacFall, *To Please a Child*, 171-72.

43. Ibid., 11-12.

44. Ibid., 12, 14-15.

45. Ibid., 12.

46. Quoted in Daniel P. Mannix, "'Off to See the Wizard'—1903: Part Two," *Baum Bugle* 13 (Spring 1969): 7.

47. Daniel P. Mannix, "'Off to See the Wizard'—1903: Part One," *Baum Bugle* 12 (Christmas 1968): 6-7.

48. Quoted in Baum and MacFall, *To Please a Child*, 13-14.

49. Mannix, "'Off to See the Wizard': Part One," 5.

50. Mannix, "'Off to See the Wizard': Part Two," 9.

51. Ibid., 7.

52. Fred Stone, *Rolling Stone* (New York: Whittlesey House, McGraw-Hill, 1945), chap. 11.

53. Baum and MacFall, *To Please a Child*, 138-39.

54. In his introduction to *The Life and Adventures of Santa Claus*, by L. Frank Baum (New York: Dover, 1976), Martin Gardner traces how the American idea of Santa Claus came from writers such as Washington Irving and Clement Clarke Moore and from illustrators such as Thomas Nast.

55. L. Frank Baum, *The Life and Adventures of Santa Claus*, with Pictures by Mary Cowles Clark (Indianapolis: Bowen-Merrill, 1902): Water Sprites . . . Light Elves (179-81); wood nymphs (4); ryls (17-18); knooks (18); Fairies (19).

56. Ibid., 182.

57. Ibid., 185.

58. Ibid., 166.

59. Ibid., 142-43.

60. Ibid., 1-2.

61. Ibid., 113.

62. Ibid., 2.

63. Ibid., 194.

64. Ibid., 5.

65. Ibid., 35.

66. Ibid., 36.

67. Ibid., 95.

68. Ibid., 108.

69. Ibid., 35, 36.

70. Ibid., 117.

71. Baum and MacFall, *To Please a Child*, 173.

72. Eunice Tietjens, *The World at My Shoulder* (New York: Macmillan, 1938), 14–15, quoted in Baum and MacFall, *To Please a Child*, 173–74.

73. L. Frank Baum, *The Enchanted Island of Yew*, illustrated by Fanny Y. Cory (Indianapolis: Bobbs-Merrill, 1903), 5.

74. Ibid., 1.

75. Ibid., 1–3. Baum's concern about "flying-machines" was far-sighted, since the Wright brothers' first flight occurred the year this book was published.

76. "There are instances on record where the Fairies have shown themselves to human beings, and have even conversed with them" (Baum, *Life and Adventures of Santa Claus*, 19).

77. The fairy said, "Mortals can't become fairies, you know—although I believe there was once a mortal [Santa Claus] who was made immortal" (Baum, *Enchanted Island of Yew*, 14).

78. Ibid., 13.

79. Ibid., 242.

80. Hearn, *Annotated Wizard of Oz*, 371.

81. Michael Patrick Hearn, David L. Greene, and Peter E. Hanff, "The Faltering Flight of Prince Silverwings," *Baum Bugle* 18 (Autumn 1974): 4–10. See also L. Frank Baum, *Scenario and General Synopsis of "Prince Silverwings,"* based on the Stories by Edith Ogden Harrison (Douglasville, Ga.: Pamami Press, 1982).

82. Hearn, Greene, and Hanff, "Faltering Flight of Prince Silverwings," 10.

83. L. Frank Baum to Emerson Hough, 15 March 1904, quoted in Olsen, "Coronado Fairyland," 2–3.

84. L. Frank Baum, *Queen Zixi of Ix; or, The Story of the Magic Cloak*, with Illustrations by Frederick Richardson (New York: Century, 1905), 301.

85. Ibid.

86. Baum had not named the Queen of the Fairies in *The Life and Adventures of Santa Claus*, only the Queen of the Wood Nymphs, Queen Zurline. But see Ruth Berman, "Lurline's Source," *Baum Bugle* 26 (Autumn 1982): 2–3. Berman thinks that there was a European source for the fairy queen, the opera *Lurline* (1860) by the Irish composer William Vincent Wallace. She believes that "clearly, Zurline, Lulea, and Lurline [who will be discussed later] are basically the same individual." I would also mention another similar name, the Forest of Lurla mentioned in *The Enchanted Island of Yew*, as one of the other places besides Burzee where fairies live.

87. Quoted in Olsen, "Coronado Fairyland," 2.

Chapter 4:
FURTHER EXPLORATION

1. L. Frank Baum, *The Marvelous Land of Oz*, pictured by John R. Neill (Chicago: Reilly & Britton, 1904), 3.

2. From an advertisement in "Oz Under Scrutiny: Early Reviews of The Marvelous Land of Oz," *Baum Bugle* 23 (Spring 1979): 13.

3. Frank Joslyn Baum and Russell P. MacFall, *To Please a Child: A Biography of L. Frank Baum, Royal Historian of Oz* (Chicago: Reilly & Lee, 1961), 210.

4. Gore Vidal, "The Oz Books," in *United*

States: Essays, 1952–1992 (New York: Random House, 1993), 1108.

5. Baum, *Marvelous Land of Oz*, 283.

6. Ibid., 285.

7. Ibid., 34.

8. Ibid., 121.

9. Ibid.: "mighty Sorceress" (238); "magic . . . Oz" (253).

10. Ibid., 210.

11. Ibid.: "golden . . . stalks" (9); "everything . . . purple" (35); "noticed . . . city" (59); "the houses . . . trees" (236); "upon . . . lawn" (237).

12. Ibid., 68.

13. Ibid.: "it . . . Oz" (35); "the former . . . me" (185–86).

14. L. Frank Baum, *The Wonderful Wizard of Oz*, with pictures by W. W. Denslow (Chicago: Hill, 1900), chap. 2, 27, chap. 15, 189.

15. According to Baum, "The name was so catchy that the same evening my wife told me I should put the Wogglebug in *The Marvelous Land of Oz*. The book was one-third written and Jack Pumpkinhead was the hero, but I brought in the Wogglebug right away. After that H. M. Wogglebug, T. E. was the hero and has become my most popular character" (*Philadelphia North American*, 3 October 1904, quoted in Scott Olsen, "The Coronado Fairyland," *Baum Bugle* 20 [Winter 1976]: 4). It is doubtful that the Wogglebug was ever Baum's "most popular character," and the Wogglebug is certainly *not* the hero of the book. At the time of this interview, however, Baum was already preparing the stage version of *The Marvelous Land of Oz*, and it was titled *The Woggle-Bug*.

16. "Oz Under Scrutiny," 13.

17. Olsen, "Coronado Fairyland," 2.

18. Review in *Cleveland Leader*, 6 November 1904, reprinted in "Oz Under Scrutiny," 13.

19. Douglas G. Greene, letter to the author, 21 March 1990.

20. C. Warren Hollister, "Criticism Criticized," *Baum Bugle* 16 (Spring 1972): 25.

21. L. Frank Baum, "Proclamation Extraordinary," *Baum Bugle* 29 (Spring 1985): 8.

22. Ibid. Also see L. Frank Baum, "Planet in a Panic over Queer Visitor," *Baum Bugle* 29 (Spring 1985): 3–7. The proclamation merely states, "They should arrive upon your Earth Planet within a brief space of Time." The promotional material, however, details the panic that the Gump causes on several other planets, except Mars, where it is reported that

> the great bird of the air which has visited a great many planets in the universe arrived here today.
> We are surprised that the natives of other planets should have been frightened, as it was simply the Gump from the "Land of Oz." . . .
> Of course the natives of other planets are not familiar with the funny things that take place on Earth, and for that reason they were probably frightened.

This indicates that the Gump's point of origin, the Land of Oz, is on the earth.

23. L. Frank Baum, *The Woggle-Bug Book (1905)*, with an introduction by Douglas G. Greene (Delmar, N.Y.: Scholars' Facsimiles & Reprints, 1978), 6.

24. Michael Patrick Hearn, "How Did the Woggle-Bug Do?" *Baum Bugle* 18 (Christmas 1974): 17–18. Baum signed two contracts: the first with the Minerva Company of Chicago and, when that one did not work out, the second with E. D. Sellman, guaranteeing him the same terms.

25. Daniel P. Mannix, "'Off to See the Wizard'—1903: Part Two," *Baum Bugle* 13 (Spring 1969): 9.

26. Quoted in Hearn, "How Did the Woggle-Bug Do?" 19.

27. There was a tenth story, "The Tiger's Eye," which was first published in *American Book Collector* 13 (December 1962): 21–24.

28. L. Frank Baum, *Animal Fairy Tales*, with illustrations by Dick Martin and an introduction by Russell P. MacFall (Chicago: International Wizard of Oz Club, 1969), 16.

29. Douglas G. Greene, "The Periodical Baum: An Annotated Checklist," *Baum Bugle* 19 (Autumn 1975): 7. "Nelebel's Fairyland" was published in the *Russ,* which Baum described "as a San Diego 'College Paper.'" Greene now believes that Baum may have been using college "in an older sense," since the *Russ* was actually a high-school paper (letter to the author).

30. L. Frank Baum, "A Kidnapped Santa Claus," with drawings by Fred Richardson, *Delineator,* December 1904, reprinted in *Baum Bugle* 12 (Christmas 1968): 13.

31. "Nelebel's Fairyland" was probably written as a gesture of good-will to Coronado.

32. David L. Greene, "L. Frank Baum's Later Oz Books: 1914–1920," *Baum Bugle* 16 (Spring 1972): 18.

33. Michael Patrick Hearn, David L. Greene, and Peter E. Hanff trace this incident back to one Baum had created for his stage adaptation of Edith Ogden Harrison's stories. They also point out that he again used the incident in *Tik-Tok of Oz,* which owes much of its plot to *Ozma of Oz* ("The Faltering Flight of Prince Silverwings," *Baum Bugle* 18 [Autumn 1974]: 4–10).

34. L. Frank Baum, *Rinkitink in Oz,* illustrated by John R. Neill (Chicago: Reilly & Britton, 1916), 246–47.

35. L. Frank Baum, *Ozma of Oz,* illustrated by John R. Neill (Chicago: Reilly & Britton, 1907), 169–70.

36. *Baum Bugle* 12 (Christmas 1968): 21.

37. Martin Gardner, introduction to *John Dough and the Cherub,* by L. Frank Baum (New York: Dover, 1974), vii.

38. L. Frank Baum, *John Dough and the Cherub,* illustrated by John R. Neill (Chicago: Reilly & Britton, 1906), 282.

39. David L. Greene, "The Writing of Two L. Frank Baum Fantasies," *Baum Bugle* 15 (Autumn 1971): 15–16. Also see the interesting discussion of the possible origin of the character of John Dough in Hearn, Greene, and Hanff, "Faltering Flight of Prince Silverwings," 9.

40. Edward Wagenknecht believes that the source for this character is Edgar Allan Poe's "The Man that Was Used Up" ("'Utopia Americana,' a Generation Afterwards," *American Book Collector* 13 [December 1962]: 12).

41. Baum, *John Dough,* 106.

42. Ibid., 65.

43. Ibid., 173.

44. Ibid., 303.

45. Ibid., 245.

46. Ibid., 233.

47. L. Frank Baum, "Nelebel's Fairyland," *Baum Bugle* 6 (Christmas 1962): 11; see also *Nelebel's Fairyland* (Douglasville, Ga.: Pamami Press, 1978), 7.

48. "The Twinkle Tales" were published in one volume in 1911 under the title *Twinkle and Chubbins. Policeman Bluejay* was issued under Baum's name as *Babes in Birdland* in 1917.

49. Laura Bancroft [L. Frank Baum], *Twinkle and Chubbins: Their Astonishing Adventures in Nature-Fairyland,* illustrated by Maginel Wright Enright (Chicago: Reilly & Britton, 1911), 137.

50. Ibid., 265, 266.

51. Ibid., 227.

52. Michael Patrick Hearn, "When L. Frank Baum was 'Laura Bancroft,'" *American Book Collector,* n.s., 8 (May 1987): 12.

53. L. Frank Baum [Laura Bancroft, pseud.], *Policeman Bluejay (1907),* with an introduction

by David L. Greene (Delmar, N.Y.: Scholars' Facsimiles & Reprints, 1981), [7].

54. Ibid., 41.

55. Bulwer-Lytton's *The Coming Race*, which describes an advanced, underground civilization where logic rules the emotions, may well have inspired some of the episodes in Baum's *Dorothy and the Wizard in Oz* (1908).

56. Edwin M. Eigner, *The Metaphysical Novel in England and America: Dickens, Bulwer, Melville, and Hawthorne* (Berkeley: University of California Press, 1978), 9.

Chapter 5:
CONCENTRATION ON OZ

1. J. R. R. Tolkien, "On Fairy-Stories," in *Tree and Leaf* (Boston: Houghton Mifflin, 1965), 9.

2. *Queen Zixi* was the last published use of this form; *King Rinkitink* was his last actual use of it.

3. David L. Greene, introduction to *Policeman Bluejay (1907)*, by L. Frank Baum [Laura Bancroft, pseud.] (Delmar, N.Y.: Scholars' Facsimiles & Reprints, 1981), vii.

4. L. Frank Baum, *Ozma of Oz*, illustrated by John R. Neill (Chicago: Reilly & Britton, 1907), [11].

5. J. R. R. Tolkien, foreword to *The Fellowship of the Ring: Being the First Part of The Lord of the Rings*, 2nd ed. (Boston: Houghton Mifflin, 1965), 6.

6. L. Frank Baum, *The Emerald City of Oz*, illustrated by John R. Neill (Chicago: Reilly & Britton, 1910), 29.

7. Also see Michael Patrick Hearn, David L. Greene, and Peter E. Hanff, "The Faltering Flight of Prince Silverwings," *Baum Bugle* 18 (Autumn 1974): 9-10. The authors of this article believe that the Nome King's character was also influenced by the Gnome King in the play *Prince Silverwings.*

8. L. Frank Baum, *The Marvelous Land of Oz,*

pictured by John R. Neill (Chicago: Reilly & Britton, 1904), 211.

9. L. Frank Baum, *Ozma of Oz*, illustrated by John R. Neill (Chicago: Reilly & Britton, 1904), 26.

10. Ibid., 38.

11. Ibid., 42.

12. Ibid., 39.

13. Ibid., 104.

14. Ibid., 112.

15. Ibid., 255-56.

16. Ibid., 135-37.

17. Ibid., 255.

18. Ibid., 260.

19. This was quite a topical reference, since the great San Francisco earthquake had occurred in 1906. The Baums were in Europe when it happened, but undoubtedly they saw the aftermath when they were in California again the next winter.

20. L. Frank Baum, *Dorothy and the Wizard in Oz*, illustrated by John R. Neill (Chicago: Reilly & Britton, 1908), 24.

21. Baum, *Ozma of Oz*, 267; Baum, *Dorothy and the Wizard in Oz*, 179.

22. Baum, *Dorothy and the Wizard in Oz*, 195.

23. Ibid., 218.

24. Ibid., 190-91.

25. Ibid., 185.

26. Ibid., 195-96.

27. Ibid., 180, 191, 195, 197.

28. Ibid., 196.

29. Ibid., 197.

30. Ibid.

31. Ibid., [11], 253 (the color plates are included in the pagination).

32. For an interesting discussion of this idea as applied to *The Wonderful Wizard of Oz,* see Earle J. Coleman, "Oz as Heaven and Other Philosophical Questions," *Baum Bugle* 24 (Autumn 1980): 18–20.

33. In the nineteenth century, many older books that had originally been written for adults were now considered "children's books." *Gulliver's Travels, Pilgrim's Progress, Robinson Crusoe,* and versions of *The Divine Comedy, The Iliad, The Odyssey,* and *The Aeneid* would all have been familiar to an imaginative child reader. In fact, Louisa May Alcott in the first part of *Little Women* (1868) and Frances Hodgson Burnett in *Two Little Pilgrims' Progress* (1895) took for granted their readers' familiarity with John Bunyan's *Pilgrim's Progress.* Burnett's story, incidentally, uses the great White City of the 1893 World's Columbian Exposition in Chicago to represent the Celestial City and is a story Baum would have known. For Baum's possible use of Bunyan, see J. Karl Franson, "From Vanity Fair to Emerald City: Baum's Debt to Bunyan," *Children's Literature* 23 (1995): 91–114.

34. Hearn, Greene, and Hanff, "Faltering Flight of Prince Silverwings," 10.

35. Baum, *Dorothy and the Wizard in Oz,* 21.

36. Richard A. Mills, "The Fairylogue and Radio Plays of L. Frank Baum," *Baum Bugle* 14 (Christmas 1970): 4.

37. Russell P. MacFall, "L. Frank Baum and the Radio-Plays," *Baum Bugle* 6 (August 1962): 3.

38. Reproduced in Michael Patrick Hearn, *The Annotated Wizard of Oz* (New York: Potter, 1973), facing 32.

39. MacFall, "Baum and the Radio-Plays," 3.

40. L. Frank Baum, *The Road to Oz,* illustrated by John R. Neill (Chicago: Reilly & Britton, 1909), 42–43.

41. Ibid., 260.

42. Ibid., 196.

43. Ibid., 184.

44. Ibid., 206.

45. Ibid., 126.

46. Ibid., 143.

47. This is especially apparent in the description of the room in the palace given to the Shaggy Man in ibid., 198–99.

48. Ibid., 189.

49. Ibid., 161.

50. Ibid., 164.

51. Ibid., 164–65.

52. Ibid., 191.

53. Ibid., 172.

54. Ibid., 176.

55. Ibid., 152.

56. Ibid., 241.

57. Ibid., 222, 225, 230, 231, 234.

58. Ibid., [9–10].

59. L. Frank Baum, *The Emerald City of Oz,* illustrated by John R. Neill (Chicago: Reilly & Britton, 1910), 29–33.

60. Ibid., 238.

61. Ibid., 268.

62. Ibid., 269.

63. Ibid., 290.

64. Ibid., 293.

65. Ibid., 295.

66. Ibid., 31, 253.

67. Ibid., 45–46. In Chapter 1, it is also stated that Ozma "has certain fairy powers" (17). It is not clear if Baum meant the Magic Picture and the Magic Belt or some kind of inherent magic power; Ozma certainly does not display any personal ability with magic in this story, although it is an idea that Baum would take up and develop in a later book.

68. Ibid., 59–60 (emphasis added).

69. Frank Joslyn Baum and Russell P. MacFall, *To Please a Child: A Biography of L. Frank Baum, Royal Historian of Oz* (Chicago: Reilly & Lee, 1961), 250.

Chapter 6:
BEGINNING AGAIN

1. Frank Joslyn Baum and Russell P. MacFall, *To Please a Child: A Biography of L. Frank Baum, Royal Historian of Oz* (Chicago: Reilly & Lee, 1961), 250–51.

2. Michael Patrick Hearn, David L. Greene, and Peter E. Hanff point out that a "Mayre" was the American girl character in the play *Prince Silverwings* and that the Mermaid Queen in the play was the probable source of the similar character in *The Sea Fairies* ("The Faltering Flight of Prince Silverwings," *Baum Bugle* 18 [Autumn 1974]: 8).

3. Trot says: "Then you must be fairies, if you've lived always," and a mermaid answers, "We are dear; we are the water fairies" (L. Frank Baum, *The Sea Fairies,* illustrated by John R. Neill [Chicago: Reilly & Britton, 1911], 27).

4. David L. Greene, "The Writing of Two L. Frank Baum Fantasies," *Baum Bugle* 15 (Autumn 1971): 14.

5. Although Oz is linked to Sky Island by the presence of Button-Bright and Polychrome, Baum also later linked Sky Island to Oz in *The Magic of Oz* (1919), 89.

6. Greene, "Writing of Two Baum Fantasies," 14.

7. Quoted in Michael Patrick Hearn, introduction to *Little Wizard Stories of Oz,* by L. Frank Baum, illustrated by John R. Neill (New York: Schocken Books, 1985), ix.

8. L. Frank Baum, *The Patchwork Girl of Oz,* illustrated by John R. Neill (Chicago: Reilly & Britton, 1913), 62.

9. Ibid., 174.

10. L. Frank Baum, *The Emerald City of Oz,* illustrated by John R. Neill (Chicago: Reilly & Britton, 1910), 30, 33.

11. Baum, *Patchwork Girl of Oz,* 235, 241.

12. Baum, *Emerald City of Oz,* 32.

13. Baum, *Patchwork Girl of Oz,* 269.

14. Ibid., 241.

15. Ibid., 230.

16. L. Frank Baum, *The Marvelous Land of Oz,* pictured by John R. Neill (Chicago: Reilly & Britton, 1904), 7–8.

17. Baum, *Patchwork Girl of Oz,* 163.

18. C. Warren Hollister, "Criticism Criticized," *Baum Bugle* 16 (Spring 1972): 24.

19. "She found the Wizard of Oz, who was planting shoe-trees in the garden . . . " (L. Frank Baum, *Rinkitink in Oz,* illustrated by John R. Neill [Chicago: Reilly & Britton, 1916], 277).

20. Baum, *Patchwork Girl of Oz,* 93.

21. Ibid., 304.

22. Michael Patrick Hearn, *The Annotated Wizard of Oz* (New York: Potter, 1973), 371.

23. Louis F. Gottschalk would later write the film score for D. W. Griffith's masterpiece *Broken Blossoms* (1919).

24. Alla T. Ford and Dick Martin, *The Musical Fantasies of L. Frank Baum* (Chicago: Wizard Press, 1958), 22.

25. L. Frank Baum, *Tik-Tok of Oz,* illustrated by John R. Neill (Chicago: Reilly & Britton, 1914), 15.

26. Ibid., 49.

27. Ibid., 64.

28. Ibid., 130.

29. Ibid., 131.

30. Ibid., 241.

31. Dorothy's dog, Toto, had been changed to a pet cow in the stage version of *The Wizard of Oz;* Billina was probably changed to a mule in *The Tik-Tok Man of Oz* so that the character could be played by an actor in costume.

32. Baum, *Tik-Tok of Oz,* 64.

33. Hearn, Greene, and Hanff, "Faltering Flight of Prince Silverwings," 8.

34. The maps were in color in the first two printings of this book; they were in green and white in the third printing; and the endpapers were blank in later printings. At various times, the publisher printed the maps separately to be given away with each Oz book purchased.

35. "That color can only be found in the yellow country of the Winkies, West of the Emerald City" (Baum, *Patchwork Girl of Oz,* 62).

36. Baum, *Tik-Tok of Oz,* 259.

37. Ibid., 257.

38. L. Frank Baum, *The Scarecrow of Oz,* illustrated by John R. Neill (Chicago: Reilly & Britton, 1915), 279.

39. Martin Gardner and Russel B. Nye, *The Wizard of Oz and Who He Was* (East Lansing: Michigan State University Press, 1957), 30.

40. Baum, *Scarecrow of Oz,* 84.

41. Ibid., 125.

42. Ibid., 109–10.

43. Ibid., 120.

44. Ibid., 121.

45. Douglas Greene to the author, 21 March 1990.

46. Baum, *Scarecrow of Oz,* 152.

47. Ibid., 254.

48. Ibid., 256.

49. In *The Patchwork Girl of Oz,* Baum wrote: "Yet with all her queenly qualities Ozma was a real girl and enjoyed the things in life that other real girls enjoy." And "in the banquet hall to-night were gathered only old and trusted friends, so here Ozma was herself—a mere girl" (216).

50. Baum and MacFall, *To Please a Child,* 257. The full name of the club was the Lofty and Exalted Order of Uplifters.

51. Richard Mills, "The Oz Film Manufacturing Company: Part One," *Baum Bugle* 16 (Christmas 1972): 5.

52. Ibid., 8; Richard A. Mills and David L. Greene, "The Oz Film Manufacturing Company: Part Two," *Baum Bugle* 17 (Spring 1973): 6.

53. Mills and Greene, "Oz Film Manufacturing Company: Part Two," 5.

54. L. Frank Baum to F. K. Reilly, 21 December 1914, quoted in David L. Greene, "L. Frank Baum on His Films," *Baum Bugle* 17 (Autumn 1973): 14.

55. Baum and MacFall, *To Please a Child,* 258; Hearn, *Annotated Wizard of Oz,* 372.

56. Baum and MacFall, *To Please a Child,* 269–70.

57. Baum, *Rinkitink in Oz,* [13].

Chapter 7:
RESOLUTION OF CONFLICT

1. Frank Joslyn Baum and Russell P. MacFall wrote that "his blooms won so many awards in strong competition in that land of flowers that he was often described as the champion amateur horticulturist of Southern California" (*To Please a Child: A Biography of L. Frank Baum, Royal Historian of Oz* [Chicago: Reilly & Lee, 1961], 22, 268).

2. Ibid., 270.

3. Ibid., 271.

4. L. Frank Baum, *The Lost Princess of Oz,* illustrated by John R. Neill (Chicago: Reilly & Britton, 1917), [14].

5. L. Frank Baum, *The Emerald City of Oz,* illustrated by John R. Neill (Chicago: Reilly & Britton, 1910), [7].

6. Baum, *Lost Princess of Oz,* [14].

7. Ibid., 57–58.

8. David L. Greene, "L. Frank Baum's Later Oz Books: 1914–1920," *Baum Bugle* 16 (Spring 1972): 19. Greene quotes a letter of 6 September 1916 from Baum to his publisher: "You will find a 'Map of the Search for the Lost Princess,' which I would like to have redrawn and printed in black-and-white and placed in the fore part of the book."

9. Baum, *Lost Princess of Oz,* 20.

10. Baum and MacFall, *To Please a Child,* 273.

11. L. Frank Baum, *The Wonderful Wizard of Oz,* with pictures by W. W. Denslow (Chicago: Hill, 1900), chap. 5, 58–61.

12. L. Frank Baum, *The Tin Woodman of Oz,* illustrated by John R. Neill (Chicago: Reilly & Britton, 1918), 156–58.

13. George MacDonald, "The Fantastic Imagination," in *The Gifts of the Child Christ: Fairytales and Stories for the Childlike,* edited by Glenn Edward Sadler (Grand Rapids, Mich.: Eerdmans, 1973), 1:23–24.

14. Baum, *Tin Woodman of Oz,* 157.

15. Ibid., 156.

16. Ibid., 207.

17. Ibid., 158.

18. For another possibility, see Ruth Berman, "Lurline's Source," *Baum Bugle* 26 (Autumn 1982): 2–3.

19. L. Frank Baum, *The Magic of Oz,* illustrated by John R. Neill (Chicago: Reilly & Lee, 1919), 240–41. Baum explains why Ozma, now a fairy, celebrates her birthdays:

> It seems odd that a fairy should have a birthday, for fairies, they say, were born at the beginning of time and live forever. Yet, on the other hand, it would be a shame to deprive a fairy, who has so many other good things, of the delights of a birthday. So we need not wonder that the fairies keep their birthdays just as other folks do, and consider them occasions for feasting and rejoicing.

20. Ibid., 266.

21. Ibid., 55.

22. Ibid., 30.

23. L. Frank Baum, *Glinda of Oz,* illustrated by John R. Neill (Chicago: Reilly & Lee, 1920), 36.

24. According to Scott Olsen, "[Baum] did manage to make major trips to the south and west in 1903 and 1904" ("The Coronado Fairyland," *Baum Bugle* 20 [Winter 1976]: 2n).

25. Baum, *Glinda of Oz,* 56, 141.

26. Ibid., 27, 58.

27. Ibid., 139.

28. Ibid., 37.

29. Ibid., 264.

30. L. Frank Baum, *The Master Key: An Electrical Fairy Tale,* illustrations by F. Y. Cory (Indianapolis: Bowen-Merrill, 1901), 237.

31. Martin Gardner and Russel B. Nye, *The Wizard of Oz and Who He Was* (East Lansing: Michigan State University Press, 1957), 40.

32. Baum and MacFall, *To Please a Child,* 274–75.

33. On the 1914 maps, Baum included places inside and outside Oz that had not yet appeared in his published stories. The Kingdom of Dreams was the only one of those places that he failed to incorporate into subsequent stories.

34. Edward Wagenknecht, *Utopia Americana* (Seattle: University of Washington Book Store, 1929; reprint, n.p.: Folcroft Press, 1970), 40.

Epilogue:
OZ AFTER BAUM

1. Edward Wagenknecht, *Utopia Americana* (Seattle: University of Washington Book Store, 1929; reprint, n.p.: Folcroft Press, 1970).

2. Frank Joslyn Baum and Russel P. MacFall, *To Please a Child: A Biography of L. Frank Baum, Royal Historian of Oz* (Chicago: Reilly & Lee, 1961), 277. The name of Reilly & Britton was changed to Reilly & Lee in 1919.

3. L. Frank Baum [Ruth Plumly Thompson], *The Royal Book of Oz*, illustrated by John R. Neill (Chicago: Reilly & Lee, 1921), [9].

4. Baum and MacFall, *To Please a Child*, 277; Douglas G. Greene and Peter E. Hanff, *Bibliographia Oziana: A Concise Bibliographical Checklist of the Oz Books by L. Frank Baum and His Successors*, rev. and enl. ed. ([Kinderhook, Ill.:] International Wizard of Oz Club, 1988), 87.

5. Allen Eyles, *The World of Oz* (Tucson: HPBooks, 1985), 63.

6. Michael O. Riley, review of *The Curious Cruise of Captain Santa*, by Ruth Plumly Thompson, *Baum Bugle* 30 (Autumn 1986): 18.

7. Eloise Jarvis McGraw and Lauren McGraw Wagner, *Merry Go Round in Oz*, designed and illustrated by Dick Martin (Chicago: Reilly & Lee, 1963), 13, 27.

8. Edward Wagenknecht, "Lyman Frank Baum—1959," *Baum Bugle* 3 (August 1959): 4.

9. *Tik-Tok of Oz* was essentially the same story as *Ozma of Oz*, with the American character's name changed from Dorothy to Betsy. In *The Scarecrow of Oz*, Baum added to Oz the characters from his short lived "Trot" series.

10. L. Frank Baum, *The Road to Oz*, illustrated by John R. Neill (Chicago: Reilly & Britton, 1909), 161.

11. Baum and MacFall, *To Please a Child*, 277. Maud Baum was herself reluctant to allow the continuation of the series, but agreed when a contract was offered guaranteeing "a fixed royalty for her and Baum's heirs on every Oz book."

12. Robert Wauchope and Virginia Wauchope, "Invisible Inzi of Oz," *Baum Bugle* 24 (Winter 1980–1981): 8–11, 14–16, and 25 (Summer 1981): 10–17. Additional information given in the second part of this reprint states that when he grew up, Robert Wauchope "became Professor of Anthropology at Tulane University, director of the Middle American Archaeology Institute, and author of nine books on archeology."

13. Stephen J. Teller, "The Other Oz: Oz Apocrypha Beyond the Forty Books," *Baum Bugle* 33 (Spring 1989): 10–13. Teller, "A Checklist of Published Oz Apocrypha," *Baum Bugle* 34 (Autumn 1990): 14–21. These articles give a fairly complete picture of the unofficial Oz books published in some form through 1990. No one knows how many exist in manuscript.

14. Sir Edward Bulwer-Lytton, *The Caxtons: A Family Picture* (Edinburgh: William Blackwood and Sons, 1849), 1:25–26.

15. "My explanation begins with an endorsement of the statement that a child learns more in the first five years of its life than in the next fifty years" ("Interview with Mr. Frank G. [*sic*] Baum," *Advance*, 22 July 1909, reprinted in *Baum Bugle* 30 [Autumn 1986]: 9).

16. Edward Wagenknecht, "To the Readers of This Book," afterword to *The Wizard of Oz*, by L. Frank Baum, illustrated by Dale Ulrey (Chicago: Reilly & Lee, 1956), 238.

17. Gore Vidal, "The Oz Books," in *United States: Essays, 1952–1992* (New York: Random House, 1993), 1095. Vidal adds: "Recently I was sent an academic dissertation. Certain aspects of Baum's *The Land of Oz* had reoccurred in a book of mine. Was this conscious or not? (It was not.) But I was intrigued. I reread *The Land of Oz.* Yes, I could see Baum's influence" (1096).

18. Baum and MacFall, *To Please a Child*, 20.

Bibliography

THE WORKS OF LYMAN FRANK BAUM

This is an area in which much of the work has already been done. Of the many bibliographies of Baum's works that have appeared, the most important are the catalogue prepared for the centenary celebration of Baum's birth in 1956 by Roland Baughman, Head of Special Collections, Columbia University Libraries; the bibliography in Martin Gardner and Russel B. Nye's *The Wizard of Oz and Who He Was* (1957); the bibliography in Alla T. Ford and Dick Martin's *The Musical Fantasies of L. Frank Baum* (1958); the "Chronological Checklist" prepared by Dick Martin for the special number of the *American Book Collector* (December 1962); and the excellent and exhaustive bibliography in Michael Patrick Hearn's *The Annotated Wizard of Oz* (1973). In addition to those, the *Baum Bugle* is publishing an ongoing series of bibliographic articles, and Douglas G. Greene's "The Periodical Baum: An Annotated Checklist" (Autumn 1975) has conveniently organized Baum's newspaper and magazine publications.

This bibliography differs from the earlier ones in one major respect—its arrangement. Without exception, the other bibliographies have placed Baum's works in categories: books under his own name, pseudonymous books, magazine stories, and so on. That is, of course, the most convenient method for presenting such diverse material, but I have chosen a different arrangement—a purely chronological one—in the attempt to present a clearer idea of the incredible quantity of work that Baum produced during his writing career.

All his various works are presented together without separate categories, including the uncompleted play projects, with the following exceptions: some of the short stories that immediately appeared in book form after their appearances in newspapers and magazines are not listed separately, and stories and poems reprinted in anthologies are omitted. Some works are either lost or impossible to date, and they are listed at the end. The pseudonyms under which Baum published many of his works are given in brackets before the name of the work, and the works discussed in the text of this study will be indicated by (*) before the title.

1873

Baum's Complete Stamp Dealers Directory. Compiled and published by Baum, Norris & Co., Syracuse, N.Y. Syracuse: Hitchcock & Tucker, Printers and Binders, 1873.

1882

[Louis F. Baum.] *The Mackrummins* [comedy-drama in three acts]. Copyright Richburg, N.Y., 1882. Unpublished.

(*) [Louis F. Baum.] *The Maid of Arran* [Irish idyll in five acts]. Produced 1882. Unpublished.

Louis F. Baum's Popular Songs as Sung with Immense Success in His Great 5 Act Irish Drama, Maid of Arran. New York: J. G. Hyde, 1882.

[Louis F. Baum.] *Matches* [comedy-drama in three acts]. Performed in 1882 and 1883. Unpublished.

1883

[Louis F. Baum.] *Kilmourne; or, O'Connor's Dream* [Irish drama]. Performed in 1883. Unpublished.

1885

The Queen of Killarney [Irish drama]. Not performed. Unpublished.

1886

The Book of the Hamburgs, a brief treatise upon the mating, rearing and management of the different varieties of Hamburgs. Hartford, Conn.: H. H. Stoddard, 1886.

1890

(*) "Our Landlady." The ongoing column that appeared in Baum's newspaper, the *Aberdeen Saturday Pioneer* (1890–1891). The extant columns have been published as *Our Landlady.* Edited and annotated by Nancy Tystad Koupal. Lincoln: University of Nebraska Press, 1996.

1895

"La Reine est Morte—Vive La Reine!" [poem]. *Chicago Times-Herald,* 23 June 1895.

"Farmer Benson on the Motocycle" [poem]. *Chicago Times-Herald,* 4 August 1895.

1896

(*)*Adventures in Phunniland.* Copyright 1896. Published as *A New Wonderland* in 1900.

(*)*Tales from Mother Goose.* Copyright 1896. Published as *Mother Goose in Prose* in 1897.

"Who Called 'Perry'?" *Chicago Times-Herald,* 19 January 1896.

(*)"Yesterday at the Exposition [From the *Times-Herald,* June 27, 2090]." *Chicago Times-Herald,* 2 February 1896.

"Two Pictures" [poem]. *Chicago Times-Herald,* 17 May 1896.

"The Latest in Magic" [poem]. *Chicago Times-Herald,* 31 May 1896.

"My Ruby Wedding Ring." Copyright October 12, 1896, by the Bacheller Syndicate. The newspaper in which the story appeared is unknown.

"The Man with the Red Shirt." Ca. 1896–1897. *Baum Bugle* 17 (Spring 1973): 21. This story exists only in the version that Baum's niece, Matilda J. Gage, wrote down after he told it to her.

1897

(*)*Mother Goose in Prose.* Illustrated by Maxfield Parrish. Chicago: Way & Williams, 1897.

"The Extravagance of Dan." *National Magazine,* May 1897.

"How Scroggs Won the Reward." Copyright May 5, 1897, by the Bacheller Syndicate. It is not known where this story was published.

"The Return of Dick Weemins." *National Magazine,* July 1897.

"The Suicide of Kiaros." *White Elephant,* September 1897.

"A Shadow Cast Before." *Philosopher,* December 1897.

1898

(*)*By the Candelabra's Glare.* Chicago: Privately Printed By L. Frank Baum In His Own Workshop, 1898.

"The Mating Day." *Short Stories,* September 1898.

1899

(*)*Father Goose, His Book.* Pictures by Wm. W. Denslow. Chicago: Hill, 1899.

"Aunt Hulda's Good Time." *Youth's Companion,* 26 October 1899.

1900

The Army Alphabet. Illustrated by Harry Kennedy. Chicago: Hill, 1900.

The Navy Alphabet. Illustrated by Harry Kennedy. Chicago: Hill, 1900.

The Art of Decorating Dry Goods Windows and Interiors. Chicago: Show Window, 1900.

(*)*A New Wonderland.* Illustrated by Frank Verbeck. New York: R. H. Russell, 1900.

The Songs of Father Goose, for the Home, School and Nursery. Music by Alberta N. Hall. Pictures by Wm. W. Denslow. Chicago: Hill, 1900.

(*)*The Wonderful Wizard of Oz.* With Pictures by W. W. Denslow. Chicago: Hill, 1900.

"The Loveridge Burglary." *Short Stories,* January 1900.

"The Real 'Mr. Dooley'" [article]. *Home Magazine,* January 1900.

"Our Den once made a picture . . . " [poem about Denslow]. January 1, 1900. *Baum Bugle* 8 (Spring 1964): 13.

"To the Grand Army of the Republic August 1900" [poem]. *Chicago Times-Herald,* 26 August 1900.

1901

(*)*American Fairy Tales.* Cover, title page, and borders designed by Ralph Fletcher Seymour. Illustrations by Ike Morgan, Harry Kennedy, and N. P. Hall. Chicago: Hill, 1901. First published weekly from March 3 through May 19, 1901, in the *Chicago Chronicle,* the *Boston Post,* and other newspapers.

(*)*Dot and Tot of Merryland.* Pictures by W. W. Denslow. Chicago: Hill, 1901.

(*)*The Master Key: An Electrical Fairy Tale.* Illustrations by F. Y. Cory. Indianapolis: Bowen-Merrill, 1901.

"The Bad Man." *Home Magazine,* February 1901.

"Strange Tale of Nursery Folk." *Chicago Times-Herald,* 3 March 1901. Attributed to Baum. First published separately as *Strange Tale of Nursery Folk.* Douglasville, Ga.: Pamami Press, 1978.

(*)"The Runaway Shadows." From an undated and unidentified newspaper clipping, ca. 1901. This story was written as one of the *American Fairy Tales,* but not included in the book edition. Another unidentified proof of this story exists with the title "A Trick of Jack Frost's." Both titles were used when it was first published separately as *The Runaway Shadows; or, A Trick of Jack Frost's.* Douglasville, Ga.: Pamami Press, 1979.

"The King Who Changed His Mind." From an unidentified newspaper clipping. According to the *Baum Bugle,* this story dates from 1901, but Douglas Greene would place it nearer the time of the *Animal Fairy Tales*—that is, 1903–1904. First published in book form in *The Purple Dragon and Other Fantasies,* by L. Frank Baum. Selected and annotated by David L. Greene. Illustrated by Tim Kirk. Lakemont, Ga.: Fictioneer Books, 1976.

King Midas [comic opera]. Music by Paul Tietjens. Not completed.

The Octopus; or, The Title Trust [comic opera]. Music by Paul Tietjens. Not produced.

The Wonderful Wizard of Oz [play]. Music by Paul Tietjens. Baum's first, rejected script from his story.

1902

(*)*The Life and Adventures of Santa Claus.* With Many Pictures by Mary Cowles Clark. Indianapolis: Bowen-Merrill, 1902.

"An Easter Egg." *Sunny South* [supplement to the *Atlanta Constitution*], 29 March 1902.

(*)*The Wizard of Oz* [musical extravaganza]. Music by Paul Tietjens. Staged by Julian Mitchell. Produced 1902.

The Wizard of Oz [book of selections and ten pieces of sheet music published separately]. Music by Paul Tietjens. New York: M. Whitmark & Sons, 1902.

1903

(*)*The Enchanted Island of Yew.* Illustrated by Fanny Y. Cory. Indianapolis: Bobbs-Merrill, 1903.

(*)*The Surprising Adventures of The Magical Monarch of Mo and His People.* With Pictures by Frank Verbeck. Indianapolis: Bobbs-Merrill, 1903. Reissue of *A New Wonderland,* with the first chapter rewritten and the name of the valley changed from Phunnyland to Mo.

"The Ryl of the Lilies." From an unidentified newspaper clipping, 12 April 1903.

The Maid of Athens: A Musical Comedy in Three Acts [play prospectus], by L. Frank Baum and Emerson Hough. [Chicago]: Privately printed, 1903. In Alla T. Ford and Dick Martin. *The Musical Fantasies of L. Frank Baum.* Chicago: Wizard Press, 1958.

The Maid of Athens [college fantasy in three acts], by L. Frank Baum and Emerson Hough. Not completed.

Scenario and General Synopsis of "Prince Silverwings": A Musical Fairy Spectacle in Three Acts and Eight Scenes, by L. Frank Baum and Edith Ogden Harrison. [Chicago]: A. C. McClurg, 1903. This prospectus is solely Baum's work and was reprinted as such in the second edition: *Scenario and General Synopsis of "Prince Silverwings": A Musical Fairy Spectacle in Three Acts and Eight Scenes.* Based on the Stories by Edith

Ogden Harrison. Douglasville, Ga.: Pamami Press, 1982.

Prince Silverwings [children's fantasy]. Music by Paul Tietjens. Completed. Not produced.

King Jonah XIII [comic opera in two acts]. Music by Nathaniel D. Mann. Not produced.

The Whatnexters. Book and lyrics by L. Frank Baum and Isidore Witmark. Not completed.

"Down Among the Marshes; The Alligator Song." Words and music by L. Frank Baum. New York: M. Whitmark & Sons, 1903.

1904

(*)*The Marvelous Land of Oz.* Pictured by John R. Neill. Chicago: Reilly & Britton, 1904.

"Queer Visitors from the Marvelous Land of Oz." A prologue and twenty-six stories that appeared in various newspapers from August 28, 1904, through February 26, 1905. Syndicated by the *Philadelphia North American.* First published in book form (with *The Woggle-Bug Book*) under the title *The Third Oz Book.* Edited by Martin Williams. Illustrated by Eric Shanower. Savannah, Ga.: Armstrong State College Press, 1986. The original promotional material for the series, which appeared from August 18 to August 28, 1906, was reprinted as " 'Planet in a Panic Over Queer Visitor' . . . and Other Little-Known Writings of L. Frank Baum." *Baum Bugle* 29 (Spring 1985): 3–8. About half these tales were heavily rewritten and published as *The Visitors from Oz.* Pictured by Dick Martin. Chicago: Reilly & Lee, 1960.

"What Did the Woggle-Bug Say?" [song]. Music by Paul Tietjens. Chicago: Reilly & Britton, 1904.

(*)"Queen Zixi of Ix" [serial]. *St. Nicholas,* November 1904–October 1905.

"A Kidnapped Santa Claus." *Delineator,* December 1904. First published separately as *A Kidnapped Santa Claus.* Introduction by Martin Williams. Illustrated by Richard Rosenbloom. Indianapolis: Bobbs-Merrill, 1969.

Father Goose [play]. Music by Paul Tietjens. Not completed.

The Pagan Potentate [play]. Music by Paul Tietjens. Not completed.

1905

(*)*Queen Zixi of Ix; or, The Story of the Magic Cloak.* With Illustrations by Frederick Richardson. New York: Century, 1905.

(*)*The Woggle-Bug Book.* Pictures by Ike Morgan. Chicago: Reilly & Britton, 1905.

(*)*King Rinkitink.* Unpublished.

[Schuyler Staunton.] *The Fate of a Crown.* Illustrated by Glen C. Sheffer. Chicago: Reilly & Britton, 1905.

(*)"Animal Fairy Tales." A prologue and nine stories serialized in the *Delineator,* January–September 1905. First published in book form as *Animal Fairy Tales.* With Illustrations by Dick Martin and an Introduction by Russell P. MacFall. Chicago: International Wizard of Oz Club, 1969. The first of these stories was rewritten by an editor and published as *Jaglon and the Tiger Fairies.* Illustrated by Dale Ulrey. Chicago: Reilly & Lee, 1953.

"The Tiger's Eye" [tenth *Animal Fairy Tale*]. *American Book Collector* 8 (December 1962): 21–24.

"Coronado, 'the Queen of Fairyland' " [poem]. *San Diego Union,* 5 March 1905.

(*)"Nelebel's Fairyland." *Russ,* June 1905. First published separately as *Nelebel's Fairyland.* Douglasville, Ga.: Pamami Press, 1978.

"Fairy Tales on Stage" [article]. *Chicago Record-Herald,* 18 June 1905.

"Jack Burgitt's Honor." Copyright August 1, 1905, by the American Press Association.

"In Memorium [*sic*]" [poem]. *San Diego Union,* ca. 1905.

"Well, Come!" [poem]. From an unidentified newspaper clipping (possibly *San Diego Union*), ca. 1905.

"Christmas Comin'!" [poem]. Ca. 1905. *Baum Bugle* 16 (Christmas 1972): 3.

The King of Gee-Whiz [musical extravaganza in three acts], by L. Frank Baum and Emerson Hough. The play was not completed, but the "Scenario and general synopsis" is in Alla T. Ford and Dick Martin. *The Musical Fantasies of L. Frank Baum*. Chicago: Wizard Press, 1958. Hough later used the title for a children's book.

(*)*The Woggle-Bug* [musical extravaganza in three acts]. Music by Frederic Chapin. Staged by Frank Smithson. Produced.

The Woggle-Bug [book of selections and twelve pieces of sheet music published separately]. Music by Frederic Chapin. New York: M. Whitmark & Sons, 1905.

Introduction to *The Christmas Stocking Series* [six small volumes of traditional rhymes and stories]. Chicago: Reilly & Britton, 1905–1906. Baum's introduction was first published separately as *The Christmas Stocking*. Douglasville, Ga.: Pamami Press, 1980.

1906
(*)*John Dough and the Cherub*. Illustrated by John R. Neill. Chicago: Reilly & Britton, 1906.

(*)[Laura Bancroft.] *The Twinkle Tales*. Six small volumes: *Mr. Woodchuck, Bandit Jim Crow, Prairie-Dog Town, Prince Mud-Turtle, Twinkle's Enchantment*, and *Sugar-Loaf Mountain*. Illustrated by Maginel Wright Enright. Chicago: Reilly & Britton, 1906.

[Capt. Hugh Fitzgerald.] *Sam Steele's Adventures on Land and Sea*. Illustrated by Howard Heath. Chicago: Reilly & Britton, 1906.

[Suzanne Metcalf.] *Annabel, a Novel for Young Folks*. Illustrated by H. Putnam Hall. Chicago: Reilly & Britton, 1906.

[Schuyler Staunton.] *Daughters of Destiny*. Illustrated by Thomas Mitchell Pierce and Harold DeLay. Chicago: Reilly & Britton, 1906.

[Edith Van Dyne.] *Aunt Jane's Nieces*. Illustrated by Emile A. Nelson. Chicago: Reilly & Britton, 1906.

[Edith Van Dyne.] *Aunt Jane's Nieces Abroad*. Illustrated by Emile A. Nelson. Chicago: Reilly & Britton, 1906.

"The Yellow Ryl." Ca. 1906. *Child's Garden for Cheerful and Happy Homes*, August and September 1925.

1907
Father Goose's Year Book: Quaint Quacks and Feathered Shafts for Mature Children. Illustrated by Walter J. Enright. Chicago: Reilly & Britton, 1907.

(*)*Ozma of Oz*. Illustrated by John R. Neill. Chicago: Reilly & Britton, 1907.

[Laura Bancroft.] *Policeman Bluejay*. Illustrated by Maginel Wright Enright. Chicago: Reilly & Britton, 1907.

[John Estes Cooke.] *Tamawaca Folks: A Summer Comedy*. n.p.: Tamawaca Press, 1907. A privately published novel that Baum wrote for his friends at Macatawa Park, Michigan, where he had his summer home.

[Capt. Hugh Fitzgerald.] *Sam Steele's Adventures in Panama*. Illustrated by Howard Heath. Chicago: Reilly & Britton, 1907.

"To Macatawa, a Rhapsody" [poem]. *Grand Rapids Herald*, 1 September 1907.

Preface to *In Other Lands Than Ours*, by Maud Gage Baum. Illustrated with photographs by Baum. Chicago: Privately printed, 1907. An account of the Baums' trip to Egypt and Europe.

1908
Baum's American Fairy Tales: Stories of Astonishing Adventures of American Boys and Girls with the Fairies of their Native Land. With Illustrations by George Kerr. Indianapolis: Bobbs-Merrill, 1908. Rearranged version of *American Fairy Tales*, with a new preface and three additional stories: "The Witchcraft of Mary-Marie," "The Adventures of an Egg" (first published in 1903 as "An Easter Egg"), and "The Ryl" (first published in 1903 as "The Ryl of the Lilies").

(*)*Dorothy and the Wizard in Oz*. Illustrated by John R. Neill. Chicago: Reilly & Britton, 1908.

[Anonymous.] *The Last Egyptian: A Romance of the Nile.* Illustrated by Francis P. Wightman. Philadelphia: Edward Stern, 1908.

[Floyd Akers.] *The Boy Fortune Hunters in Alaska.* Illustrated by Howard Heath. Chicago: Reilly & Britton, 1908. Reissue of the first Sam Steele book by "Capt. Hugh Fitzgerald."

[Floyd Akers.] *The Boy Fortune Hunters in Egypt.* Illustrated by Emile A. Nelson. Chicago: Reilly & Britton, 1908.

[Floyd Akers.] *The Boy Fortune Hunters in the Panama.* Illustrated by Howard Heath. Chicago: Reilly & Britton, 1908. Reissue of the second Sam Steele book by "Capt. Hugh Fitzgerald."

[Edith Van Dyne.] *Aunt Jane's Nieces at Millville.* Frontispiece by Emile A. Nelson. Chicago: Reilly & Britton, 1908.

"To the Littlefield Baby" [poem]. April 5, 1908. *Baum Bugle* 33 (Spring 1989): 9.

(*)*The Fairylogue and Radio-Plays* [motion pictures and slides]. Narration by L. Frank Baum. Filmed by William Nicholas Selig, Chicago.

1909

(*)*The Road to Oz.* Illustrated by John R. Neill. Chicago: Reilly & Britton, 1909.

[Floyd Akers.] *The Boy Fortune Hunters in China.* Frontispiece by Emile A. Nelson. Chicago: Reilly & Britton, 1909.

[Edith Van Dyne.] *Aunt Jane's Nieces at Work.* Frontispiece by Emile A. Nelson. Chicago: Reilly & Britton, 1909.

(*)"Modern Fairy Tales" [article]. *Advance,* 19 August 1909.

"The Fairy Prince" [short play based on *The Enchanted Island of Yew*]. *Entertaining,* December 1909.

The Koran of the Prophet [musical extravaganza]. Not completed.

(*)*The Rainbow's Daughter; or, The Magnet of Love* [musical extravaganza in two acts]. Possibly not completed.

Ozma of Oz [musical extravaganza]. Music by Manuel Klein. Scenic effects by Arthur

Voegtlin. The second version of *The Rainbow's Daughter.* Not produced.

Peter and Paul [opera]. Music by Arthur Pryor. Possibly not completed.

The Pipes O' Pan [musical comedy in three acts], by L. Frank Baum and George Scarborough. Music by Paul Tietjens. Not produced. The first act is in Alla T. Ford and Dick Martin. *The Musical Fantasies of L. Frank Baum.* Chicago: Wizard Press, 1958.

The Girl from Oz [comedy]. Ca. 1909. Not produced. Later rewritten as a radio operetta by Baum's son.

1910

(*)*The Emerald City of Oz.* Illustrated by John R. Neill. Chicago: Reilly & Britton, 1910.

L. Frank Baum's Juvenile Speaker: Readings and Recitations in Prose and Verse, Humorous and Otherwise. Illustrated by John R. Neill and Maginel Wright Enright. Chicago: Reilly & Britton, 1910. Mostly selections from previously published works.

[Floyd Akers.] *The Boy Fortune Hunters in Yucatan.* Frontispiece by George A. Rieman. Chicago: Reilly & Britton, 1910.

[Edith Van Dyne.] *Aunt Jane's Nieces in Society.* Frontispiece by Emile A. Nelson. Chicago: Reilly & Britton, 1910.

"Juggerjook." *St. Nicholas,* December 1910.

"The Man Fairy." *Ladies' World,* December 1910.

"Verse Letter to Mrs. C. B. Boothe." June 26, 1910. *Baum Bugle* 1 (October 1957): 4.

"Gee, There's been a lot of fuss . . . " [poem]. 1910. *Baum Bugle* 25 (Summer 1981): 17.

The Wonderful Wizard of Oz [motion picture]. Scenario by L. Frank Baum. Filmed by William Nicholas Selig, Chicago.

Dorothy and the Scarecrow in Oz [motion picture]. Scenario by L. Frank Baum. Filmed by William Nicholas Selig, Chicago.

The Land of Oz [motion picture]. Scenario by L. Frank Baum. Filmed by William Nicholas Selig, Chicago.

John Dough and the Cherub [motion picture].

Scenario by L. Frank Baum. Filmed by William Nicholas Selig, Chicago.

The Pea-Green Poodle [play]. Not produced.

The Clock Shop [play]. Ca. 1910. Not produced.

1911

(*)*The Sea Fairies.* Illustrated by John R. Neill. Chicago: Reilly & Britton, 1911.

The Daring Twins: A Story for Young Folk. Illustrated by Pauline M. Batchelder. Chicago: Reilly & Britton, 1911.

Baum's Own Book for Children: Stories and Verses from the Famous Oz Books, Father Goose, His Book, Etc., Etc., With many Hitherto Unpublished Selections. Illustrated by John R. Neill and Maginel Wright Enright. Chicago: Reilly & Britton, 1911. Reissue of *L. Frank Baum's Juvenile Speaker.*

[Floyd Akers.] *The Boy Fortune Hunters in the South Seas.* Frontispiece by Emile A. Nelson. Chicago: Reilly & Britton, 1911.

(*) [Laura Bancroft.] *Twinkle and Chubbins: Their Astonishing Adventures in Nature-Fairyland.* Illustrated by Maginel Wright Enright. Chicago: Reilly & Britton, 1911. Reissue of the six *Twinkle Tales* in one volume.

(*) [Laura Bancroft.] *Babes in Birdland.* Illustrated by Maginel Wright Enright. Chicago: Reilly & Britton, 1911. Reissue of *Policeman Bluejay.*

(*) [Edith Van Dyne.] *Aunt Jane's Nieces and Uncle John.* Frontispiece by Emile A. Nelson. Chicago: Reilly & Britton, 1911.

[Edith Van Dyne.] *The Flying Girl.* Illustrated by Joseph Pierre Nuyttens. Chicago: Reilly & Britton, 1911.

"The Tramp and the Baby." *Ladies' World,* October 1911.

"Bessie's Fairy Tale." *Ladies' World,* December 1911.

"Santa Claus was good to me . . . " [poem]. December 26, 1911. *Baum Bugle* 15 (Christmas 1971): 3.

1912

(*)*Sky Island.* Illustrated by John R. Neill. Chicago: Reilly & Britton, 1912.

Phoebe Daring. Illustrated by Joseph Pierre Nuyttens. Chicago: Reilly & Britton, 1912.

[Edith Van Dyne.] *Aunt Jane's Nieces on Vacation.* Frontispiece by Emile A. Nelson. Chicago: Reilly & Britton, 1912.

[Edith Van Dyne.] *The Flying Girl and Her Chum.* Illustrated by Joseph Pierre Nuyttens. Chicago: Reilly & Britton, 1912.

"Aunt Phroney's Boy." *St. Nicholas,* December 1912.

1913

(*)*The Little Wizard Series.* Six small volumes: *The Cowardly Lion and the Hungry Tiger, Little Dorothy and Toto, Tik-Tok and the Nome King, Ozma and the Little Wizard, Jack Pumpkinhead and the Sawhorse,* and *The Scarecrow and the Tin Woodman.* Illustrated by John R. Neill. Chicago: Reilly & Britton, 1913.

(*)*The Patchwork Girl of Oz.* Illustrated by John R. Neill. Chicago: Reilly & Britton, 1913.

Phil Daring's Experiment. Third title in the series. Not completed.

[Edith Van Dyne.] *Aunt Jane's Nieces on the Ranch.* Unsigned frontispiece. Chicago: Reilly & Britton, 1913.

[Edith Van Dyne.] *The Flying Girl's Brave Venture.* Third title in the series. Not completed.

(*)*The Tik-Tok Man of Oz* [fairyland extravaganza in three acts]. Music by Louis F. Gottschalk. Staged by Oliver Morosco. Produced. Final version of *The Rainbow's Daughter.*

The Tik-Tok Man of Oz [book of selections and fourteen pieces of sheet music published separately]. Music by Louis F. Gottschalk. New York: Jerome H. Remick, 1913.

1914

(*)*Tik-Tok of Oz.* Illustrated by John R. Neill. Chicago: Reilly & Britton, 1914.

(*)*Little Wizard Stories of Oz.* Illustrated by John R. Neill. Chicago: Reilly & Britton, 1914. Reissue of the six *Little Wizard* stories in one volume.

[Edith Van Dyne.] *Aunt Jane's Nieces out West.* Frontispiece by James McCracken. Chicago: Reilly & Britton, 1914.

Stagecraft, the Adventures of a Strictly Moral Man [play]. Music by Louis F. Gottschalk. Produced by the Uplifters for their "First Uplifter High Jinks."

The Patchwork Girl of Oz [motion picture]. Scenario by L. Frank Baum. The Oz Film Manufacturing Company. Released 1914.

The Magic Cloak [motion picture]. Scenario by L. Frank Baum. The Oz Film Manufacturing Company. Released 1914.

The Last Egyptian [motion picture]. Scenario by L. Frank Baum. The Oz Film Manufacturing Company. Released 1914.

(*)*His Majesty, the Scarecrow of Oz* [motion picture released as *The New Wizard of Oz*]. Scenario by L. Frank Baum. The Oz Film Manufacturing Company. Released 1915.

Violet's Dreams [four one-reel fairy-tale motion pictures]. Scenarios probably by L. Frank Baum. Oz Film Manufacturing Company. 1914–1915.

1915

(*)*The Scarecrow of Oz.* Illustrated by John R. Neill. Chicago: Reilly & Britton, 1915.

[Edith Van Dyne.] *Aunt Jane's Nieces in the Red Cross.* Frontispiece by Norman P. Hall. Chicago: Reilly & Britton, 1915. Reissued in 1918 with four additional chapters.

"Our Hollywood" [article]. From an unidentified newspaper clipping, ca. 1915.

The Gray Nun of Belgium [motion picture]. Scenario by L. Frank Baum. Dramatic Features Corporation. Not released.

The Uplift of Lucifer; or, Raising Hell (An Allegorical Squazosh). Music by Louis F. Gottschalk. Produced by the Uplifters for their second "High Jinks." First published as *The Uplift of Lucifer.* Los Angeles: Privately printed, 1963.

1916

(*)*Rinkitink in Oz.* Illustrated by John R. Neill. Chicago: Reilly & Britton, 1916.

The Snuggle Tales. Six small volumes: *Little Bun Rabbit, Once Upon a Time, The Yellow Hen, The Magic Cloak, The Ginger-Bread Man,* and *Jack Pumpkinhead.* Illustrated by John R. Neill and Maginel Wright Enright. Chicago: Reilly & Britton, 1916–1917. Stories from *L. Frank Baum's Juvenile Speaker.* The first four were issued in 1916 and the last two in 1917.

[Edith Van Dyne.] *Mary Louise.* Frontispiece by J. Allen St. John. Chicago: Reilly & Britton, 1916.

[Edith Van Dyne.] *Mary Louise in the Country.* Frontispiece by J. Allen St. John. Chicago: Reilly & Britton, 1916.

The Uplifters' Minstrels. Music by Byron Gay. Produced by the Uplifters for their third "High Jinks."

Snow white [musical comedy]. Not completed.

1917

(*)*The Lost Princess of Oz.* Illustrated by John R. Neill. Chicago: Reilly & Britton, 1917.

(*)*Babes in Birdland.* Illustrated by Maginel Wright Enright. Chicago: Reilly & Britton, 1917. Reissue of the "Laura Bancroft" title under Baum's name.

[Edith Van Dyne.] *Mary Louise Solves a Mystery.* Frontispiece by Anna B. Mueller. Chicago: Reilly & Britton, 1917.

The Orpheus Road Company. Music by Louis F. Gottschalk. Produced by the Uplifters for their fourth "High Jinks."

1918

(*)*The Tin Woodman of Oz.* Illustrated by John R. Neill. Chicago: Reilly & Britton, 1918.

[Edith Van Dyne.] *Mary Louise and the Liberty Girls.* Frontispiece by Alice Carsey. Chicago: Reilly & Britton, 1918.

"Mister Doodle" [poem]. *Los Angeles Times,* 5 July 1918. First published in *L. Frank Baum's Juvenile Speaker.*

1919

(*)*The Magic of Oz.* Illustrated by John R. Neill. Chicago: Reilly & Lee, 1919.

[Edith Van Dyne.] *Mary Louise Adopts a Soldier.* Frontispiece by Joseph W. Wyckoff. Chicago: Reilly & Lee, 1919. After Baum's death, this series was continued by Emma Speed Sampson.

1920

(*)*Glinda of Oz*. Illustrated by John R. Neill. Chicago: Reilly & Lee, 1920.

Oz-Man Tales. Illustrated by John R. Neill and Maginel Wright Enright. Chicago: Reilly & Lee, 1920. Reissue of the six *Snuggle Tales* under another name.

"Susan Doozan" [song]. Music by Byron Gay. Los Angeles: Cooper's Melody Shop, 1920. From the 1916 Uplifters' "High Jinks."

UNDATABLE

"Johnson" [novel]. Lost.

"Molly Oodle" [novel]. Lost.

"Chrome Yellow" [story]. Unpublished.

"The Diamondback." *Baum Bugle* 26 (Spring 1982): 7–9.

"An Oz Book" [fragment]. *Baum Bugle* 9 (Christmas 1965): 11.

"The Littlest Giant: An 'Oz' Story." *Baum Bugle* 19 (Spring 1975): 2–5. The story has little to do with Oz.

"Mr. Rumple's Chill" [story]. Lost.

"Bess of the Movies" [story]. Lost.

OZ BOOKS
BY OTHER AUTHORS

This section lists the Oz and Oz-related books by Baum's immediate family and by those authors and illustrators associated with the official series.

W. W. Denslow

Pictures from The Wonderful Wizard of Oz. Story by Thomas H. Ogilvie. Chicago: George W. Ogilvie, [1903–1904]. Denslow owned the copyright of his illustrations and published this book after his partnership with Baum broke up.

Ruth Plumly Thompson

The Royal Book of Oz. Illustrated by John R. Neill. Chicago: Reilly & Lee, 1921.

Kabumpo in Oz. Illustrated by John R. Neill. Chicago: Reilly & Lee, 1922.

The Cowardly Lion of Oz. Illustrated by John R. Neill. Chicago: Reilly & Lee, 1923.

Grampa in Oz. Illustrated by John R. Neill. Chicago: Reilly & Lee, 1924.

The Lost King of Oz. Illustrated by John R. Neill. Chicago: Reilly & Lee, 1925.

The Hungry Tiger of Oz. Illustrated by John R. Neill. Chicago: Reilly & Lee, 1926.

The Gnome King of Oz. Illustrated by John R. Neill. Chicago: Reilly & Lee, 1927.

The Giant Horse of Oz. Illustrated by John R. Neill. Chicago: Reilly & Lee, 1928.

Jack Pumpkinhead of Oz. Illustrated by John R. Neill. Chicago: Reilly & Lee, 1929.

The Yellow Knight of Oz. Illustrated by John R. Neill. Chicago: Reilly & Lee, 1930.

Pirates in Oz. Illustrated by John R. Neill. Chicago: Reilly & Lee, 1931.

The Purple Prince of Oz. Illustrated by John R. Neill. Chicago: Reilly & Lee, 1932.

Ojo in Oz. Illustrated by John R. Neill. Chicago: Reilly & Lee, 1933.

Speedy in Oz. Illustrated by John R. Neill. Chicago: Reilly & Lee, 1934.

The Wishing Horse of Oz. Illustrated by John R. Neill. Chicago: Reilly & Lee, 1935.

Captain Salt in Oz. Illustrated by John R. Neill. Chicago: Reilly & Lee, 1936.

Handy Mandy in Oz. Illustrated by John R. Neill. Chicago: Reilly & Lee, 1937.

The Silver Princess in Oz. Illustrated by John R. Neill. Chicago: Reilly & Lee, 1938.

Ozoplaning with the Wizard of Oz. Illustrated by John R. Neill. Chicago: Reilly & Lee, 1939.

Yankee in Oz. Illustrated by Dick Martin. [Kinderhook, Ill.]: International Wizard of Oz Club, 1972.

The Enchanted Island of Oz. Illustrated by Dick Martin. [Kinderhook, Ill.]: International Wizard of Oz Club, 1976.

The Cheerful Citizens of Oz. Illustrated by Rob Roy MacVeigh. [Kinderhook, Ill.]: International Wizard of Oz Club, 1992. Collection of Oz-related verse.

Frank Joslyn Baum

The Laughing Dragon of Oz. Illustrated by Milt Youngren. Racine, Wis.: Whitman, 1935. Oz book by Baum's eldest son; withdrawn as the result of a copyright lawsuit brought by Reilly & Lee.

Kenneth Gage Baum

The Dinamonster of Oz. Illustrated by Dorothy Gita Morena. Preface by Ozma Baum Mantele. Afterword by Stephen J. Teller. Albuquerque: Buckethead Enterprises of Oz, 1991. Oz book by Baum's fourth son, originally written in 1941.

John R. Neill

The Oz Toy Book Cut-outs for the Kiddies. Illustrated by John R. Neill. Chicago: Reilly & Britton, 1915.
The Wonder City of Oz. Illustrated by John R. Neill. Chicago: Reilly & Lee, 1940.
The Scalawagons of Oz. Illustrated by John R. Neill. Chicago: Reilly & Lee, 1941.
Lucky Bucky in Oz. Illustrated by John R. Neill. Chicago: Reilly & Lee, 1942.
The Runaway in Oz. Illustrated by Eric Shanower. New York: Books of Wonder, 1995. This was to be the Oz book for 1943, but Neill died before he could illustrate it.

Jack Snow

The Magical Mimics in Oz. Illustrated by Frank Kramer. Chicago: Reilly & Lee, 1946.
The Shaggy Man of Oz. Illustrated by Frank Kramer. Chicago: Reilly & Lee, 1949.
Who's Who in Oz. Illustrated by reproductions of pictures by John R. Neill, Frank Kramer, and "Dirk" [Dirk Gringhuis]. Chicago: Reilly & Lee, 1954.

Rachel R. Cosgrove [Rachel Cosgrove Payes]

The Hidden Valley of Oz. Illustrated by "Dirk" [Dirk Gringhuis]. Chicago: Reilly & Lee, 1951.
The Wicked Witch of Oz. Illustrated by Eric Shanower. Kinderhook Ill.: International Wizard of Oz Club, 1993.

Eloise Jarvis McGraw and Lauren McGraw Wagner

Merry Go Round in Oz. Illustrated by Dick Martin. Chicago: Reilly & Lee, 1963.
The Forbidden Fountain of Oz. Illustrated by Dick Martin. [Kinderhook, Ill.]: International Wizard of Oz Club, 1980.

Dick Martin

An Oz Picture Gallery. [Kinderhook, Ill.]: International Wizard of Oz Club, 1984. Picture book.
The Ozmapolitan of Oz. Illustrated by Dick Martin. [Kinderhook, Ill.]: International Wizard of Oz Club, 1986.
An Oz Sketchbook. [Kinderhook, Ill.]: International Wizard of Oz Club, 1988. Picture book.

WORKS CITED

Attebery, Brian. *The Fantasy Tradition in American Literature: From Irving to Le Guin.* Bloomington: Indiana University Press, 1980.
Baum, Frank Joslyn, and Russell P. MacFall. *To Please a Child: A Biography of L. Frank Baum, Royal Historian of Oz.* Chicago: Reilly & Lee, 1961.
Baum, L. Frank. *The Rose Lawn Home Journal,* 1 July 1871. *Baum Bugle* 30 (Spring 1986): 13–16.
Benson, Sally. *Meet Me in St. Louis.* 1942. Reprint. New York: Bantam Books, 1958.
Berman, Ruth. "Lurline's Source." *Baum Bugle* 26 (Autumn 1982): 2–3.
Bulwer-Lytton, Sir Edward. *The Caxtons: A Family Picture.* 3 vols. Edinburgh: William Blackwood and Sons, 1849.
Butterworth, Hezekiah. *Zigzag Journeys in the White City with Visits to the Neighboring Metropolis.* Boston: Estes Lauriat, 1894.
Carpenter, Humphrey. *Secret Gardens: A Study of the Golden Age of Children's Literature.* London: George Allen & Unwin, 1985.
Coleman, Earle J. "Oz as Heaven and Other Philosophical Questions." *Baum Bugle* 24 (Autumn 1980): 18–20.

"Contract with the Reilly & Britton Company, 1905." *Baum Bugle* 12 (Christmas 1968): 21.

Crowder, Richard. *Those Innocent Years: The Legacy and Inheritance of a Hero of the Victorian Era, James Whitcomb Riley.* Indianapolis: Bobbs-Merrill, 1957.

Delkin, Jay. "The Meaning of 'Oz.'" *Baum Bugle* 15 (Autumn 1971): 18–20.

Eigner, Edwin M. *The Metaphysical Novel in England and America: Dickens, Bulwer, Melville, and Hawthorne.* Berkeley: University of California Press, 1978.

Eyles, Allen. *The World of Oz.* Tucson: HPBooks, 1985.

Ford, Alla T., and Dick Martin. *The Musical Fantasies of L. Frank Baum.* Chicago: Wizard Press, 1958.

Franson, J. Karl. "From Vanity Fair to Emerald City: Baum's Debt to Bunyan." *Children's Literature* 23 (1995): 91–114.

Gage, Matilda J. "The Dakota Days of L. Frank Baum: Part I." *Baum Bugle* 10 (Spring 1966): 5–8.

———. "The Dakota Days of L. Frank Baum: Part II." *Baum Bugle* 10 (Autumn 1966): 8–9.

———. "The Dakota Days of L. Frank Baum: Part III." *Baum Bugle* 10 (Christmas 1966): 9–11.

Gardner, Martin. Introduction to *John Dough and the Cherub*, by L. Frank Baum. Illustrated by John R. Neill. New York: Dover, 1974.

———. Introduction to *The Life and Adventures of Santa Claus*, by L. Frank Baum. With all the original illustrations by Mary Cowles Clark. New York: Dover, 1976.

———. Introduction to *The Surprising Adventures of The Magical Monarch of Mo and His People*, by L. Frank Baum. With pictures by Frank Ver Beck [*sic*]. New York: Dover, 1968.

Gardner, Martin, and Russel B. Nye. *The Wizard of Oz and Who He Was.* East Lansing: Michigan State University Press, 1957.

Greene, David L. Introduction to *Policeman Bluejay (1907)*, by L. Frank Baum [Laura Bancroft, pseud.]. Facsimile Reproduction of the First Edition. Delmar, N.Y.: Scholars' Facsimiles & Reprints, 1981.

———. "L. Frank Baum on His Films." *Baum Bugle* 17 (Autumn 1973): 14–15.

———. "L. Frank Baum's Later Oz Books: 1914–1920." *Baum Bugle* 16 (Spring 1972): 17–20.

———. "The Writing of Two L. Frank Baum Fantasies." *Baum Bugle* 15 (Autumn 1971): 14–16.

Greene, David L., and Peter E. Hanff. "Baum and Denslow: Their Books, Part One." *Baum Bugle* 19 (Spring 1975): 7–11.

Greene, Douglas G. Introduction to *The Woggle-Bug Book (1905)*, by L. Frank Baum. Facsimile Reproduction. Delmar, N.Y.: Scholars' Facsimiles & Reprints, 1978.

———. "The Periodical Baum: An Annotated Checklist." *Baum Bugle* 19 (Autumn 1975): 3–9.

Green, Douglas G., and Peter E. Hanff. *Bibliographia Oziana: A Concise Bibliographical Checklist of the Oz Books by L. Frank Baum and His Successors.* Rev. and enlarged ed. [Kinderhook, Ill.]: International Wizard of Oz Club, 1988.

Green, Douglas G., and Michael Patrick Hearn. *W. W. Denslow.* Mt. Pleasant: Clarke Historical Library, Central Michigan University, 1976.

Hanff, Peter E. Introduction to *By the Candelabra's Glare (1898)*, by L. Frank Baum. Facsimile Reproduction. Delmar, N.Y.: Scholars' Facsimiles & Reprints, 1981.

Hearn, Michael Patrick. *The Annotated Wizard of Oz.* New York: Potter, 1973.

———. "How Did the Woggle-Bug Do?" *Baum Bugle* 18 (Christmas 1974): 16–23.

———. Introduction to *Little Wizard Stories of Oz*, by L. Frank Baum, Illustrated by John R. Neill. New York: Schocken Books, 1985.

———. "L. Frank Baum: Amateur Printer." *Baum Bugle* 30 (Spring 1986): 11–18.

———. "L. Frank Baum: Chicken Fancier." *Baum Bugle* 30 (Autumn 1986): 23–25.

——. "When L. Frank Baum was 'Laura Bancroft.'" *American Book Collector*, n.s., 8 (May 1987): 11–16.

Hearn, Michael Patrick, David L. Greene, and Peter E. Hanff. "The Faltering Flight of Prince Silverwings." *Baum Bugle* 18 (Autumn 1974): 4–10.

Hoffman, Daniel G. *Paul Bunyan: Last of the Frontier Demigods*. Philadelphia: University of Pennsylvania Press for Temple University Publications, 1952.

Hollister, C. Warren. "Criticism Criticized. *Baum Bugle* 16 (Spring 1972): 24–25.

——. "Oz and the Fifth Criterion." *Baum Bugle* 15 (Christmas 1971): 5–8.

Houck, Clara M. "Journey to Oz." *Baum Bugle* 26 (Autumn 1982): 14–16.

"Interview with Mr. Frank G. [*sic*] Baum." *Advance*, 22 July 1909. Reprinted in *Baum Bugle* 30 (Autumn 1986): 9–10.

MacDonald, George. *The Gifts of the Child Christ: Fairytales and Stories for the Childlike*. Edited by Glenn Edward Sadler. 2 vols. Grand Rapids, Mich.: Eerdmans, 1973.

MacFall, Russell P. Introduction to *Animal Fairy Tales*, by L. Frank Baum. With Illustrations by Dick Martin. Chicago: International Wizard of Oz Club, 1969.

——. "L. Frank Baum and the Radio-Plays." *Baum Bugle* 6 (August 1962): 3–4.

Mannix, Daniel P. "'Off to See the Wizard'—1903: Part One." *Baum Bugle* 12 (Christmas 1968): 5–10.

——. "'Off to See the Wizard'—1903: Part Two." *Baum Bugle* 13 (Spring 1969): 5–10.

Mills, Richard A. "The Fairylogue and Radio Plays of L. Frank Baum." *Baum Bugle* 14 (Christmas 1970): 4–7.

——. "The Oz Film Manufacturing Company: Part One." *Baum Bugle* 16 (Christmas 1972): 5–11.

Mills, Richard A., and David L. Greene. "The Oz Film Manufacturing Company: Part Two." *Baum Bugle* 17 (Spring 1973): 5–10.

Moore, Raylyn. *Wonderful Wizard, Marvelous Land*. Bowling Green, Ohio: Bowling Green University Popular Press, 1974.

Morley, Christopher. Preface to *The Complete Sherlock Holmes*, by Sir Arthur Conan Doyle. Garden City, N.Y.: Doubleday, 1930.

Olsen, Scott. "The Coronado Fairyland." *Baum Bugle* 20 (Winter 1976): 2–5.

"The Original Title Page for The Wonderful Wizard of Oz." *Baum Bugle* 16 (Autumn 1972): 3 and front cover.

"Oz Under Scrutiny: Early Reviews of The Marvelous Land of Oz." *Baum Bugle* 23 (Spring 1979): 12–14.

Riley, Michael O. Review of *The Curious Cruise of Captain Santa*, by Ruth Plumly Thompson. *Baum Bugle* 30 (Autumn 1986): 18.

Stone, Fred. *Rolling Stone*. New York: Whittlesey House, McGraw-Hill, 1945.

Tarkington, Booth. *The Magnificent Ambersons*. Illustrated by Arthur William Brown. Garden City, N.Y.: Doubleday, Page, 1918.

Teller, Stephen J. "A Checklist of Published Oz Apocrypha." *Baum Bugle* 34 (Autumn 1990): 14–21.

——. "The Other Oz: Oz Apocrypha Beyond the Forty Books." *Baum Bugle* 33 (Spring 1989): 10–13.

Tietjens, Eunice. *The World at My Shoulder*. New York: Macmillan, 1938.

Tolkien, J. R. R. Foreword to *The Fellowship of the Ring: Being the First Part of The Lord of the Rings*. 2nd ed. Boston: Houghton Mifflin, 1965.

——. *Tree and Leaf*. Boston: Houghton Mifflin, 1965.

Vidal, Gore. *United States: Essays, 1952–1992*. New York: Random House, 1993.

Wagenknecht, Edward. "Lyman Frank Baum—1959." *Baum Bugle* 3 (August 1959): 4.

——. "To the Readers of this Book." In *The Wizard of Oz*, by L. Frank Baum. Illustrated by Dale Ulrey. Chicago: Reilly & Lee, 1956.

——. *Utopia Americana*. Seattle: University of Washington Book Store, 1929. Reprint. N.p.: Folcroft Press, 1970.

——. "'Utopia Americana,' a Generation Afterwards." *American Book Collector* 13 (December 1962): 12–13.

Wauchope, Robert, and Virginia Wauchope. "Invisible Inzi of Oz, Part One." Introduction by Maude [*sic*] Gage Baum. *Baum Bugle* 24 (Winter 1980–1981): 8–11, 14–16.

——. "Invisible Inzi of Oz, Part Two." *Baum Bugle* 25 (Summer 1981): 10–17.

FURTHER READING

The following is not intended to be an exhaustive list, but it is hoped that it will suggest the rich variety of Baum and Oz research.

American Book Collector 13 (December 1962). [Special issue devoted to Baum and Oz]

American Book Collector 15 (December 1964). [Special issue devoted to W. W. Denslow]

Baughman, Roland. "L. Frank Baum and the 'Oz Books.'" *Columbia University Library Columns*, May 1955, 15–35.

Baughman, Roland, and Joan Baum. *L. Frank Baum: The Wonderful Wizard of Oz: An Exhibition of His Published Writings, in Commemoration of the Centenary of His Birth, May 15, 1856*. New York: Columbia University Libraries, 1956.

Baum Bugle. Kinderhook, Ill.: International Wizard of Oz Club, 1957–present.

Baum, Frank [J.]. "The Oz Film Co." *Films in Review*, August–September 1956, 329–33.

Baum, Frank L. [*sic*]. "Why the Wizard Keeps on Selling." *Writer's Digest*, December 1952, 19, 36–37.

Baum, Roger S. *Dorothy of Oz*. Illustrated by Elizabeth Miles. New York: Books of Wonder, 1989. [Novel by Baum's great-grandson]

Beweley, Marius. "The Land of Oz: America's Great Good Place." In *Masks and Mirrors:*

Essays and Criticism, 255–67. New York: Atheneum, 1970.

Bradbury, Ray. "Two Balmy Promenades Along the Yellow Brick Road." *Los Angeles Times Books Review*, 9 October 1977, 1, 3.

Brotman, Jordan. "A Late Wanderer in Oz." In *Only Connect: Readings on Children's Literature*, edited by Sheila Egoff, G. T. Stubbs, and L. F. Ashley, 156–69. New York: Oxford University Press, 1969.

Carpenter, Angelica Shirley, and Jean Shirley. *L. Frank Baum: Royal Historian of Oz*. Minneapolis: Lerner, 1992.

Dulabone, Chris. "Why Do People Keep Writing Oz Stories?" *Baum Bugle* 34 (Autumn 1990): 12–13.

Earle, Neil. *The Wonderful Wizard of Oz in American Popular Culture: Uneasy in Eden*. Lampeter, Wales: Mellen Press, 1993.

Erisman, Fred. "L. Frank Baum and the Progressive Dilemma." *American Quarterly* 20 (Fall 1968): 616–23.

Farmer, Philip José. *A Barnstormer in Oz; or, A Rationalization and Extrapolation of the Split-Level Continuum*. New York: Berkley Books, 1982. [Adult science-fiction novel]

Gallico, Paul. "This Man's World: The Wonderful Wizard of Oz." *Esquire*, February 1957, 32, 34.

Gardner, Martin. Introduction to *American Fairy Tales*, by L. Frank Baum. Illustrated by N. P. Hall, Harry Kennedy, Ike Morgan, and Ralph Fletcher Seymour [and George Kerr]. New York: Dover, 1978.

——. Introduction to *Queen Zixi of Ix; or, The Story of the Magic Cloak*, by L. Frank Baum. Illustrated by Frederick Richardson. New York: Dover, 1971.

——. Introduction to *The Wonderful Wizard of Oz*, by L. Frank Baum. With Pictures by W. W. Denslow. New York: Dover, 1960.

——. "The Librarians in Oz." *Saturday Review*, 11 April 1959, 18–19.

——. "We're Off to See the Wizard." *New York Times Book Review*, 2 May 1971, 1, 42.

——. "Why Librarians Dislike Oz." *Library Journal*, 15 February 1963, 834–36.

Gessel, Michael. "Tale of a Parable." *Baum Bugle* 36 (Spring 1992): 19–23.

Greene, David L. "The Concept of Oz." *Children's Literature* 3 (1974): 173–76.

Greene, David L., and Dick Martin. *The Oz Scrapbook*. New York: Random House, 1977.

Greene, Douglas G., and David L. Greene. "Around the World with the Wizard of Oz." *Baum Bugle* 10 (Christmas 1966): 16–17.

Hearn, Michael Patrick. "L. Frank Baum and the 'Modernized Fairy Tale.'" *Children's Literature in Education*, Spring 1979, 57–66.

——. "Silent Oz." *Baum Bugle* 37 (Winter 1993): 4–7, 28.

——, ed. *The Wizard of Oz*, by L. Frank Baum. With Pictures by W. W. Denslow. The Critical Heritage Series. New York: Schocken Books, 1983.

Hollister, Edith, and C. Warren Hollister. Introduction to *In Other Lands Than Ours (1907)*, by Maud Gage Baum. Edited and with a preface by L. Frank Baum. Facsimile Reproduction of the First Edition. Delmar, N.Y.: Scholars' Facsimiles & Reprints, 1983.

Jackson, Shirley. "The Lost Kingdom of Oz." *Reporter*, 10 December 1959, 42–43.

Koupal, Nancy Tystad. Preface and annotations to *Our Landlady*, by L. Frank Baum. Lincoln: University of Nebraska Press, 1996.

Lanes, Selma G. *Down the Rabbit Hole*. New York: Atheneum, 1971.

Leach, William R. "The Clown from Syracuse: The Life and Times of L. Frank Baum." In *The Wonderful Wizard of Oz*, by L. Frank Baum. American Society and Culture Series. Belmont, Calif.: Wadsworth, 1991.

Littlefield, Henry M. "The Wizard of Oz: Parable on Populism." *American Quarterly* 16 (Spring 1964): 47–58.

Maguire, Gregory. *Wicked: The Life and Times of the Wicked Witch of the West*. Illustrations by Douglas Smith. New York: Regan-Books, 1995. [Adult novel]

Mannix, Daniel P. "The Father of the Wizard of Oz." *American Heritage*, December 1964, 36–47, 108–9.

Morey, Anne. "'A Whole Book for a Nickel'? L. Frank Baum as Filmmaker." *Children's Literature Association Quarterly* 20 (Winter 1995–1996): 155–60.

Nathanson, Paul. *Over the Rainbow: The Wizard of Oz as a Secular Myth of America*. McGill Studies in the History of Religion. Albany: State University of New York Press, 1991.

The Oz-Story Magazine. Edited by David Maxine. Art direction by Eric Shaower. Bloomfield, N.J.: Hungry Tiger Press, 1995–present.

Pattrick, Robert R. *Unexplored Territory in Oz*. Kinderhook, Ill.: International Wizard of Oz Club, 1963.

Rushdie, Salman. *The Wizard of Oz*. British Film Institute Film Classics. London: BFI, 1992.

Ryman, Geoff. *WAS: A Novel*. New York: Knopf, 1992. [Adult novel using Oz characters]

Sackett, S. J. "The Utopia of Oz." *Georgia Review* 14 (Fall 1960): 275–90.

St. John, Tom. "Lyman Frank Baum: Looking Back to the Promised Land." *Western Humanities Review*, Winter 1982, 349–60.

Sale, Roger. *Fairy Tales and After: From Snow White to E. B. White*. Cambridge, Mass.: Harvard University Press, 1978.

Schuman, Samuel. "Out of the Frying Pan into the Pyre: Comedy, Myth and *The Wizard of Oz*." *Journal of Popular Culture* 7 (Fall 1973): 302–4.

Seaman, Noah, and Barbara Seaman. "Munchkins, Ozophiles, and Feminists Too." *Ms.*, January 1974, 93.

Seymour, Ralph Fletcher. *Some Went This Way*. Chicago: Privately printed, 1945.

Shanower, Eric. *The Giant Garden of Oz*. Illustrated by Eric Shanower. New York: Emerald City Press, 1993.

Shulman, Alix Kates. "Ozomania Under the Rainbow." *Village Voice*, 3 March 1975, 35.

Starr, Nathan Comfort. "*The Wonderful Wizard of Oz:* A Study in Archetypal Mythic Smybiosis." *Unicorn,* Summer 1973, 13–17.

Tedrow, Thomas L. *Dorothy: Return to Oz.* New York: FamilyVision Press, 1993. [Novel]

Thurber, James. "The Wizard of Chittenango." *New Republic,* 12 December 1934, 81, 141.

Wollheim, Daniel A. Introduction to *The Wizard of Oz,* by L. Frank Baum. New York: Airmont, 1965.

The Worlds' [sic] *Columbian Exposition. Portfolio of Views.* Issued by the Department of Photography, C. D. Arnold, Chief. Chicago: National Chemigraph Company, 1893.

Index